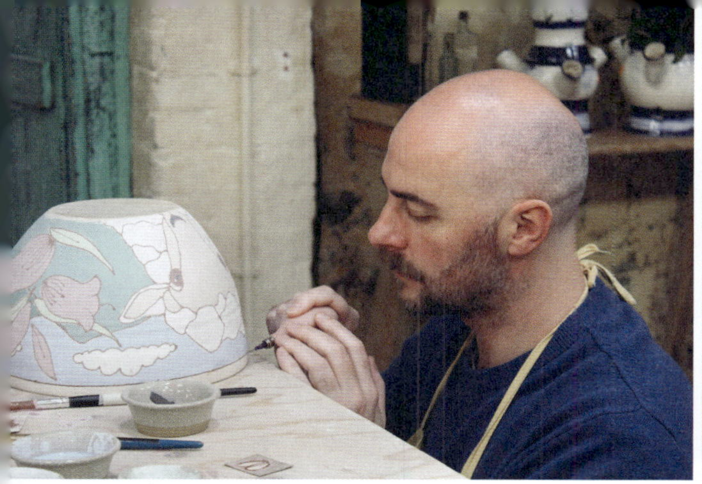

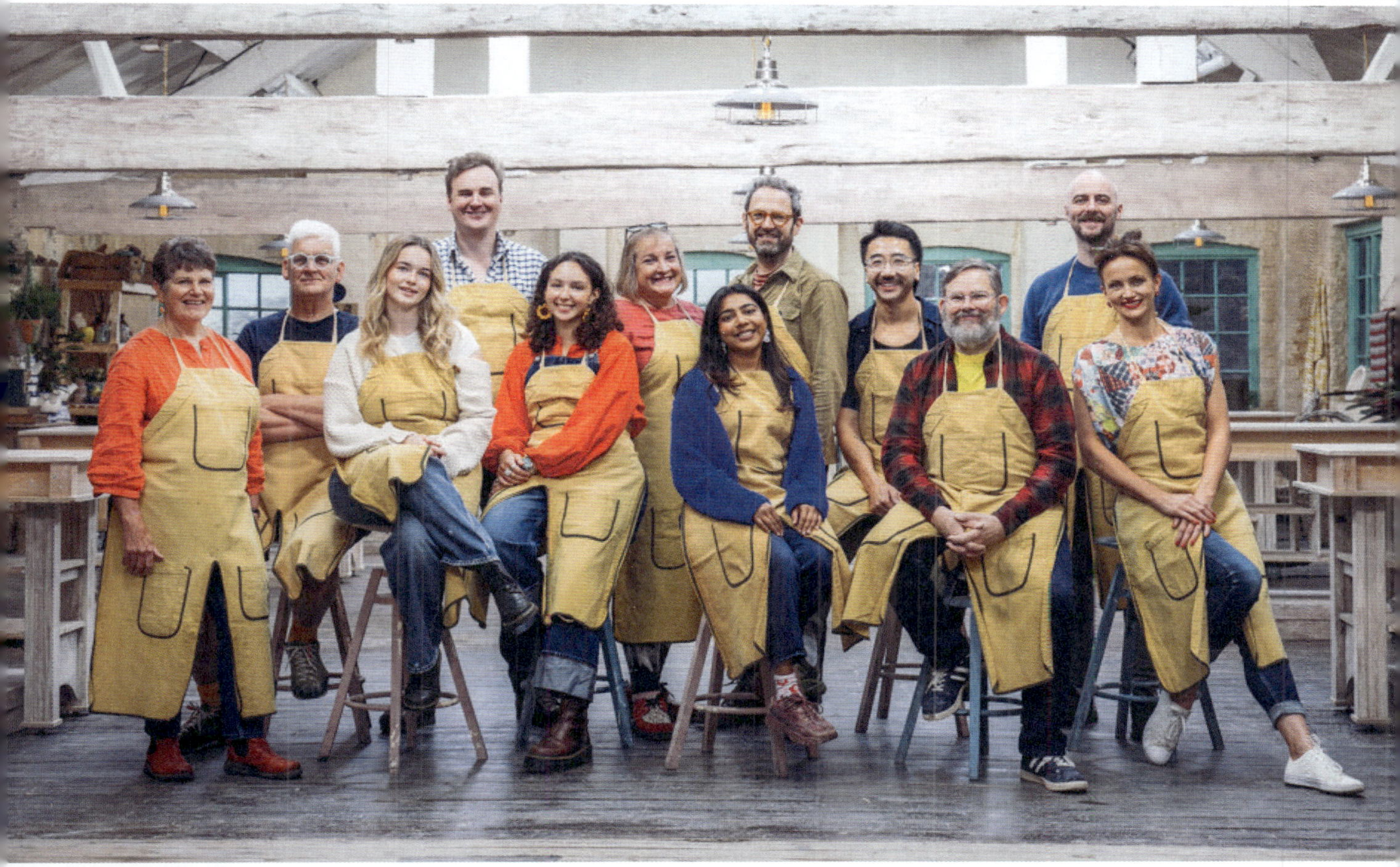

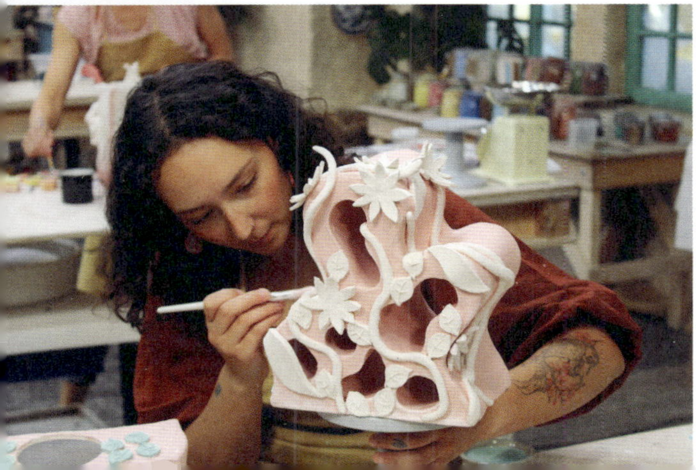

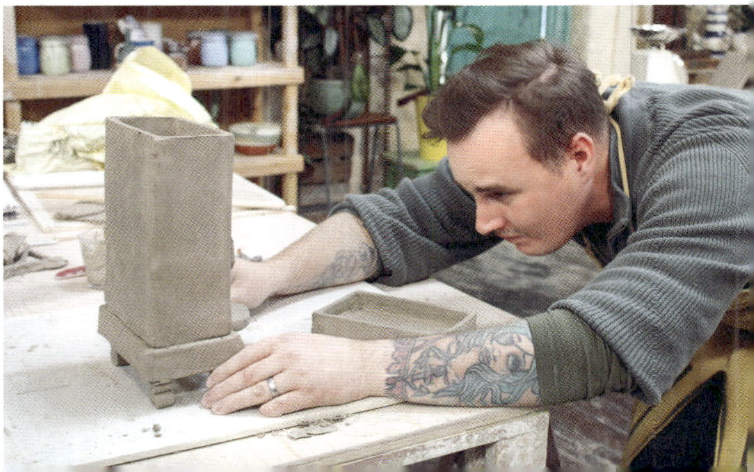

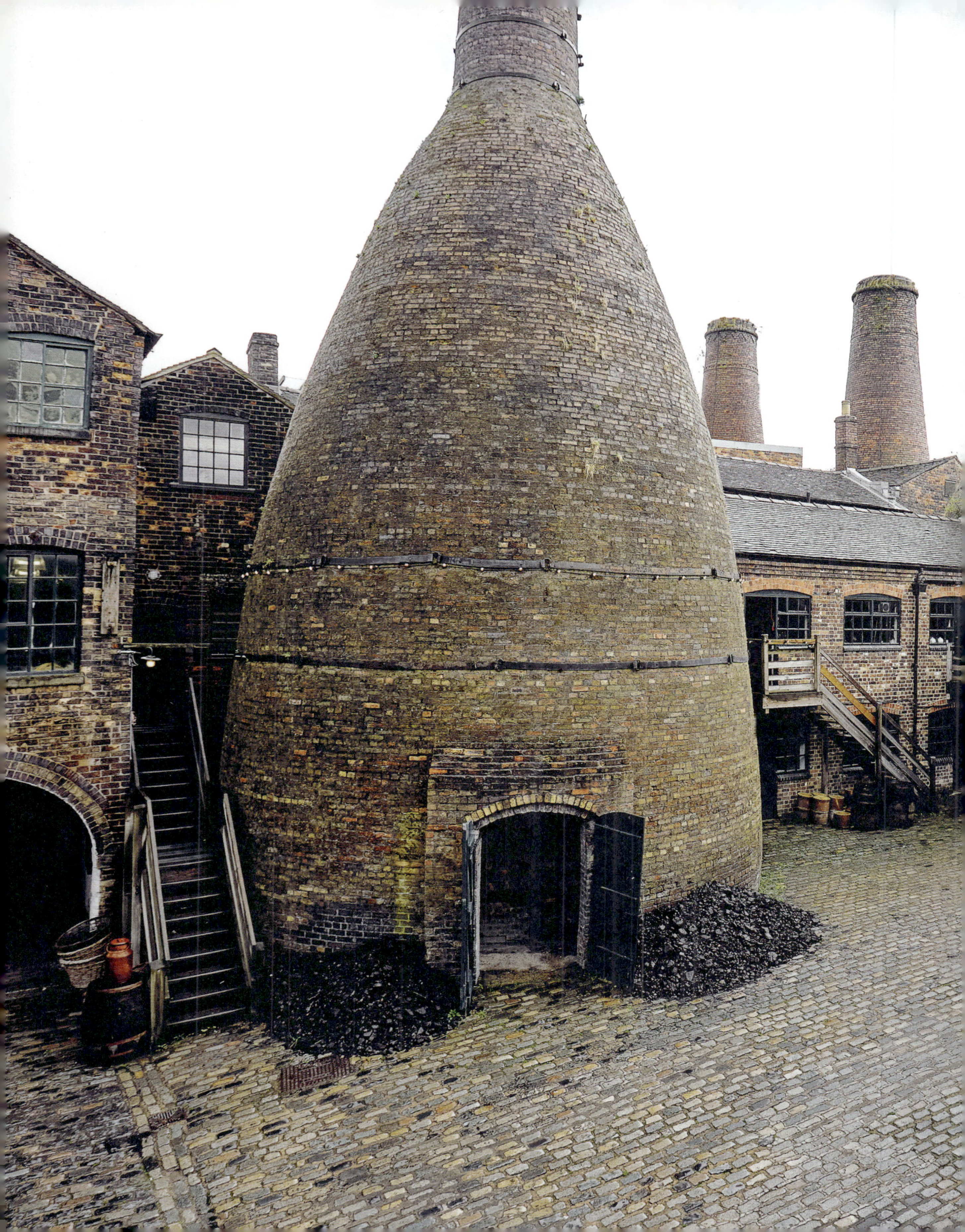

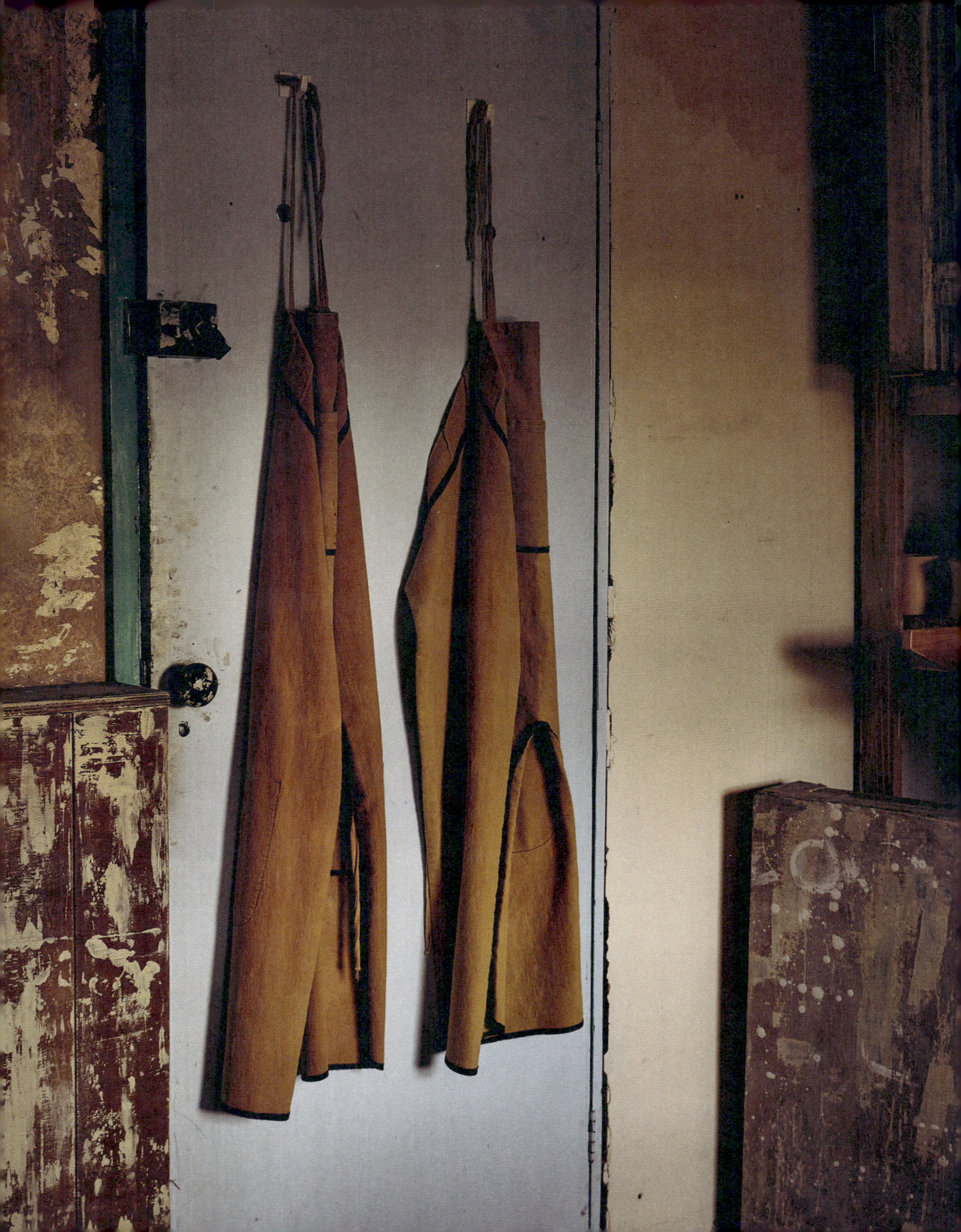

The Great Pottery Throw Down

20 Projects to Create at Home

Jacqui Atkin

Forewords by **Keith Brymer Jones** and **Rich Miller**

Project photography by Kim Lightbody
Step photography by Phil Wilkins

Quadrille

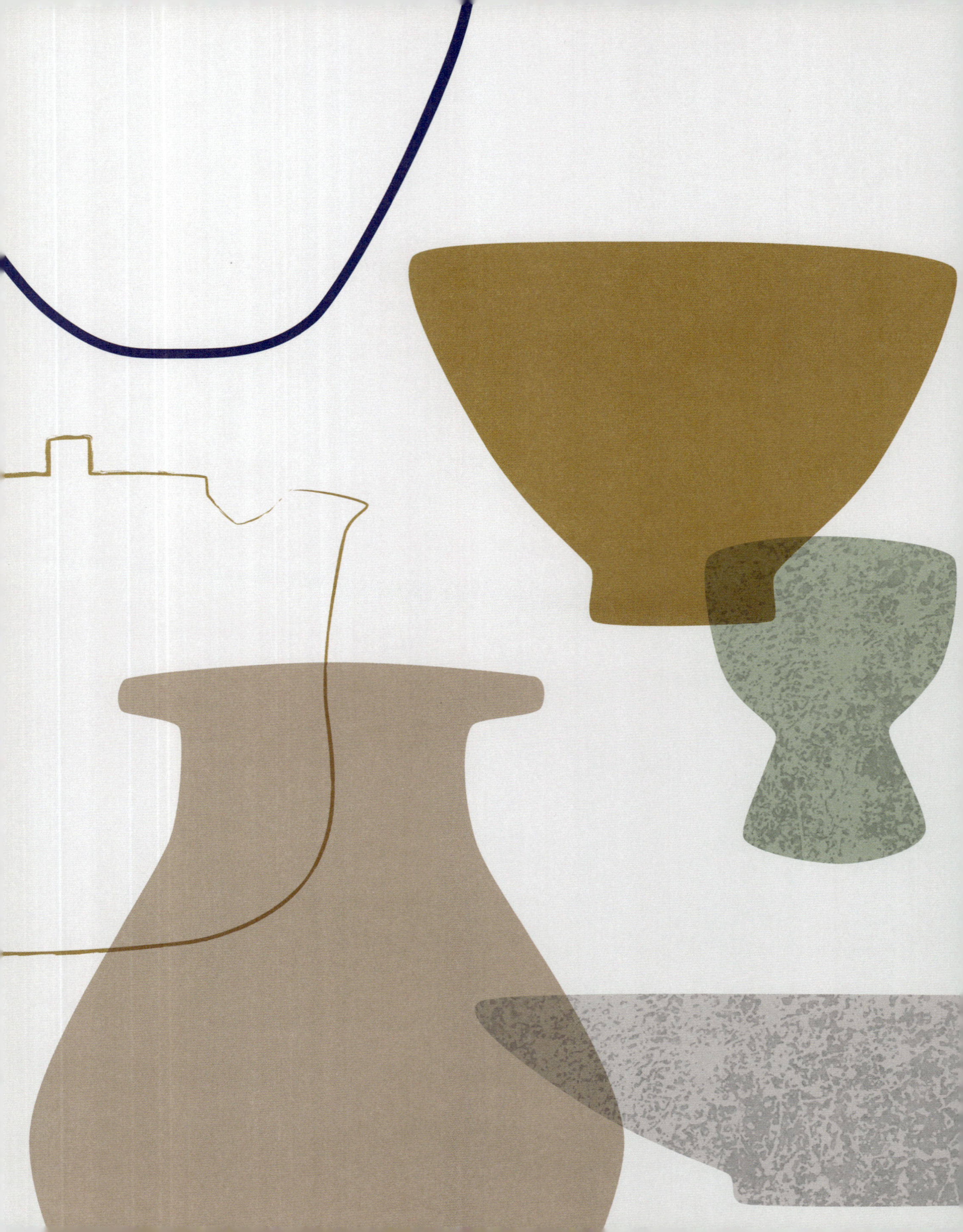

Contents

FOREWORD BY

Keith Brymer Jones

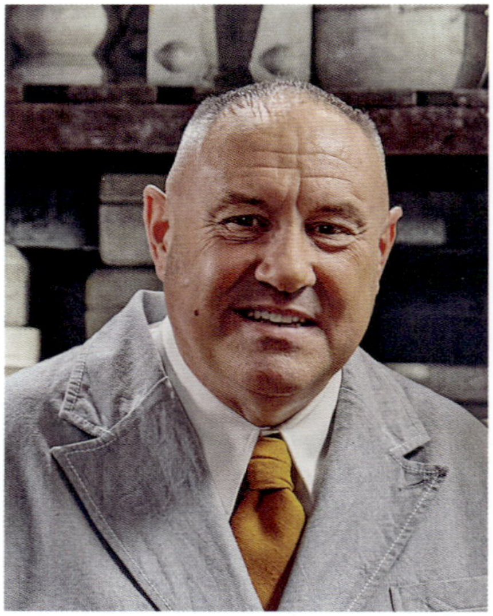

It was at the age of 11 when an inspiring art teacher called Mr Mortman handed me a lump of clay and told me to make something that my lifelong passion for pottery began. (I made a little owl, if you really want to know.) From the very first time I threw a pot, I knew that was what I was destined to do. I started an apprenticeship at the age of 16 under two gruff, old (to me) master potters who wouldn't even let me near the wheel for the first few years and I've never looked back.

I've been a judge on *The Great Pottery Throw Down* since the very first series in 2015 and I can honestly say it's been one of the most joyful experiences of my life. Not only do I get to work with a great bunch of people of all ages and from all walks of life, but I also get to see them grow in skill and confidence, taking on technical challenges that they would never have dreamed they were capable of when they first walked into the pottery.

As everyone who's watched the show knows, I can get a bit emotional sometimes. (Quite a lot of the time, actually!) That's because I know from my own work just how much of themselves the potters put into their creations. Making anything – whether it's a pot or a painting, a woven textile or a beautifully turned piece of wood – is an intensely personal experience. It's a two-way process: you're responding to the clay and the way it behaves, allowing it to almost come alive in your hands, and at the same time you're putting your own heart and soul into it, through the shapes and textures you create and the way you choose to embellish and decorate them.

That's what really moves me: the fact that our potters are prepared not just to take on the technical challenges that we throw (no pun intended) at them, but to put themselveson the line and share their stories through the medium of clay.

If you've bought this book, the chances are you're either a beginner or a relative novice. You might be thinking that you're miles away from being able to create anything like the potters on the show. But as the old Chinese proverb goes, a journey of a thousand miles starts with a single step.

So go on – give pottery a go! What have you got to lose? It could be the start of a wonderful journey, just as my little pottery owl at school was all those years ago.

FOREWORD BY

Rich Miller

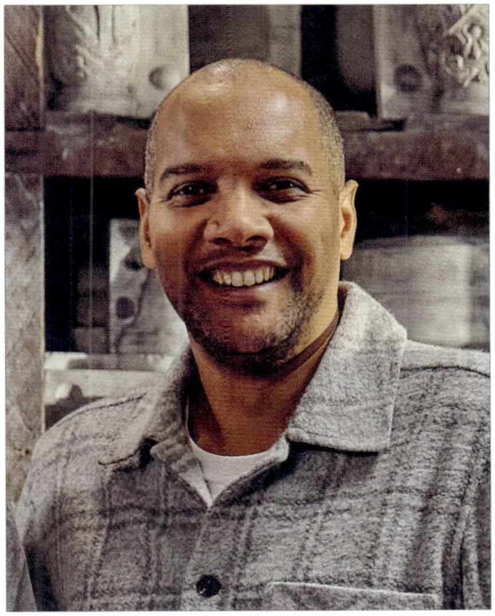

I've been involved in *The Great Pottery Throw Down* since series one, first as a kiln technician and later as a judge alongside Keith, and it's such an inspirational and positive show to be a part of. Who would have thought before that first series aired that a programme about pottery would ever make prime-time TV?!

Every year we set challenges that are designed to test the potters' skill and creativity – and every year I'm absolutely blown away by what they produce. Everyone involved has different strengths: some are amazing throwers, some are amazing hand builders, and some are amazing decorators.

As I'm a potter myself, I suppose I tend to look first of all at the technical side of things when I'm judging. After all, there's no point in creating a beautiful hand-painted teapot if it doesn't pour properly and dribbles hot tea all over your table, or in making an eye-catching vase that doesn't actually hold water! But of course, technique and design flair go hand in hand – and the real magic happens when those two elements come together. I feel really privileged to be allowed into our potters' worlds and see how they all put their unique spin on their creations, even though they're all working to the same basic brief. Although it's a competition, in my eyes every single potter is a winner.

This book is aimed at people who are just starting out in pottery and provides a solid grounding in basic techniques. Even if you've never handled clay in your life, let alone thrown a pot on the wheel or attempted to get to grips with the alchemy of glazing, I hope it will open your eyes to some of the myriad possibilities and encourage you to push yourself further than you ever believed possible.

Introduction

***The Great Pottery Throw Down* has undoubtedly created a resurgence of interest in and enthusiasm for ceramics and all things clay. Prior to the programme starting all those series ago, there had been a serious decline in teaching pottery, with schools and colleges closing departments and selling off their equipment. Many of these establishments are now looking to reintroduce the subject but progress is slow in these economically difficult times, meaning there are still few options, even to do a night class which is, for many people, the gateway to discovering this amazingly exciting and versatile material. So, we thought, what is needed is a book to sit alongside the programme that will demonstrate all the basic skills required and perhaps help to spark a new obsession.**

The journey begins here – happy potting!

About this book

Clay is a unique material that gives endless opportunity for personal expression, whether you want to create decorative, sculptural or functional work. This book aims to provide you with all the basic information you need, without overwhelming you with technical detail.

Chapter 1 is all about how to get started, including where to look for inspiration and information about tools, equipment and clays, as well as the essential stages of clay preparation and handling.

Next, we demonstrate the skills of hand building and throwing. This is followed by a series of projects inspired by *The Great Pottery Throw Down* challenges from over the years. These projects will help develop those basic skills into forms for use or decoration. Clear step-by-step photos take you through the processes from start to finish and there are lots of useful tips along the way that you can take forward into your own work.

The final chapter, 'Finishing Techniques', shows examples of the surface treatments used to decorate the various projects using simple, easy-to-achieve methods, and also includes an introduction to firing.

All the information in this book is designed to teach an understanding of the skills required to work with clay and to build up confidence. It is by no means a definitive guide, because most potters develop their own individual approach to clay after initial training and we all interpret things slightly differently as we learn. It is important to understand that the book is not an end in itself but a starting point from which we hope you will go on to develop your own methods, ideas and unique style.

Have fun – this could change your life!

The key stages of ceramics

It's useful to have an overview of the different stages involved in the creation of ceramics. The steps outlined here are the most common, though some stages may not apply depending on the route you decide to take with your work.

1. Developing ideas from sources of inspiration
2. Deciding on the best method for making
3. Preparing the clay
4. Making the form using your chosen method (including surface decoration if it is applied pre-construction – for example, texture on slabs)
5. Decorating the surface of greenware (unfired works) using a post-construction technique (for example, any slip technique)
6. Drying the form thoroughly
7. Bisque firing – the first firing that changes the clay to a permanent state
8. Decorating the surface using a post-bisque firing technique (for example, underglaze or glaze)
9. Glost firing – the final firing to the clay's optimal temperature that seals the glaze to the surface and makes it impermeable

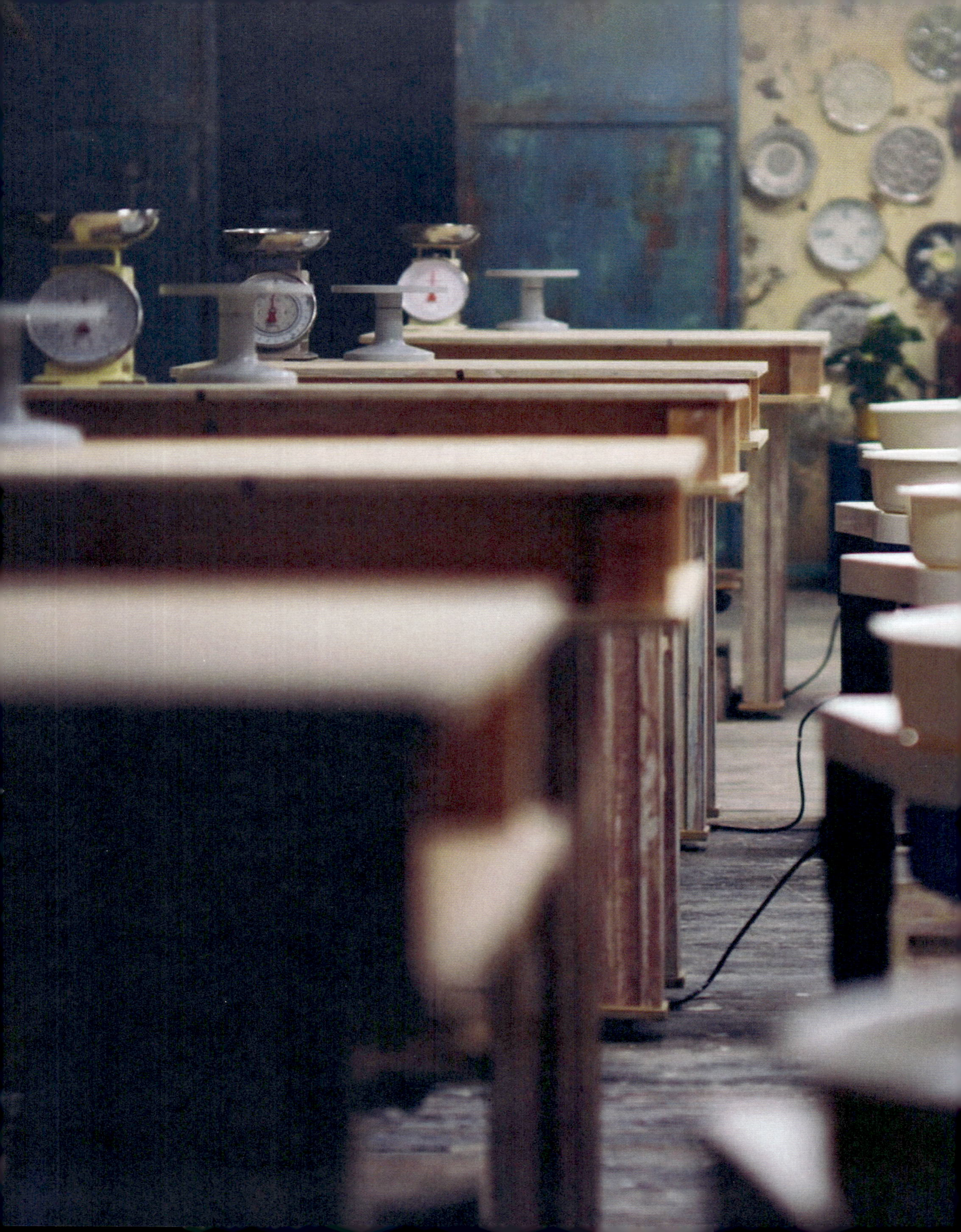

Getting started

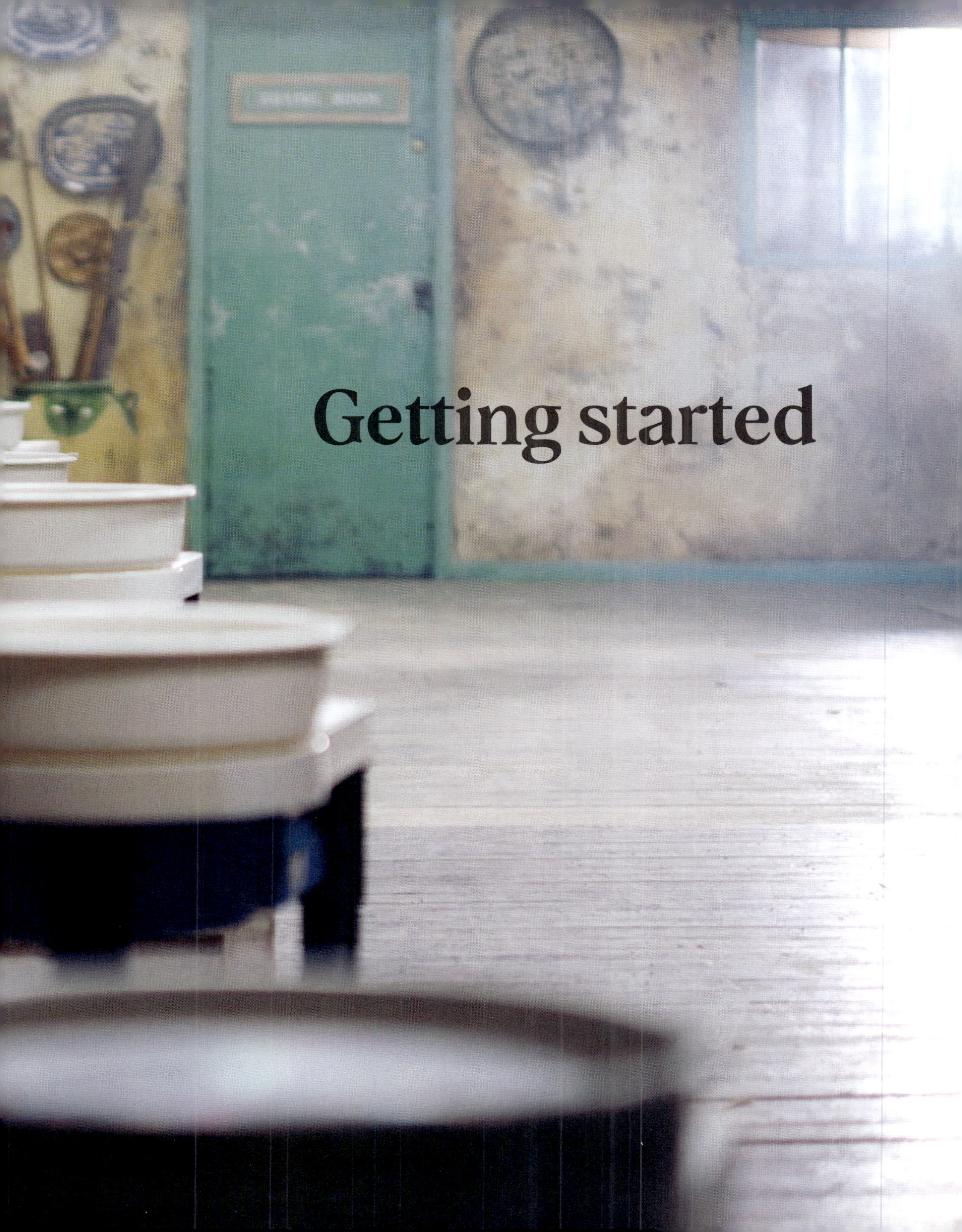

Design inspiration

Design considerations may not figure in your thoughts when you first start out on your pottery journey; in fact, you will almost certainly just want to get your hands into the clay to make something. The very word 'design' can seem daunting, because it suggests that you need a certain level of artistic ability. So where do you start?

WHERE TO FIND INSPIRATION

In reality, inspiration is all around us: everything has a shape, colour or texture, in both nature and in the man-made world. The key lies in learning to see – looking at things and recording those that excite you. So the first thing to do when something attracts your attention is to ask yourself why. Is it the shape or the colour? Maybe it has a surface quality or a pattern that particularly appeals. Or it could be simply the way that light interacts with the thing you are looking at.

Look at other potters' work, too (without copying it, of course), and record the things you like about it: shape, colour, texture, balance, small details – such as the position of a handle or spout, the angle of a rim, or the way a lid fits – and so on.

KEEP NOTES

Once you've identified something that appeals to you, make a record so that you can come back to it and refine it later. Pottery has been around for literally thousands of years, so there's a rich seam of historic artefacts to delve into as well as amazing contemporary work.

Look for inspiration outside the world of ceramics, too. The curve of a branch, the arch of a church window, geometric shapes in a modern building, the colours of lichen or autumn leaves: if something ignites a spark in you, then it's a potential source of ideas for your pottery.

Record these details either on your mobile phone or in a small sketchbook. In many ways, using a sketchbook is a better method for recording details because it requires you to look for a longer period of time and in so doing consider what you are recording – it locks an idea into the brain better. You don't need to have amazing drawing skills – the sketchbook is for you alone. Alongside your drawings, make notes about alternative ideas or details that will help to develop the idea even further.

Carry a treasure collection bag with you when you're out for a walk in the country or along a beach and fill it with things that catch your attention. It could be something with an interesting tone, angle or surface – anything you feel could translate in some way to your work.

IDENTIFY THINGS THAT ARE REALLY PERSONAL TO YOU

Many of the most memorable makes on *The Great Pottery Throw Down* have occurred when the potters have decorated their pieces in a really personal way. For example, they might incorporate something like a childhood memory, a motif that represents their home town or country, an object associated with their favourite hobby, a miniature version of their pet dog or cat, or even a particular phrase or line of poetry. Some go even further, drawing on their emotions to create semi-abstract pieces that represent a particular time in their life and how they felt. What people and experiences have shaped your own life? What objects best represent you and your personality? You don't have to make every single piece a personal statement, of course, but there will be some projects that simply cry out for this kind of approach and it will certainly make your work stand out.

TRY RECORDING IDEAS IN CLAY

The final part of developing a style of your own involves testing your ideas in clay – and this is vital because you cannot plan for all eventualities on paper. Often, details that could not have been anticipated only occur in the making process, so it is good practice to iron these out before committing to a full body of work.

Keep your experimental test pieces and record all details relating to them, such as weights of clay, type of clay, making method, firing temperature etc. If things don't work the way you had envisaged, you will then have all the information you need to make adjustments.

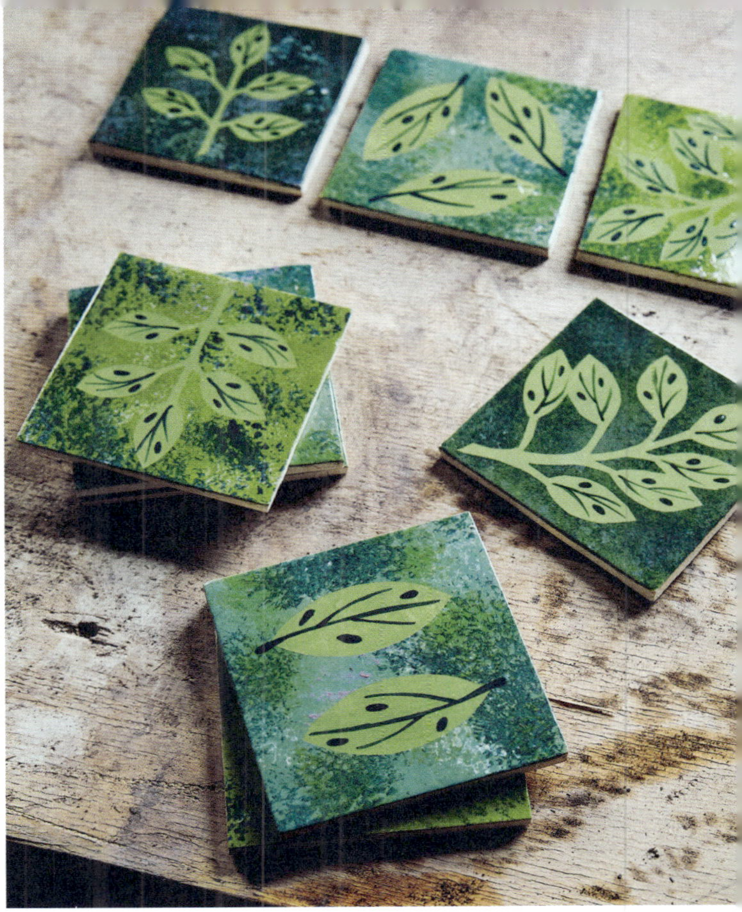

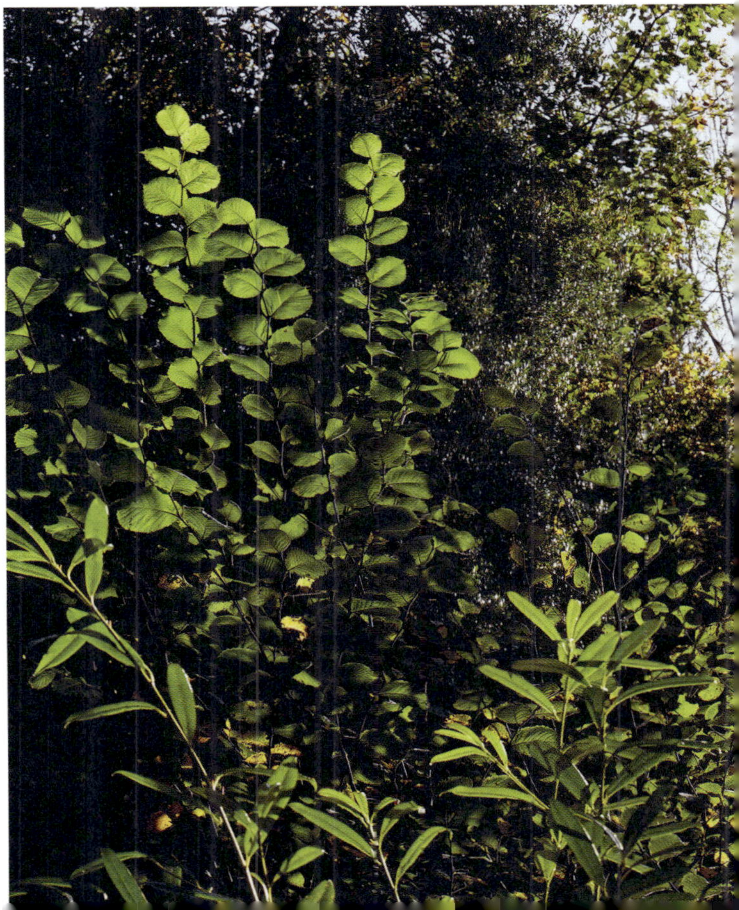

NOTE

You may not always be allowed to photograph things in museums and galleries and you should always ask permission before photographing makers' work at fairs and markets.

Setting up your space

The key to success when setting up your space is planning and being prepared. You need to have the right tools and equipment, the right clay, an organized space to work in and a good understanding of health and safety issues (see page 170). Most importantly, you need a clear idea of what you want to make, so you have everything you need at hand.

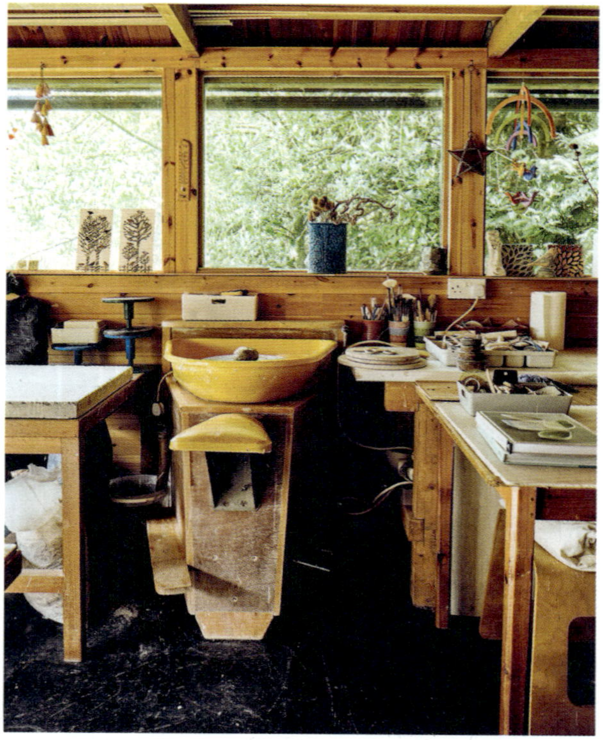

When you are just starting out you might be working at the kitchen table, but this is not ideal: clay dust is a health and safety hazard, so you will have to be meticulous in cleaning up when you have finished.

Access to water is essential. Ideally, a sink should have a sump installed below it to catch clay and other materials, but it's highly unlikely that you'll have this in a domestic situation, in which case the next best thing is a sturdy bucket of water.

A better space to work in would be a garage, cellar or garden shed, where you can set up a work bench and shelves to sit alongside any equipment you may have invested in and where you can plan the flow of your working practice to utilize its best potential.

Consider how you intend to work and plan the space accordingly. A small wheel will not be difficult to position and it may be possible to tuck it under another surface when it is not in use, so this is a good starting option. Larger wheels cannot be easily moved and can take up considerable space.

Even a small kiln must be sited on a suitable fireproof surface, away from anything flammable and with plenty of space around it.

If you are planning to spend time at the wheel, it would be helpful to have the wedging area next to it and a surface for the thrown items to sit on.

Have batts and tools close at hand so that you don't have to get up from the wheel each time you need something.

These are just a few basic considerations that should apply to any making method or task.

YOU WILL NEED

Good light
Ideally your light source should be daylight or good overhead lighting, but failing that an anglepoise lamp with a daylight bulb will work.

A work bench or sturdy table
Install a storage shelf underneath it if possible.

A surface for clay preparation
You will need this to wedge and knead your clay on (see page 26). A good surface for this is a paving slab, available from DIY stores or builder's merchants. Do not use an absorbent surface, because this will remove moisture from your clay and make it difficult to work with.

A place to store your work in progress
Adjustable shelving is ideal to accommodate different scales of work, but a cupboard (or even an old fridge) is great because it keeps the clay at a constant state to work with if you have to leave things half finished.

A place to dry your work
Open shelving positioned in an area that is not subject to draughts is vital. Drying work should have an even and consistent flow of air circulating around it.

A place to store fired work (both bisque ware and finished pieces)
Again, dedicated shelving is ideal.

An area to store your clay and other ceramic materials
Clay should be stored in a dedicated cool area if possible, but this could be in a large plastic box under your work bench if space is limited. Dry materials should be contained in airtight containers and stored in a dedicated space.

A container for recycling clay
Have a large bin or bucket for collecting clay to be reclaimed (see page 29). From this, more manageable amounts can be transferred to buckets to slake down (see page 30) so that the task does not become too onerous.

Storage for smaller items
These smaller pieces of equipment and tools could be hung on wall hooks to help keep them out of the way.

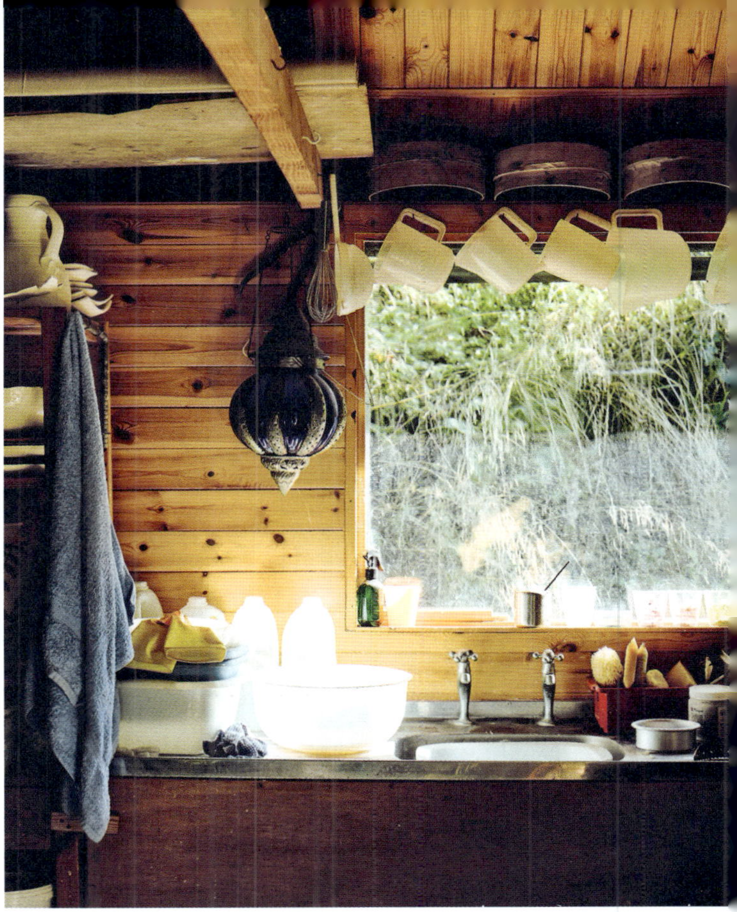

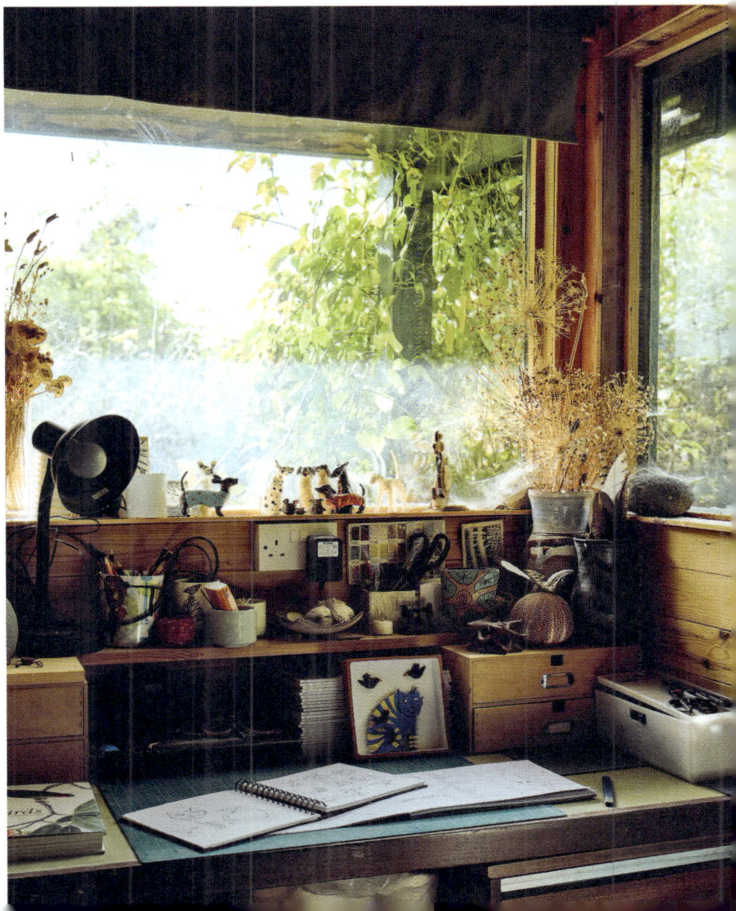

Tools

There is something very seductive about tools: they say 'buy me, buy me' – and before you know it, you have a box full of things you rarely use. The temptation is to get everything because you don't know exactly what you will need, but many items can be sourced from the kitchen and others adapted from other things. Frankly, the best tools you will ever possess are your hands – you can do most things with them and just a few tools and props.

So, if you are just starting out, here's a guide to a basic tool kit.

Essential tools

CUTTING WIRES (1)

You will need at least one of these. There are several types available to buy, including a standard version that comes in a basic kit from a pottery supplier. Made from wooden dowelling and finely twisted metal wire, it is a perfectly functional cutting wire.

Alternatively, you can make your own from wooden curtain rings and fishing wire. This is a cheap and easy alternative as one reel of fishing wire will last for many years, if not a whole career!

KIDNEYS, RIBS AND SCRAPING TOOLS

Rectangular metal scraping / smoothing tool (2)
Also known as a palette rib, this useful tool is good for angled surfaces that need a sharp edge and for smoothing the surface of large slabs.

Large red silicone or rubber rib (3)
Very flexible; ideal for smoothing rounded surfaces and cleaning the last drops of slip or glaze from buckets and bowls. Not absolutely essential, but certainly useful.

Small, flexible rubber or silicone ribs (4)
Good for smoothing the interiors of pots and difficult-to-reach areas. Very useful and available in varying degrees of firmness, from flexible to hard.

Standard rigid metal kidney (5)
Essential tool for scraping and smoothing – a tool-box must have. As Rich always says, an old bank or store card also work well as an alternative kidney.

Surform or rasp blade (6)
This is possibly one of the most useful tools you can have. Use it to level rims, reduce the thickness of clay walls, level foot rings and create textured surface detail.

Serrated metal rib (7)
A most useful tool for scoring areas before joining, scraping back surfaces both externally and internally, and for creating textured finishes.

A POTTER'S PIN (8)

Used for many purposes – from bursting air bubbles in clay to decorative techniques such as sgraffito – this is a tool-box essential but you could make your own by setting a bodkin into an old wine cork. They are available in several gauges, from fine upwards, and it is useful to have a couple of sizes.

KNIFE (9)

Essential tool at all stages of making, its uses are obvious. You do not need to buy a specialist knife – a craft knife works well as an alternative.

Continued overleaf

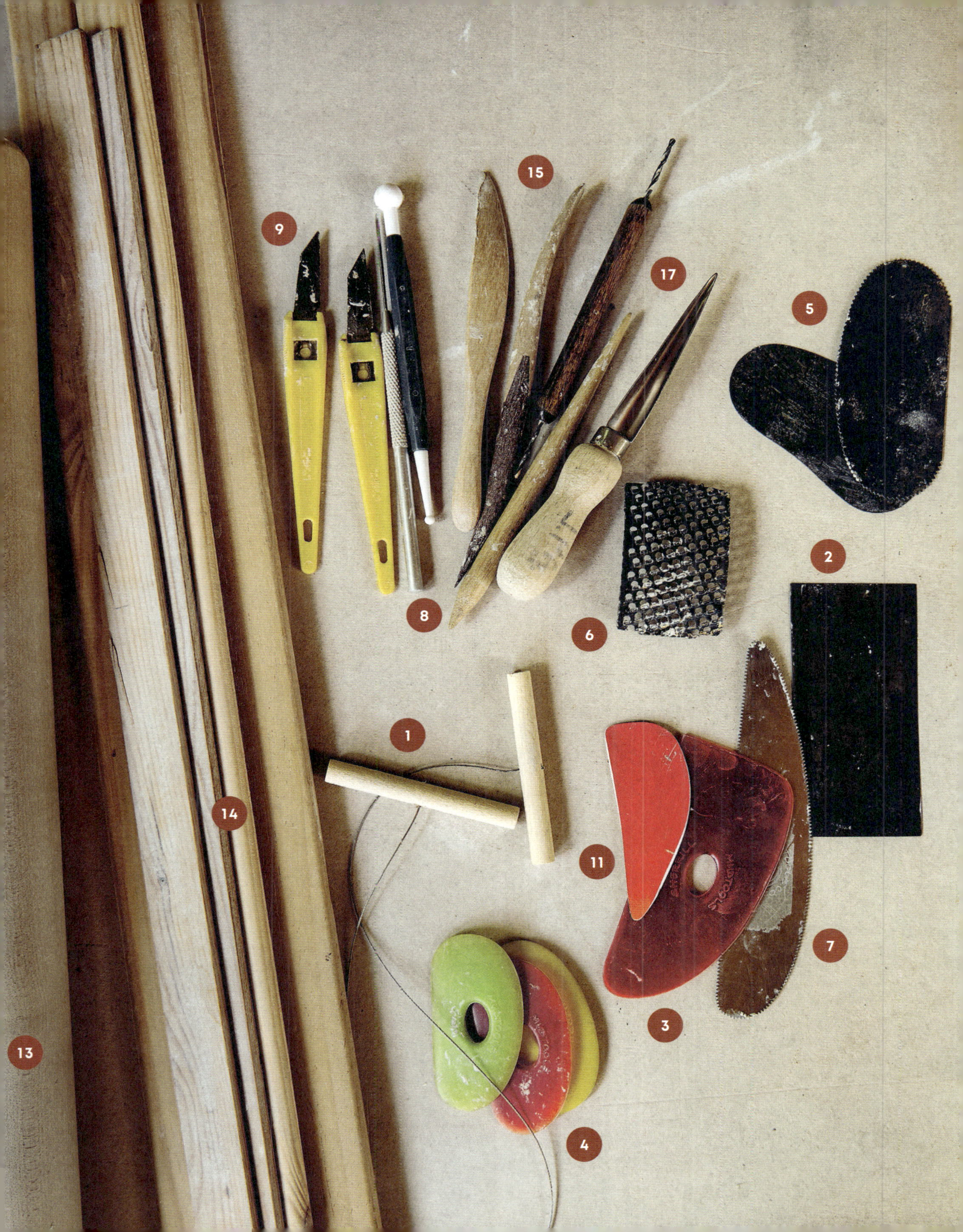
15
9
17
5
2
8
6
1
14
11
7
3
13
4

SPONGES (10)

These are always handy for mopping up and applying surface treatments such as slip and sometimes glaze. When throwing they are useful for removing surplus water from interiors. Beware of overusing them, though, because they can remove the fine clay particles from a surface, leaving heavier content such as grog (ground-down fired clay added to strengthen soft clay) exposed.

Natural sponges are the best choice for even slip application. It's useful to have a selection of sizes, from very small for fine detail to palm-sized for quick application over larger areas.

Non-essential but handy-to-have tools

HOME-MADE RIBS (11)

Useful for interior surfaces where access is limited. Make your own from old bank or store cards cut to shape with a pair of scissors. The red one shown in the image has a narrow end (useful for difficult and restricted angles), a straight edge (useful for right-angled edges) and a curved edge for rounded interior or concave surfaces.

WOODEN THROWING RIB (12)

Again, these are available in a huge range of shapes and sizes, but you could easily improvise with ribs of other types.

Tools for slabbing

ROLLING PIN (13)

Choose a long wooden pin without handles – pins with handles are not wide enough to roll a decent slab and using them often results in fingers getting snagged in the clay.

ROLLER GUIDES (14)

These allow you to roll even slabs to specific thicknesses. Available in long, thin strips from DIY stores. Choose a depth of thickness to meet your slabbing needs and cut pairs of the same length to accommodate the size of slab you are likely to roll. You will find it useful to have a range of thicknesses to suit different clay types. For instance, porcelain is usually better in thin sections, so the guides need only be millimetres thick, but a large sculptural item needs a thicker wall to support it so thicker guides are needed.

PLASTIC SHEETING/FABRIC

Plastic is the best surface to roll out on because it allows you to both lift the slab in place without it falling off, and easily lift the clay off when required. You will see plastic being used for rolling slabs in the projects in this book. The advantage of using plastic instead of fabric is that it does not texture the surface in any way. Fabric is a good alternative if you want to incorporate the surface texture as part of the overall design.

Modelling and trimming tools

WOODEN MODELLING TOOLS (15)

These are the only tools that individual makers will need to match to their needs. Where possible, choose ones with different

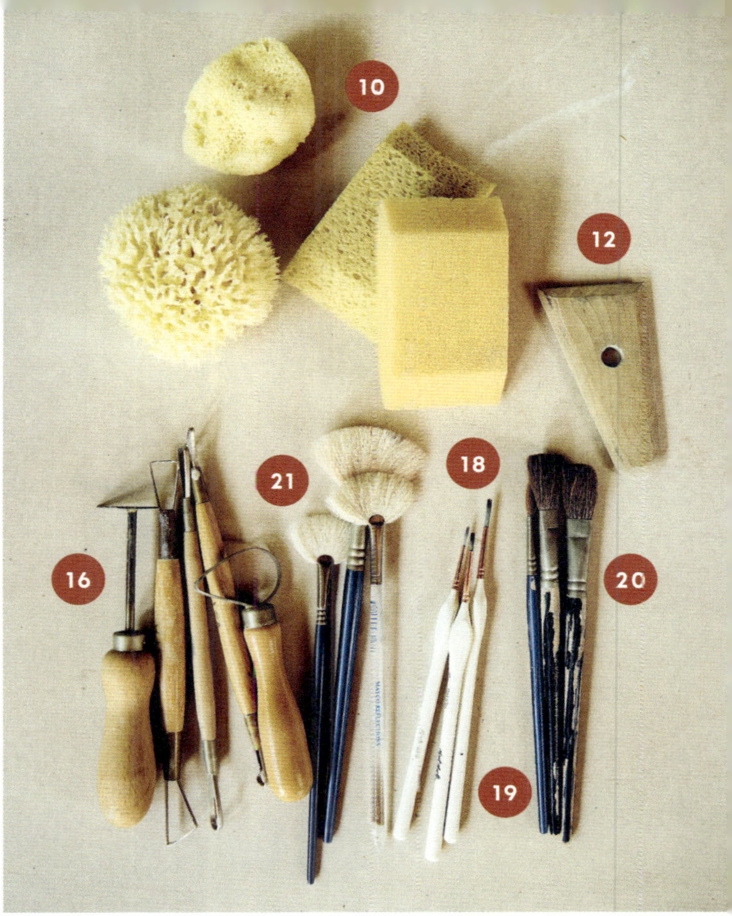

tools at each end for different jobs. Maybe go for three or four of this type of tool to begin with and build up more as your experience increases. You will find there is little value in buying the multi-packs of tools available because you will probably only use a few of them.

LOOP TOOLS (16)

These are most often used for turning the surfaces of thrown pots, but are also useful for scraping excess clay from specific areas and certain decorative techniques. Buy just one to begin with – a medium-sized tool with one loop and a squared-off end should be all you require until you have a specific need for another shape.

HOLE-MAKING TOOLS (17)

These are very useful to have. Choose one that can make a range of hole sizes and another that looks like it has a different-size drill bit attached to each end of a wooden stem. You could, of course also make one yourself from old drill bits and a short length of dowel.

Brushes

Brushes are required for so many things when working with clay and you should have a selection for different purposes:

GENERAL-PURPOSE BRUSH FOR APPLYING JOINING SLIP

It doesn't have to be the best quality.

FINE TIPS (18)

For specific decorative tasks such as slip work and other surface decoration applications.

MEDIUM TIPS (19)

For applications on larger areas and bold surface treatments.

WIDE HEADS (20)

For applying slips or glaze to large areas.

FAN-TYPE (21)

Particularly useful for applying brush-on glaze.

AN OLD TOOTHBRUSH

Brilliant for both slipping and scoring. Simply dip in water, then brush over the surface in the same way you would if brushing your teeth – the action creates the slip and the bristles score the surface.

Kilns

Once you've decided that pottery is something you want to pursue, some pieces of equipment are essential. And the kiln – along with a wheel for those who want to throw – is the most important. These will be the most expensive items you need to buy, so it's important to make sure they meet all your requirements.

Not ready to buy?

If you are doing an evening class or short course in pottery, you will likely have access to a kiln to fire your work. Failing this, if you don't want to go to the expense of buying a kiln of your own you could use a site such as kilnshare.com, which shows local potters who have kiln space to rent out. Alternatively, you could approach a local college or school with a kiln and offer them a small fee to fire your work.

DON'T GO MAD BUYING EQUIPMENT!

Ceramic equipment can be expensive to purchase new and you should only consider buying it when you are sure you want to pursue your interest in pottery. There are several platforms that advertise and sell second-hand pottery equipment and are worth looking at as an alternative to new.

Choosing a kiln

Kilns are available in a large range of sizes, from small mains-operated hobby kilns to massive commercial ones that require a special power supply. Not all kilns are electric – gas is also a popular choice for those without an electricity supply at their kiln site or who want to make reduction stoneware. Then there are kilns for raku firing and wood-firing kilns that are generally built *in situ* in rural areas because of the fumes they emit. However, for beginners the easiest and most obvious first choice is an electric kiln and this is what we will focus on here.

UNDERSTAND THE OPTIONS

Electric kilns are generally the best choice for beginners, especially for those living in urban environments, because they burn cleanly and are available in many sizes – some of them small enough to fire in a domestic situation.

Sophisticated controllers / programmers allow you to avoid having to 'kiln-sit' (attend or oversee the firing) as the programme automatically turns up the temperature at the right time for the kiln to fire smoothly.

Top-loading kilns are usually less expensive than front loaders, easily fit into small-scale workshops, and are simple to install.

Front-loading kilns usually have a solid metal framework with a more substantial firebrick wall. As a result they are heavier and retain heat for much longer. They are more expensive to buy and install, but much harder wearing than top loaders.

QUESTIONS TO ADDRESS

Space to house the kiln This will to a large extent dictate the size of the kiln you buy.

Accessibility to the kiln site A large kiln will not fit through a little door. Similarly, moving a heavy kiln from the delivery vehicle to site can be a nightmare if you live on the side of a hill and it has to be carried some distance!

Power supply Obviously, an electric kiln needs an electricity supply – and large kilns often need a bigger supply than most domestic situations provide. Make sure your supply is adequate for the kiln's needs.

Scale of work It goes without saying that the scale of your work will dictate the size of the kiln you require, but be aware that if you need to fire something in a hurry and your kiln is big, you will waste precious energy. It is far better, and more economical, to fire a small kiln more often.

Safety Ideally, the kiln should not be sited in the room where you work – but if it has to be, fire your pieces overnight to avoid breathing in potentially toxic fumes given off in the process.

Kiln site The kiln should be sited away from flammable materials or structures, with enough space to move around and access it easily.

Floor Make sure the floor of your workshop can support the weight of the kiln and tolerate heat.

VERY IMPORTANT

A top-loading kiln can be hazardous for people who suffer with back problems – especially when lifting large or heavy work up, then over and down into the firing chamber. A front loader would be a safer choice in this case.

New versus old

If you can afford it, buy a new kiln because older kilns tend to be heavier, less efficient and thus more expensive to fire. They can also often be a false economy because they may need expensive overhauling. However, great bargains can be had from people who bought new kilns then lost interest in pottery. There are also excellent websites specializing in second-hand pottery equipment and materials.

If you decide to buy new, most pottery suppliers will have a good range of kilns to choose from and be able to advise you on the best size and type to meet your needs. However, it pays to shop around before committing yourself to a purchase – often a supplier will do a deal if you say you have found something similar elsewhere that is cheaper! They may, for example, throw the kiln furniture into the price if it was not included initially, or upgrade a controller to a more sophisticated model. Nothing is lost by asking to negotiate.

Kiln furniture

Kiln interiors are equipped with shelves and supports and these often come as part of the package with a new kiln. Tubular props are available in different sizes and are stackable to allow you to adjust the height of the shelves.

Triangular star or pin stilts are a popular method of raising earthenware and glazed pottery wares off the kiln shelf. Each stilt has three arms with an upward and and downward point which give minimal contact with a surface and are knocked off after firing. Star stilts have short metal pins and are reusuable.

Ask the kiln supplier for suitable furniture for your model if it is not included in the price.

Wheels

Throwing wheels are available in many sizes and shapes, but when choosing one your main consideration should be comfort, especially if this is going to be your primary making method because it can be a great strain on the back. An electric wheel is the most practical choice for beginners and established potters alike for producing large batches of work. Some people choose a momentum wheel for the particular aesthetic qualities it can give to work, but this is not the easiest choice to begin with, as it requires both body and hand co-ordination (a bit like driving a car).

Electric wheels

RANGE AVAILABLE

Available in table-top types, small models that can be stored under a surface when not in use, and in large wooden-framed versions with or without seats.

USES

Throwing, turning or trimming production tableware or decorative forms; turning clay models for plaster mould making, or as a banding wheel for the application of slip, underglaze or glaze on greenware or bisque-fired forms.

Whirlers, lining/banding wheels

These wheels are not powered by a motor but are essential pieces of equipment for hand building and decorating.

RANGE AVAILABLE AND THEIR USES

Bench whirler
A small wheel that sits on the work surface for rotating forms as they are constructed. They are available in several heights for different types of work, but a generic-sized option is a good choice to begin with and is an almost essential requirement for hand builders.

Lining or banding wheels
These are floor standing and adjustable, allowing you to set the work at exactly the right height as a form grows in size during construction. Both types of wheel are generally made from steel or aluminium and are available from most pottery suppliers.

Choosing the right clay

Having a basic understanding of the origins of clay and the qualities that define each type is useful, but in truth the vast majority of makers just purchase clay from a ceramic supplier to meet their specific requirements and get on with the job of making, knowing that the outcome is more or less guaranteed.

Information about clay is widely available for those who want to learn more, but for the purposes of this book the emphasis is on choosing the right clay from the vast number available when you are starting out.

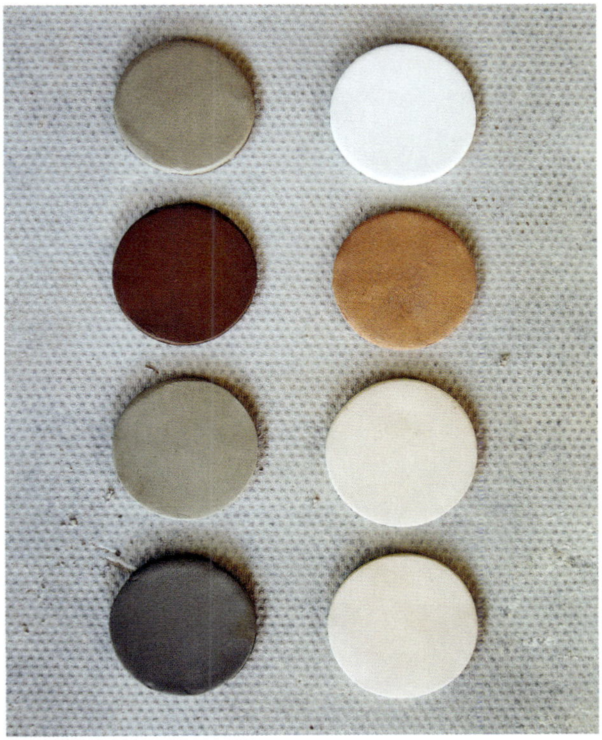

Clay categories

Clay is generally classified into three main categories – earthenware, stoneware and porcelain – each defined by the temperature it is fired to and the consequent density and strength of the body.

When you look in your clay catalogue, however, you will see lists of clays that have a very wide firing range, enabling them to be fired at earthenware (1080–1180°C/1976–2156°F); middle temperature (1080–1250°C/1976–2282°F); stoneware (1120–1280°C/ 2048–2336°F); and porcelain (up to 1300°C/2372°F) temperature ranges. So how do you choose?

The projects in this book use different types of clay, which are all shown in the image on the left in both their green (formed but unfired) and fired states. Until you become more experienced, these four types should cover all your needs. We have not included porcelain, because it can be a difficult clay to master.

Top row: Wide firing white/cream body that can be fired at earthenware or stoneware temperatures. It is a good throwing body and a great choice for colourful surface decoration. It has a firing range of 1080–1250°C (1976–2282°F).

Second row: Red earthenware, also referred to as terracotta. It needs a white slip covering before colourful decoration is applied. It has a firing range of 1080–1180°C (1976–2156°F).

Third row: Buff stoneware – an excellent, smooth, general-purpose clay, suitable for throwing or hand building. It has a firing range of 1120–1280°C (2048–2336°F).

Fourth row: Speckled stoneware – good for throwing or hand building. The speckle can react with glazes to give lovely surface qualities. It has a firing range of 1120–1280°C (2048–2336°F).

Choosing a clay that is right for you

Deciding on the right clay can be difficult, because the choice is so great, but here are some basic questions to help you narrow down your options.

FIRING TEMPERATURE

This choice will be dictated by your kiln's firing capability, but the higher the firing temperature, the more expensive the cost, no matter what fuel is used.

FIRING METHOD – ELECTRIC OR GAS?

For those just starting out these are the two main options. Of the two, electric is the easiest choice for most people. However, gas may be the only option, and will enable you to carry out reduction firing for specific glaze and body finishes. Some clays are more suited to reduction firings than others – the manufacturer's catalogue will guide you to suitable clays for each type.

CLAY COLOUR

Your choice will be mainly influenced by the surface decoration you want to apply. Red clay bodies will influence the final fired colour of the underglaze or glaze, however you could apply a light coloured slip background to help neutralise this effect. This is a good option if you want a contrast between clay colour and glaze colour.

Alternatively, if you want a vibrant colour response, choose a white clay and you will avoid having to apply slip.

A final option are clays with additions that give them a speckled appearance when fired – the speckles themselves will react with a glaze to produce a very distinctive surface. Manufacturers often suggest glazes to fit well with these types of clay.

MAKING METHOD

Your making method will directly influence the type of clay you choose. Throwing is generally easier with a smooth, plastic clay. Hand-building clays benefit from the addition of some grog, which gives increased resistance to warping and cracking, but be aware that fine detailing or turning can be compromised.

Most clay manufacturer's catalogues have a suitability code to further help you decide. It may read something like this:

- **a.** Clays good for general domestic ware
- **b.** Clays suitable for larger domestic wares
- **c.** Clays suitable for big pots – bread crocks etc.
- **d.** Clays for general-purpose use – throwing, slabbing, coiling, etc.
- **e.** Especially good for throwing
- **f.** Especially good for slabbing and hand building
- **g.** Clays for larger constructions and tiles needing good warp resistance

Buying and storing clay

The amount of clay you should buy will depend on your intended output and the way you work. Throwers generally get through clay much quicker than hand builders, because the process is faster. When hand building, a few bags of clay will last quite a long time, especially if you reclaim all your scraps. However, one of the main factors for how much you purchase will be storage space.

You will find that clay is generally cheaper to buy in large quantities, but if you have not tested the clay, resist the temptation to do this. Ask for a sample first and test to check that it meets your requirements – then buy in quantities that you can practically store.

Keep clay in tightly sealed bags to retain moisture, preferably in a dark, frost-free place.

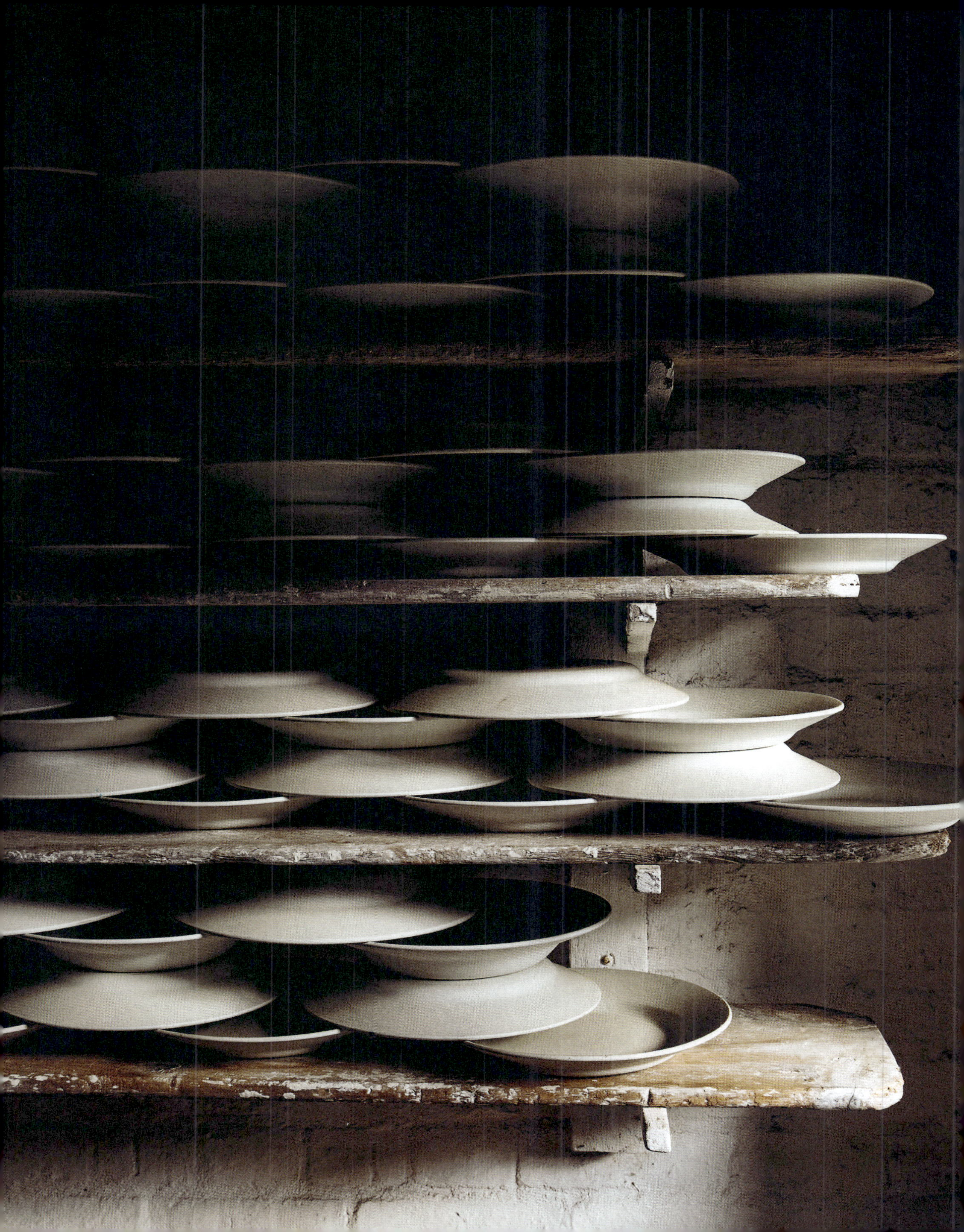

Clay preparation

The single most important consideration for a successful outcome is the preparation and treatment of your clay. New bags of clay will have been de-aired in the manufacturing process and generally be ready to use, but most potters still wedge or knead their clay before commencing work to make sure there are no pockets of trapped air that could cause work to blister, crack or even explode during firing.

JUDGES' TIP

If possible, wedge your clay on a sturdy work bench that is just below waist height. The process involves a lot of force and this allows the clay to fall from a greater height, thus enabling you to save energy.

Wedging

Wedging is an essential process for several reasons but, most basically, it serves to mix the clay thoroughly and remove air bubbles that can cause the form to explode or shatter when fired. It is also an essential step in the reclaiming process and the first step to prepare clay for use, whatever the making method you are planning to employ. It is also the best way of mixing clay bodies for specific effects.

1. Whether you are beginning with clay straight from the bag or reclaimed, form the mass into a brick shape, then lift it with one hand and allow the front end to fall onto the wedging bench so that the back end remains raised slightly.

   Position the cutting wire under the raised end of the clay mass as close to the centre as possible and cut it in half by drawing the wire upwards.

2. Lift the front half of the brick (photo 2A) and turn it so that when placed on top of the other half the two cut faces are the same way around (photo 2B).

3. Now raise it to shoulder height and slam it back down on top of the other half forcibly, allowing the weight of the clay to do the work for you. Neaten the clay mass back to the original brick shape by beating it with your hand, then repeat the process until the clay has an even consistency and colour, and is air free. It will take some time and probably involve at least 20 cut and lifts, but keeping control of the shape will make the job faster and easier.

1

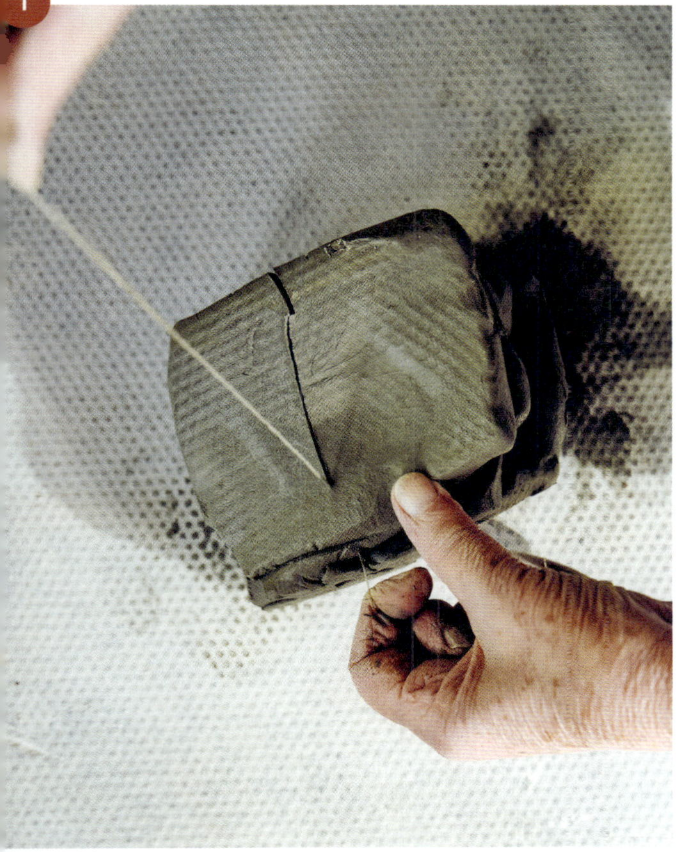

2A

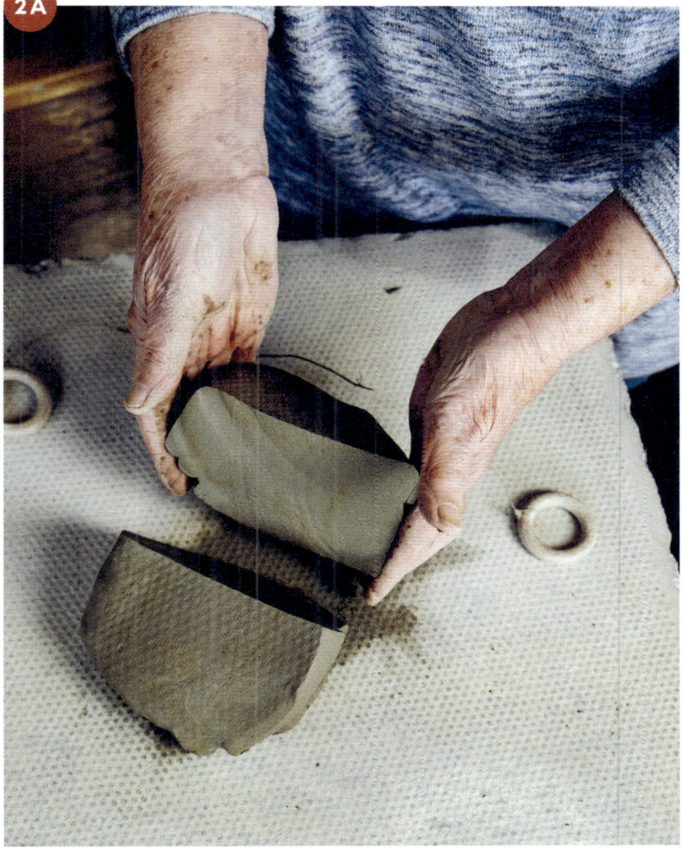

2B

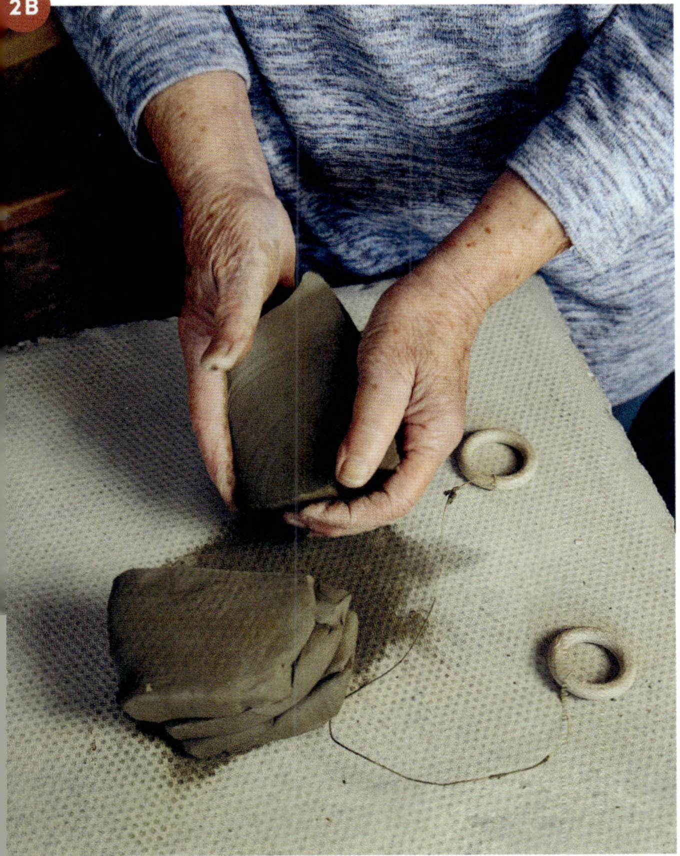

3

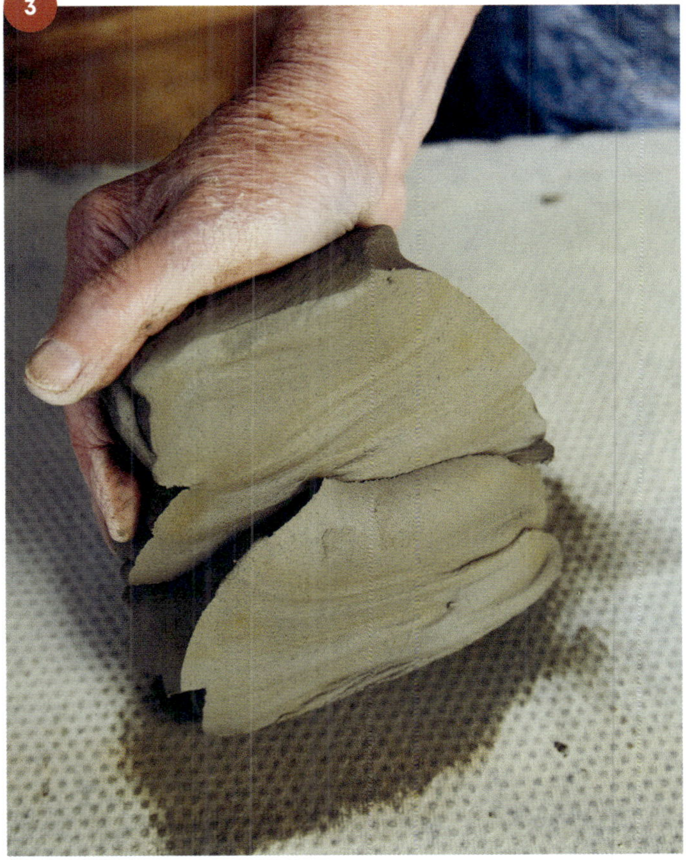

Kneading

Kneading is another vital step in the preparation of clay and is helpful to even out the clay body and remove any air bubbles left behind after wedging. However, properly wedged clay will need only minimal kneading, so it is worth perfecting the technique to save time and effort at this stage.

WHY KNEAD?

Water is constantly evaporating from clay, making it appear wet around the edges but much drier in the middle. Kneading the clay redistributes the water, but the evaporation process starts again almost immediately, so a good tip is to only prepare enough clay to complete the project you are working on and keep it sealed in plastic at all times until required.

Generally, kneading is done immediately prior to starting work and it should become an integral part of your working practice.

OX-HEAD KNEADING

This method is named after the shape that is formed as the clay is kneaded. Many potters find it the easier of the two methods outlined here.

Position your hands on opposite sides of the clay mass, with the heels of your hand over the top and your fingers wrapped around the sides to contain it. Push the clay down and away from your body, digging your palms into the clay so that a raised mass remains in the centre. Roll the clay back towards your body and reposition your hands slightly forward on the clay. Repeat the rolling and pushing action, trying not to fold the clay because this will re-introduce air into the body, which will defeat the object of the exercise.

As you knead the clay, the ox-head shape will develop, with the hands forming the eye sockets.

Continue to knead the clay by rocking and pushing until it is smooth and thoroughly mixed, with no air pockets. Cut through the kneaded clay from time to time to check progress.

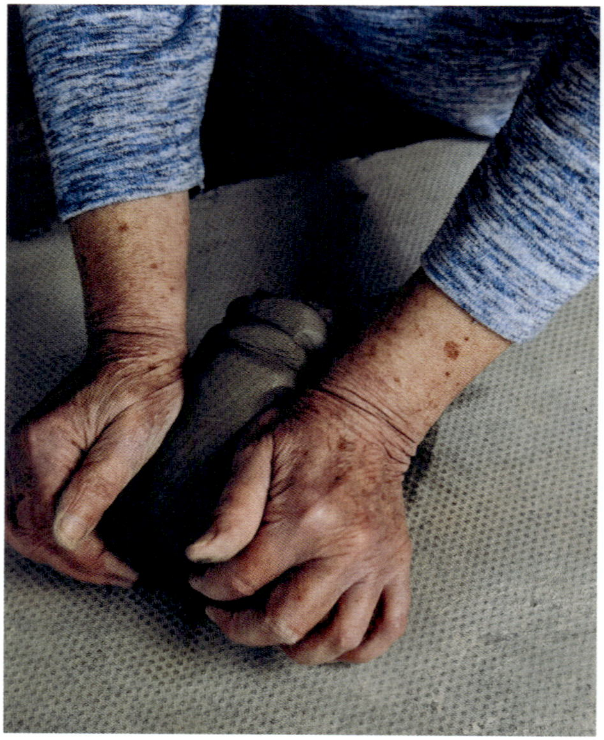

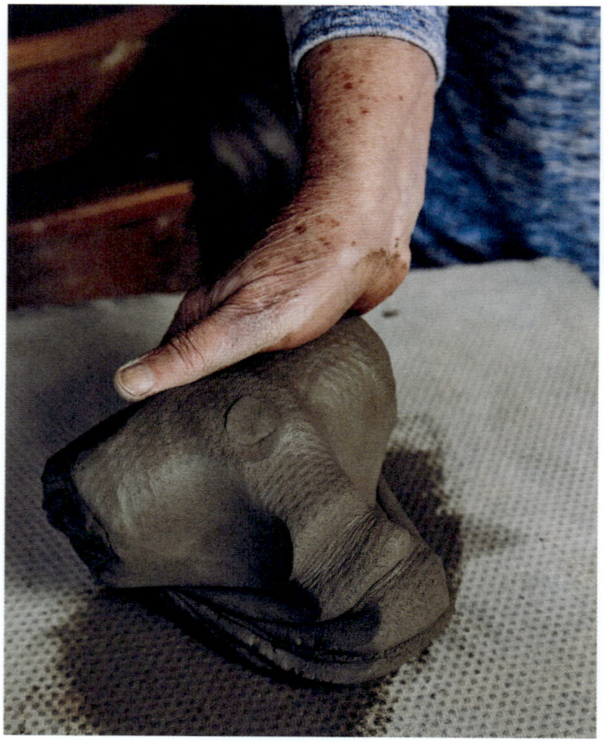

SPIRAL KNEADING

A spiral shape is formed as the clay is processed using this technique. It is more difficult to master than ox-head kneading, but is useful for larger amounts of clay.

Place your hands on opposite sides of a roughly rounded mass of clay. Use your right hand to push down on the clay while rolling it forwards and your left hand to contain the clay from the side and prevent sideways movement. Also use your left hand to rotate the clay mass after each forward movement. This action creates the spiral. Use the weight of your upper body rather than your wrist to keep control of the shape.

You will see the spiral begin to develop as you knead, but cutting through the clay mass from time to time will better show the developing spiral and whether or not you are performing the process correctly.

Continue to rotate the clay anticlockwise, moving your right hand into position for each downward push. The clay is ready when it is smooth and there are no air pockets.

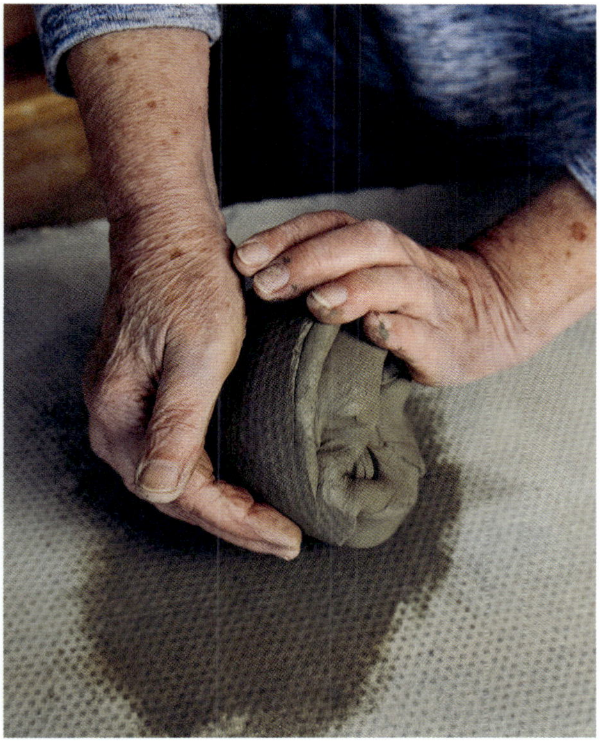

Reclaiming clay

The great thing about clay is that it never needs to be wasted and can be recycled with very little effort. The process for making slip (page 30) demonstrates how to slake clay down, but the method is largely the same for reclaiming greater amounts.

1. Slake down a manageable amount of clay in hot water – leave for at least 24 hours.
2. Siphon off the excess water covering the clay using a slip trailing bulb or soft squeezy bottle.
3. Mix the slurry, then transfer it to an absorbent surface such as a plaster batt to form a layer about 5 cm (2 in.) thick.
4. Check the clay from time to time. When it has dried to a stage where it can be lifted easily from the batt, turn the clay over so that the wetter surface comes into contact with the plaster.
5. Still working on the plaster batt, work the clay into a large brick shape and wedge it thoroughly (see page 26).

JUDGES' TIPS

› **Reclaim clay regularly in smallish amounts to avoid the job becoming onerous.**

› **If you use warm water rather than cold, the clay will slake down much faster.**

› **Reclaimed clay needs to be stored for at least a few weeks to restore plasticity. Keep it in sealed plastic bags and label the bags with dates and clay type. Store in a cool but dry place until ready to use.**

Slip

Slip is simply liquid clay – that is to say, in its simplest form, a clay body mixed with a lot of water to create a fluid that can be used to join sections when constructing a form or mixed with oxides or commercial stains to create colours for surface decoration.

Making a joining slip

A joining slip must be made from the same clay body that you are working with. If you are using several different clays, a separate slip should be made from each.

1. Allow your clay to dry out completely, then break it down into small pieces and place it in a plastic bowl. Crush the clay into small pieces using the end of your rolling pin.
2. Cover the clay in warm water and allow it to break down overnight – this process is called 'slaking down'.
3. Using a spoon, mix the clay thoroughly to form a smooth slurry with no lumps.
4. Transfer the slip to a sealable container and label it accordingly.

Coloured slips

Coloured slips are used for decorating a clay surface and are often best made from the clay body itself – white clays are the most responsive. Suggestions for stain or oxide additions can be found opposite.

1. Wearing a dust mask, crush a small bowl of dried white earthenware clay to dust and weigh out the amount so that you can easily work out how much body stain or oxide to add to colour it.
2. Weigh out the colour accordingly, then transfer it to a pestle and mortar.
3. Add a little water, then thoroughly grind and blend it. Note – some stains or oxides can speckle when used if you miss this step out.
4. Combine the colourant with the dry clay, add more water and mix to the consistency of thick cream.
5. Push the slip through a 60- or 80-mesh sieve suspended on battens over a bowl. If the slip is very liquid, leave it overnight and then siphon off the excess using a slip trailer before transferring the contents to a sealable container and labelling.

OXIDES

0.2–2.5% for light tones
2.5–5% for medium tones
5–10% for dark tones

STAINS

2–5% for light tones
5–10% for medium tones
10–15% for dark tones

Slip made from materials other than a clay body

Slip can be made from materials other than your clay – useful if, for instance, your body of choice is red. There are many recipes to be found on ceramic forums and in books. However, coloured decorating slips can be bought ready mixed from clay suppliers if you don't want to go to the trouble of making your own.

MAKING A JOINING SLIP

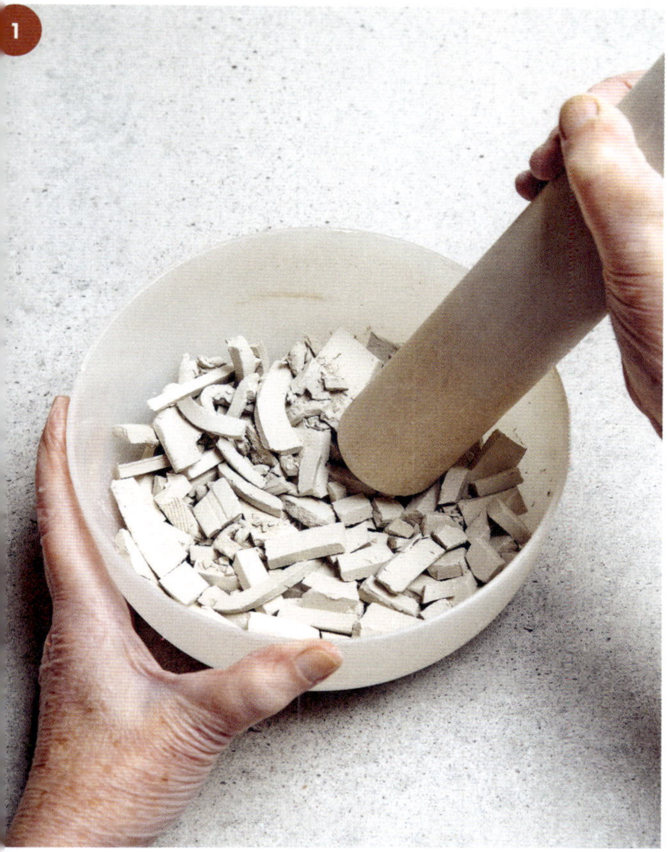

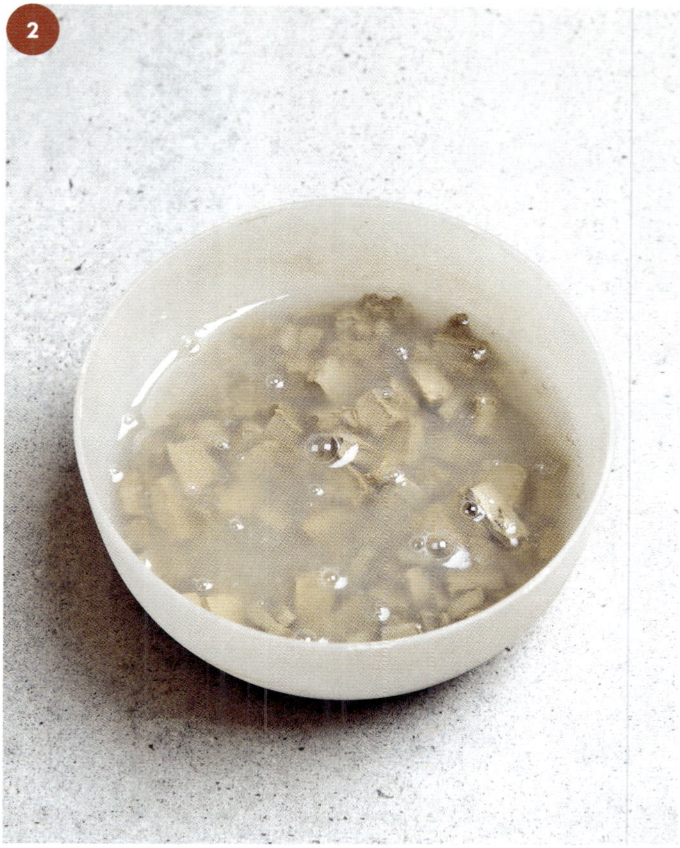

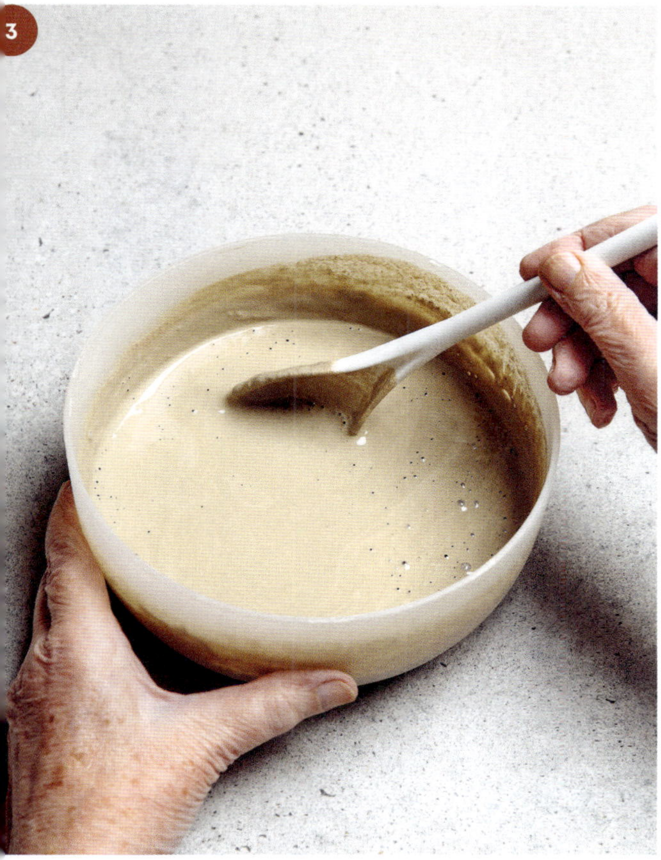

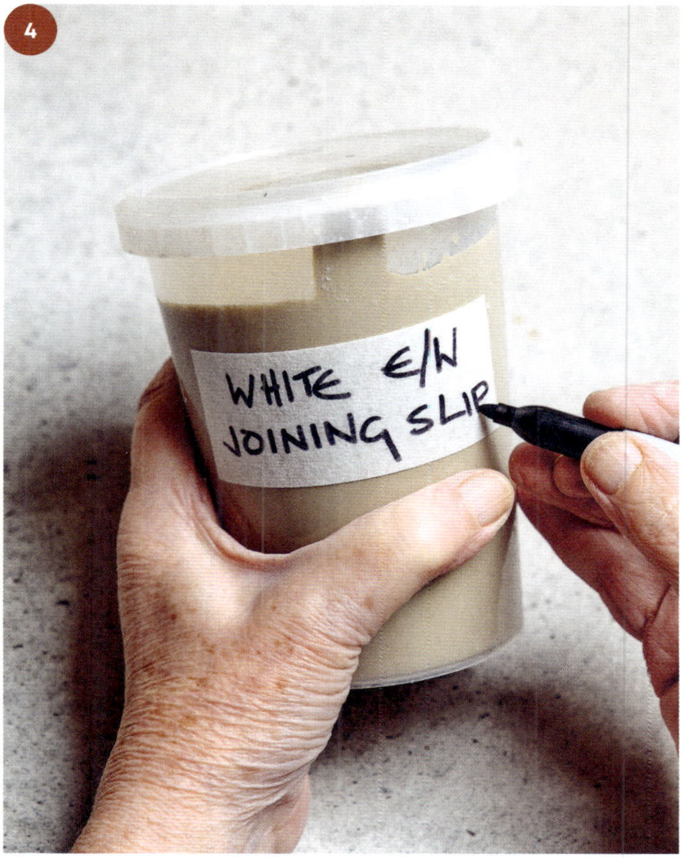

Using moulds

Moulds are wonderfully versatile bits of kit and every maker should have at least a couple of them in their studio.

There are different kinds of moulds for certain ceramic applications – namely press moulds, hump moulds and others for slip casting. However, many moulds are multifunctional and one made for pressing, for example, could also be used for casting. Here we show how to use press moulds and hump moulds, which are the ones you are most likely to use when beginning pottery.

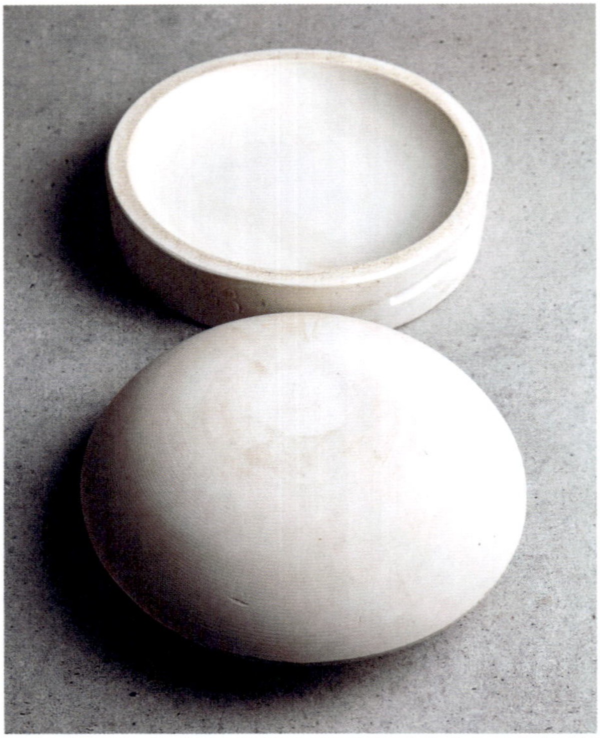

Press mould

1. Roll out a slab of clay large enough to fit your mould on a plastic sheet (see page 40).

   Lift the rolled slab on the plastic sheet and position it over the mould carefully. Release the plastic sheet, then gently ease the clay into the mould using a barely damp sponge, rather than your fingers, to avoid distorting it.

2. Remove the surplus clay at the rim using the side of a batten held flat on the surface of the mould. Still holding the clay in place with the sponge in one hand, carefully draw the batten sideways and backwards in small stages until all the clay is removed and the rim is level.

3. Allow to firm to leather hard in the mould before removing.

Hump mould

1. Roll out a slab of clay large enough to cover your mould on a plastic sheet (see page 40).

   Lift the rolled slab on the plastic sheet and position it over the mould, correcting it as required until the surface is fully covered. Peel the sheet off when ready, then ease the slab to fit the mould, using a barely damp sponge.

   Smooth over the surface of the slab with a soft rib to compress the clay.

2. Place the mould on a whirler, then remove the surplus clay at the rim using a long-bladed knife held level with the underside of the plaster. The rim can be fully refined later when the form is removed from the mould.

3. Allow to firm to leather hard on the mould before removing.

PRESS MOULD

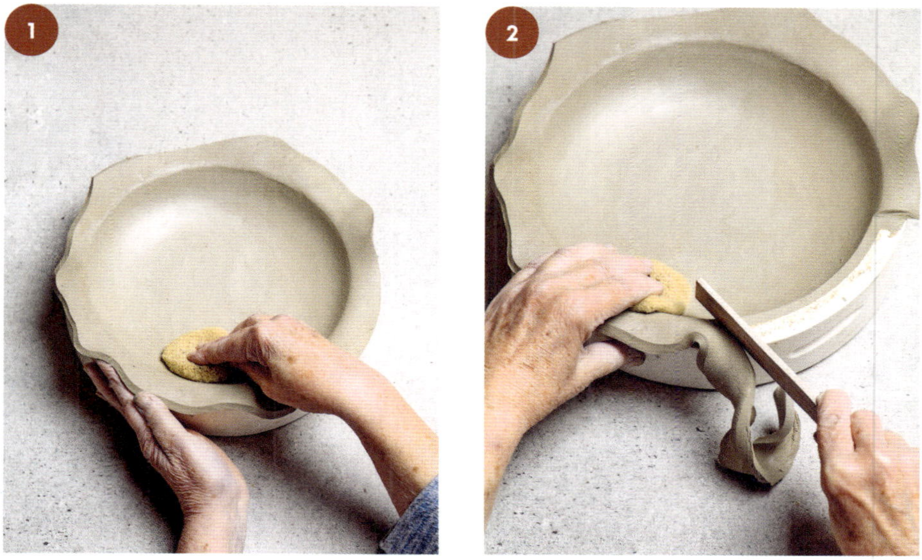

HUMP MOULD

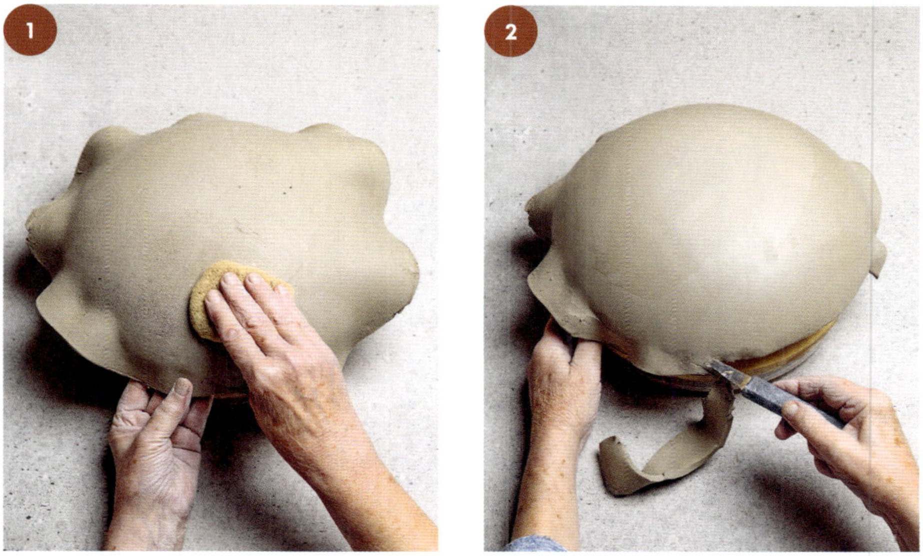

Other ways of using moulds

Moulds can be used for more things than just making a given form. For example, they can be used as a base for composite forms in which the body is built up using another method such as coiling, pinching or slabbing. You can also join moulded parts together to create new forms: for instance, two shallow dishes put together might form the body of a vase, onto which you could add other features.

JUDGES' NOTE

A bowl form like this could have a coiled or slabbed foot ring added to it, before removing it from the mould if required.

Ready-made moulds can be purchased in a wide range of shapes and sizes. Try using different types to gain experience until you are ready to make your own.

Hand-building and throwing techniques

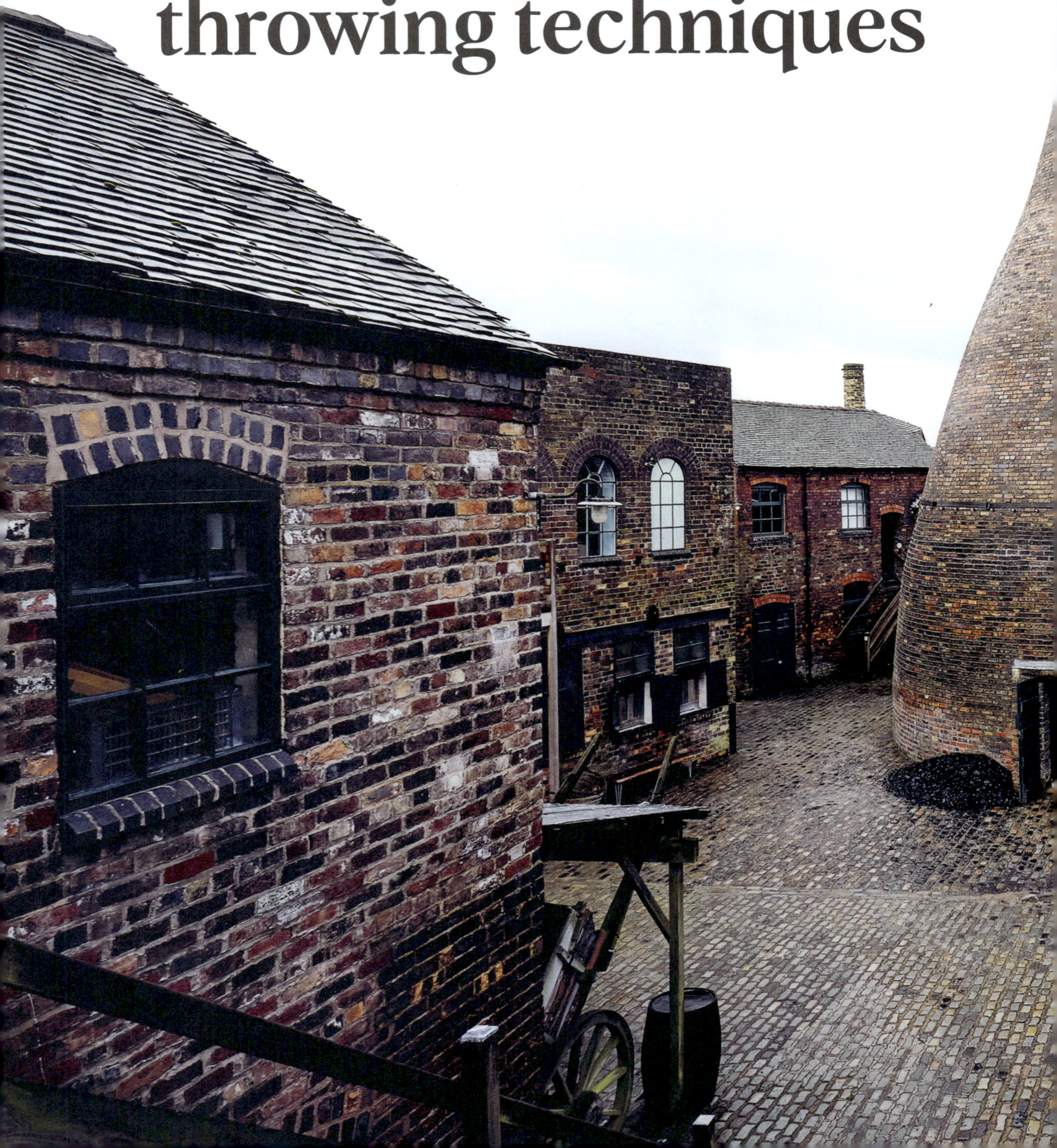

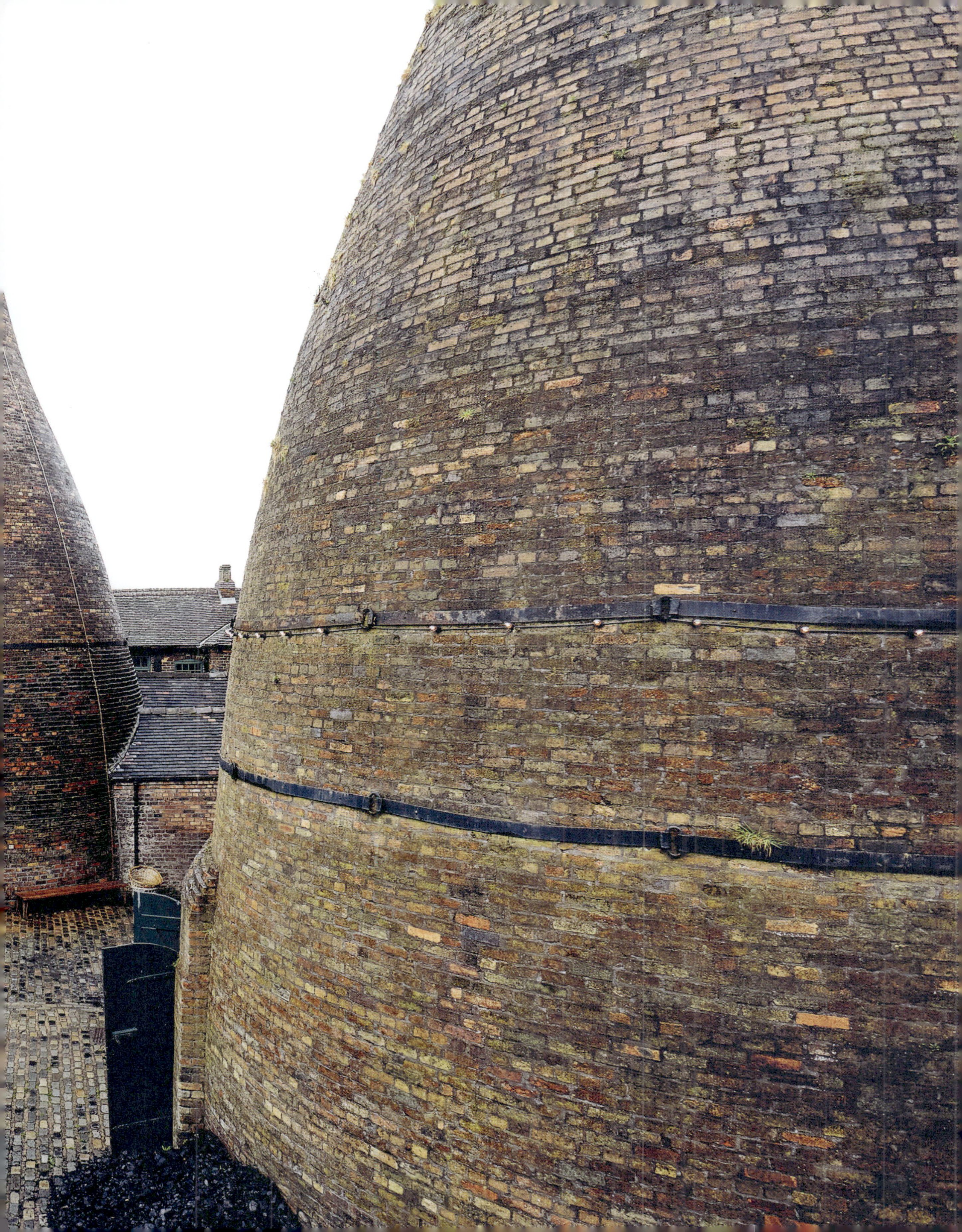

Hand building

Hand building is a slower making process than throwing and requires patience, which some people have more of than others. As a result, many argue that it is a more contemplative way of working – though throwers would say there is a certain sense of Zen in repeating a form many times over and seeing the shelves stack up quickly. One thing is for sure, there is nothing that you can't make using a hand-building process. Ultimately, the making technique you choose should best suit your personality – you will know which gives you the greatest joy.

Pinching

In contemporary terms, pinching seems to be a less well-regarded making method than others, maybe because of its association with early learning, or perhaps because it is seen as a rudimentary technique from which you graduate to other, more sophisticated technical methods. However, many people struggle with the complexities of pinching and find it has challenges like any other technique. Mastering pinching will teach tactile sensitivity better than any other making method, because it requires careful control of the clay. Once mastered, it is possible to make wonderful, innovative forms for practical or decorative use that rival anything made by other methods, even those on the wheel.

The basic method demonstrated here forms the starting point for main makes in this book and is worth taking the time to perfect before attempting anything more challenging – you will find it will not take long to master.

Some practical tips to get started

› Almost any clay body can be pinched – even porcelain can be mastered with practice but for the best chance of early success start with a basic red or white earthenware.

› Softer clay is easier to pinch than hard clay.

› If you're pinching for the first time, begin with grogged (textured) clay. It has greater strength to hold its shape without cracking. As you gain experience and a better understanding of clay behaviour, you can progress to smoother samples with finer particles that will pinch out to a thinner section.

› Some people don't like the feel of grogged clay but this can be overcome by mixing it half and half with a smooth clay that fires to the same temperature. It will retain its strength for building but have a better surface quality and pinch out a litter thinner.

› Long nails are no good at all for pinching – they get in the way by cutting into the clay.

› Hot hands will dry clay out quickly and cause cracking – the problem gets worse the more time you take to work on a piece. Cooling your hands under cold water periodically and working as quickly as possible will go some way to remedying the problem.

› A small amount of clay will pinch out a long way and the technique is generally not suitable for very large amounts. You will find you can increase the starting weight of clay as you gain experience, but forms can be enlarged in other ways to overcome the issue. It is best to start with an amount that sits comfortably in the palm of your hand.

› If you want to make the same form several times, weigh your clay before pinching so you always start with the same amount.

1

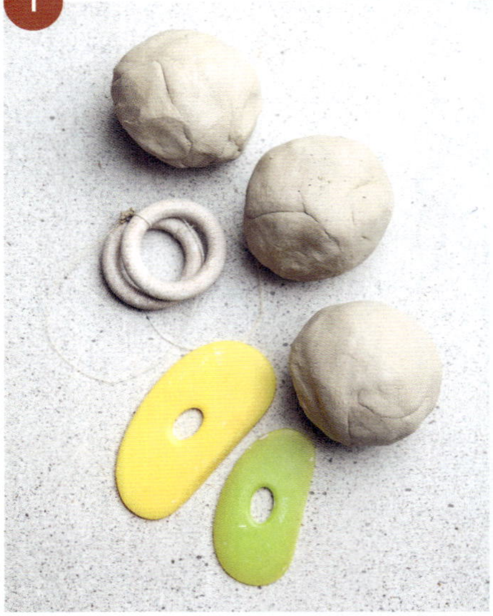

2

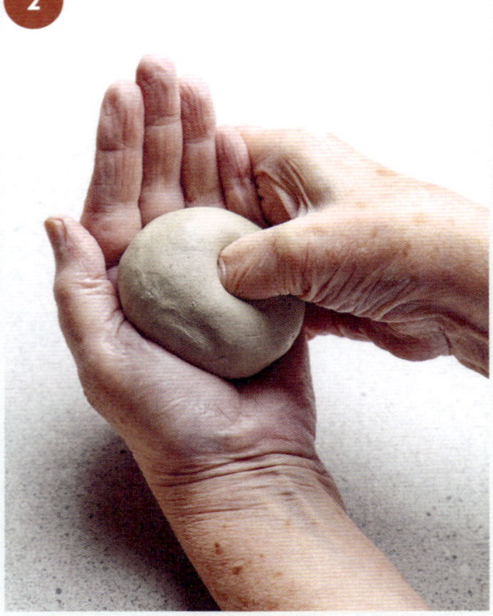

3

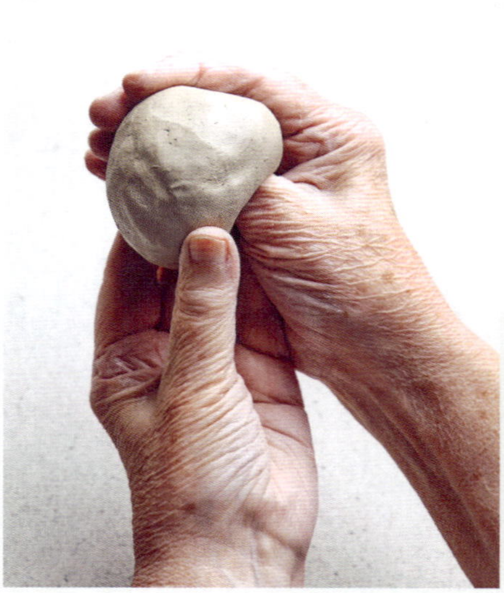

4

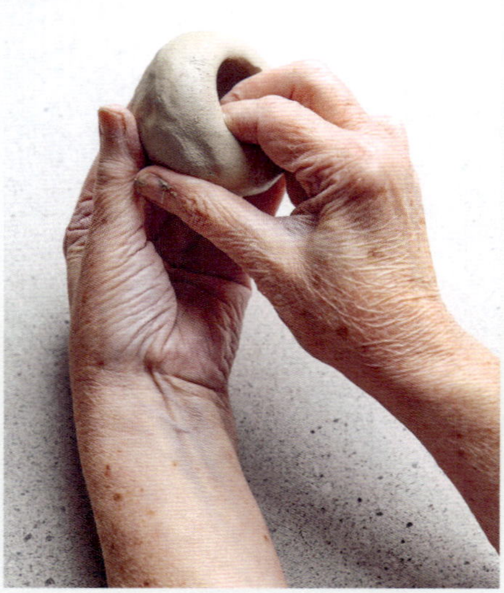

5

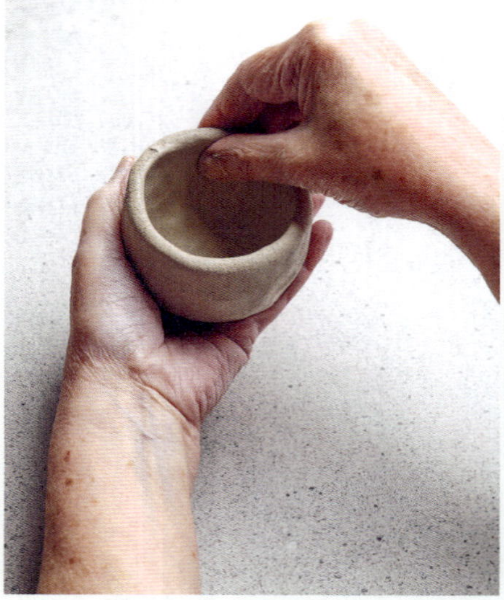

6

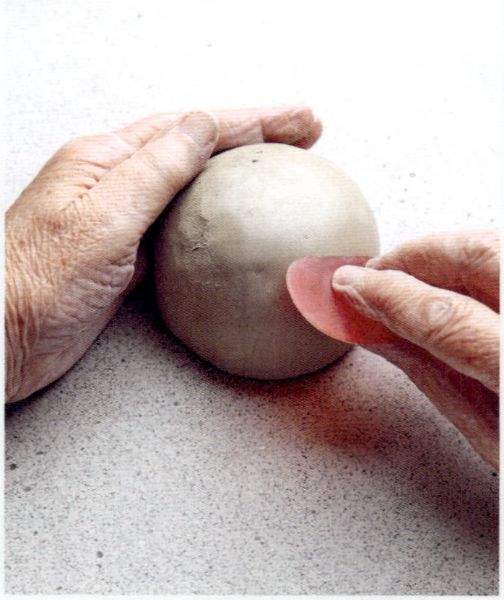

1. To get started, you need a cutting wire for your clay and ribs to work on the pinched surface. Weigh your clay and form it into a ball – 200 g (8 oz) is a good weight to begin with. Prepare a few balls and keep them under plastic until you are ready to use them. When you're beginning, it's a good exercise to pinch several forms to the same dimensions so you know you can repeat a shape.

2. Position the first ball of clay in one hand, then press down into the centre with the thumb of your other hand until you can feel some pressure in your palm.

3. Pinch out the base of the pot first, because it becomes difficult to reach as the shape grows. Work around the wall in small pinches for even thickness, pinching the clay between your fingers and thumb, which should be held in a crooked position. Work up to but not including the rim, which should remain slightly closed at this stage.

4. Turn the bowl over to rest in the palm of your hand again, then pinch the wall in small stages, working rhythmically around the circumference and turning the pot continuously.

   Maintain control of the rim it is important to keep it from flaring outwards until you have almost finished pinching the body.

5. Continue to pinch the wall until it is an even 5 mm (¼ in.) thick and cup shaped, with straight walls and a round base.

   Finally, pinch the rim to the same thickness and diameter as the wall.

6. Smooth over the surface of the form, inside and out, using a kidney to remove lumps and bumps.

   The process demonstrated here is all that is required to complete the pinched projects in the book.

Slabbing

Slabbing is a versatile way of working at any scale. Some makers choose to work with soft slabs that allow a form to be manipulated in the construction process, while others choose firm slabs that can be constructed in a more engineered way. Many makers who use slabbing purchase a slab rolling machine, but this is an expensive piece of equipment that takes up a lot of space in the studio. The following method is the most suitable when testing the technique for the first time.

Some practical tips to get started

› Purchase some lengths of batten in different thicknesses. These are widely available from DIY stores. Look for thicknesses from 2–10 mm (⅛–⅜ in.) and cut them into pairs of equal length. A good general thickness to work with is 5 mm (¼ in.). These battens will become your roller guides.

› Slabbing really exposes trapped air in clay, so it is important to prepare your clay well.

› Many people like to roll clay on fabric sheeting, which gives it some texture, but rolling on a plastic sheet provides far more flexibility when it comes to handling the slab, especially when positioning it over a mould. The slab will stick to the plastic until you are ready to release it, whereas it will fall off fabric.

› If you want to work with firm slabs, it is handy to have an absorbent surface to place the slab on once rolled. Sheets of fireboard, available from DIY stores, are perfect for this job.

YOU WILL NEED

Clay of choice

Plastic sheet or a piece of fabric

Roller guides

Rolling pin

Palette rib or similar

1. Prepare a block of clay large enough to create the parts of the project you will be working on.

   Place the clay on your sheet of plastic or piece of fabric between the roller guides and reduce its bulk by beating it with the side of your rolling pin. Work in measured, even strokes from one side of the clay to the other, to avoid making deep grooves in the surface.

2. Roll out the clay between your roller guides, beginning at the centre and rolling outwards from that point.

3. You will find that turning the slab periodically makes rolling much easier and gives you more control to achieve the approximate shape that you require. Lift the plastic sheet and allow the slab to sit on your hand as you peel it off. Turn the slab through 90°, place it back on the sheet between the guides and roll again.

   Repeat this until the rolling pin glides over the clay easily.

4. Once you've rolled it out, smooth over the surface of the slab with a rib to compact the clay.

5. Turn the slab over onto an absorbent board and peel off the plastic sheet. Smooth over the exposed surface with a rib again.

1

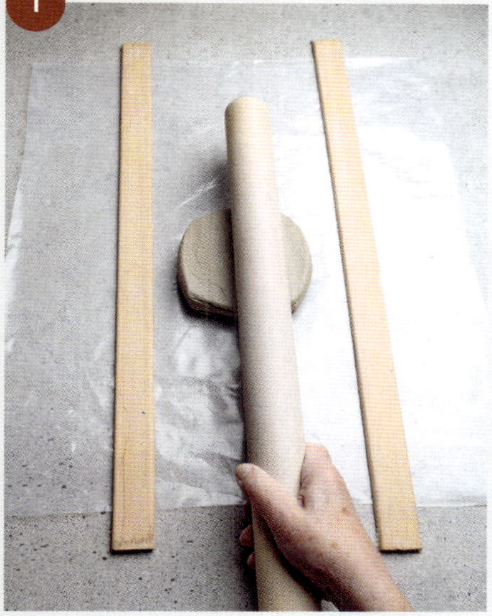

2

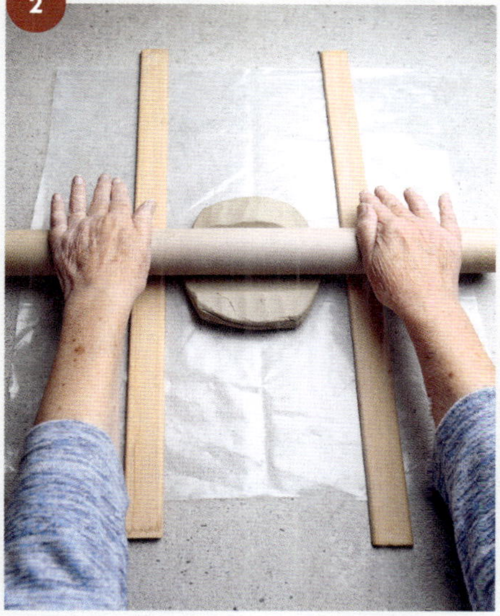

3

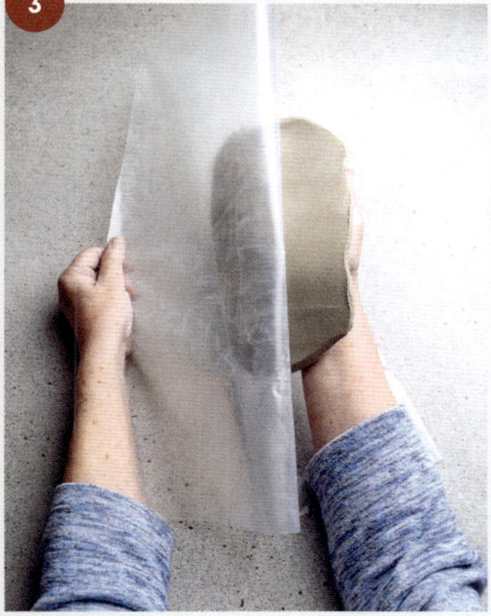

4

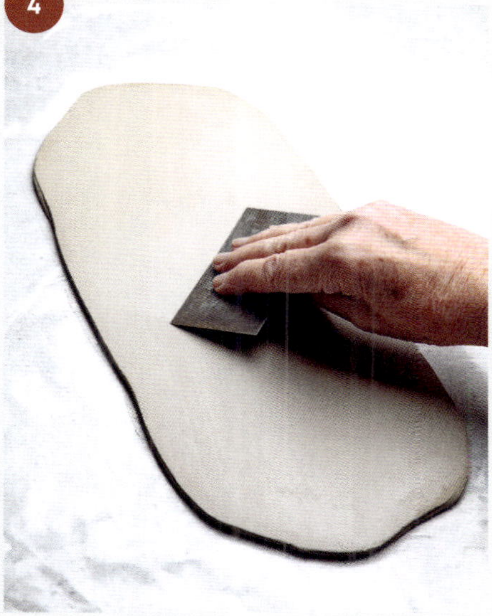

5

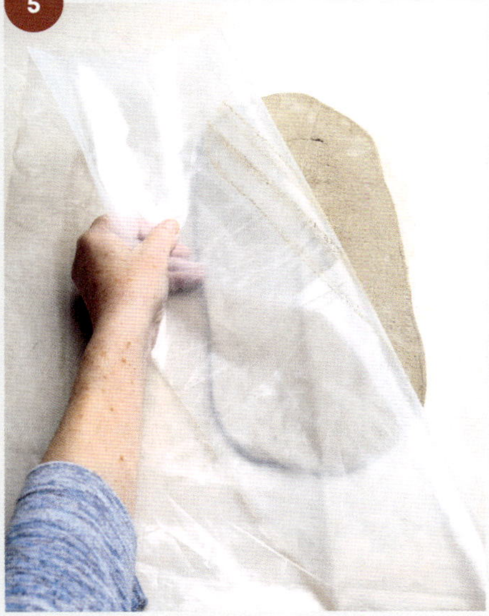

Coiling

Coiling is one of the most traditional methods of constructing pots from clay, but rolling coils requires practise. Spend some time learning to do this well, because evenly rolled coils build pots with walls of an even thickness. You can practise with any type of clay, as almost all are suitable for coiling.

1. Begin by forming the clay into a thick, rough coil shape between both hands. Ease the shape out gently from the centre towards each end to form a manageable size for rolling. Try not to squeeze the shape so that it has deep finger marks in it because this will cause problems when rolling. The coil should be as even as possible.
2. Lay the coil on a clean, dry, non-absorbent surface then, using your palms rather than your fingers, roll the coil gently but firmly back and forth, beginning at the centre and working out towards each end.
3. One of the problems most often encountered when rolling coils is that they tend to lose their shape in the rolling process and flatten in parts. To correct the shape, hold the coil at each end and twist it gently in opposite directions until it returns to a rounded shape; then re-roll it to size. You can repeat this process as often as required.

Adapting a rounded coil

Coils can be used to construct either in their rounded form or in a flattened version, which speeds up the process a little and gives greater control over the thickness of the clay wall. Flattened coils also help reduce the amount of scraping back or refining of the wall at a later stage, because they are more uniform to begin with.

1. Form a thick rounded coil using the method described previously. Lay one end of the coil on a sheet of plastic while holding the other end slightly elevated from the surface in your hand. Using the heel of your other hand, flatten the coil along its length by applying firm and even pressure.

   The coil will not flatten completely first time, so when you have worked along the length once, lift the coil off the plastic sheet, turn it over and repeat the process again until it is the thickness you require.
2. To help form the shape of a pot, flattened coils can be manipulated into a curved shape during the final part of the flattening process. This requires slightly more dexterity, but the process is the same as for flattening straight, except that you turn the coil gently as you press.

   Manipulating the coils in this way allows you to build the form in either an outward or an inward direction, which is particularly useful for bowls or sculptural works.
3. Work over the surface of the coil with a ribto smooth and even out the thickness before using it.

1

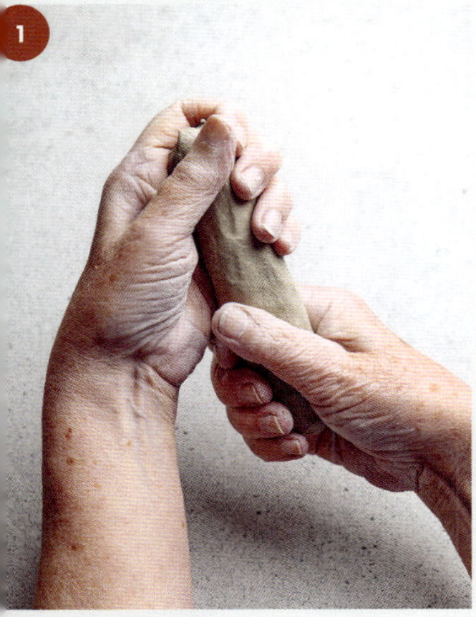

2

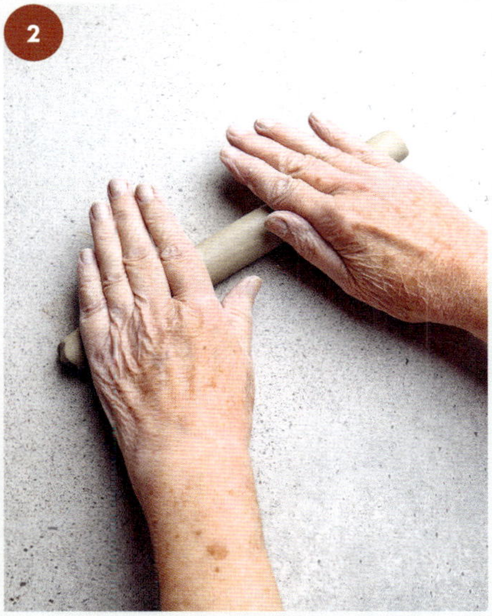

3

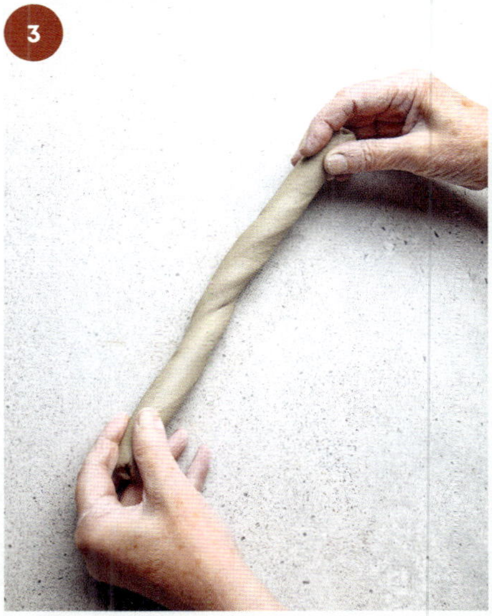

ADAPTING A ROUNDED COIL

1

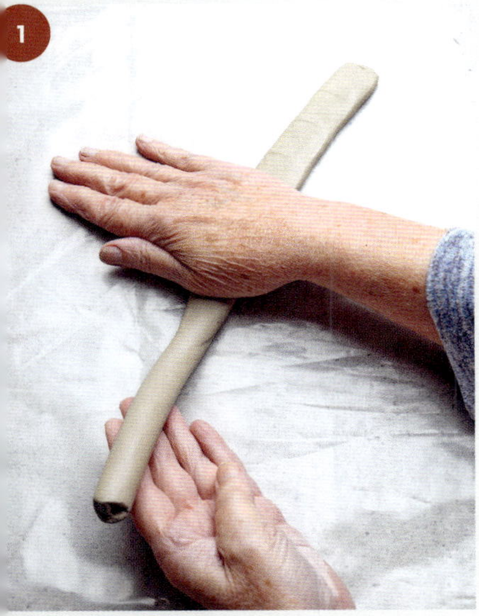

2

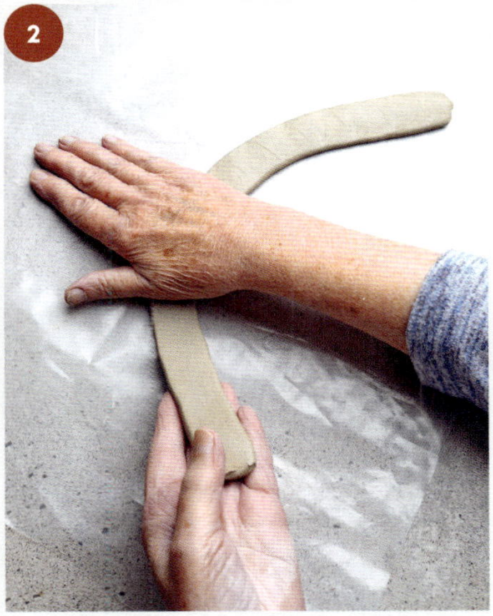

3

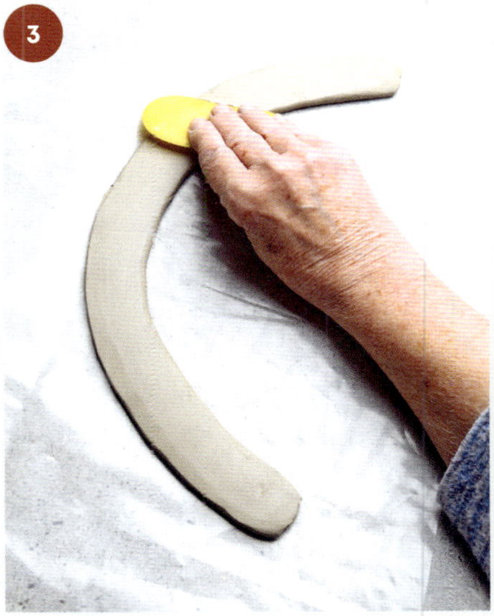

COIL THICKNESS

Do not make the coils too thin to begin with, as this makes them difficult to handle. With practice you will find that you naturally flatten the coils more, but this may take some time and it is easy enough to scrape the walls back at a later stage if you feel they are too thick.

PRACTISE MAKES PERFECT!

The final thickness of the coil depends on the type of pot you are constructing but practise rolling coils of varying sizes to begin with to get the feel of the technique. Another good exercise is to roll multiples of a particular sized coil; this will help speed up the construction process later.

Throwing

Throwing is the technique that people most associate with pottery and beginners aspire to become proficient at. However, mastering it requires endless amounts of practise and improvement often seems to come very slowly – especially if you do not have regular access to a wheel. But once mastered, though, the technique is endlessly rewarding because it allows you to produce a vast range of wares in a relatively short space of time. Perseverance and determination are the keys to success.

Using the wheel

Throwing is often considered the hardest technique to master, but in reality it is no more difficult than other making techniques. The key to success when making, no matter which method you use, lies in understanding the basic principles and then practise, practise, practise.

Before you begin

› Prepare several balls of clay – each about 900 g (2 lb) is a good starting weight.

› Wear something short sleeved when throwing to keep your hands and arms unhindered.

› Clay preparation is the key to successful centring (see page 46). Knead the clay thoroughly to eliminate air bubbles and remove any unevenness that may be present. 'Coning up' is a process that allows you to do this on the wheel itself while centring and is practised by most experienced potters, but it can be bypassed if the clay is well prepared.

Suitable clays for throwing

The most important criterion when choosing a throwing clay is good plasticity (the ability to retain its shape when worked, to produce a smooth and unbroken surface). Choose a smooth variety that is recommended as a good throwing body. Other vital decisions about clay choice can be made as you gain experience.

It easier to centre softer clay, but if it is too soft it will struggle to hold its shape as the wall is pulled up during the throwing process.

In contrast, if the clay is too hard, you will have to apply greater strength to centre it and more pressure to shape the form.

It is best to begin with a softer clay to master the initial centring technique.

JUDGES' TIP

Store your prepared clay balls in a plastic bowl with a sheet of plastic covering them – this keeps them contained and prevents the clay from drying out.

Preparing to throw

YOU WILL NEED

Ball of clay

Bowl of water

Sponge

Ribs of different shapes

Cutting wire

The wheel head must be clean, dust free and moist for the clay to adhere. Wipe over the surface with a damp sponge – be careful not to use too much water as this will cause the clay to slide off the wheel head as it gathers speed.

Have all your tools and clay close at hand so that you are comfortable in your space.

The underside of the ball of clay should be perfectly convex to prevent air from being trapped as it is placed on the wheel.

Centring

Centring – positioning the clay correctly – is the most important aspect of the throwing technique as it ensures that the wall can be lifted evenly. It is perhaps the one element of the whole process that takes the longest time to become proficient in. Again, the key to success is practise.

1. Position the ball of clay at the centre of the wheel, then pat it down with the palm of your hand to fix it in place. Use the concentric lines on the wheel head to position the ball as centrally as possible, then smooth the clay at the base of the ball with your finger to seal it to the wheel head.
2. Start the wheel spinning and dribble a small amount of water over the clay surface.
3. Brace your left arm on the side of the pan. This hand controls the side of the clay. Keep your back and shoulders rigid, with your elbows tucked into your body for support. Position your hands on opposite sides of the clay, with the thumb of your right hand supporting the left (photo 3A), then push the clay with equal pressure from both sides (photo 3B) so that it rises to a cone shape as it rotates (photo 3C).
4. Dribble a little more water over the clay, then maintaining your left hand at the side, brace your right forearm on the pan, position the side of your hand over the surface of the cone and gently push down to reduce its height and control the top of the clay.

Continued overleaf

WHEEL SPEED

Spin the wheel at speed to centre, then slow down later to open out and lift the walls of the form.

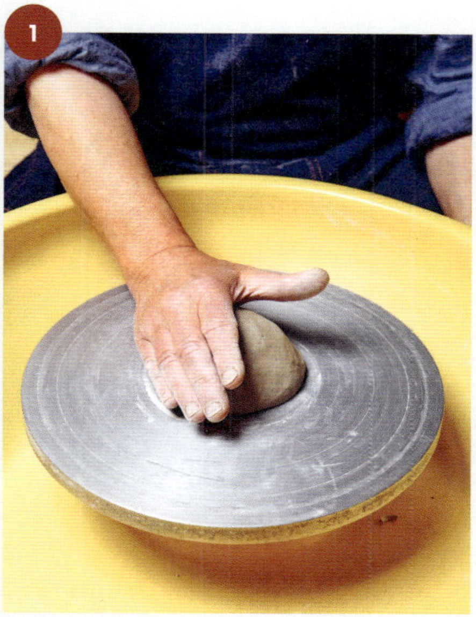
1

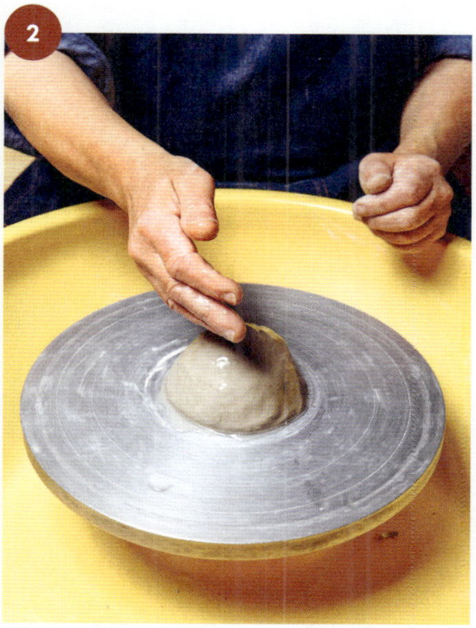
2

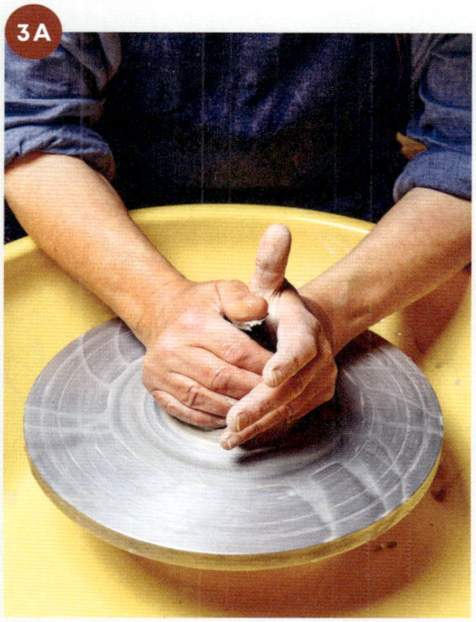
3A

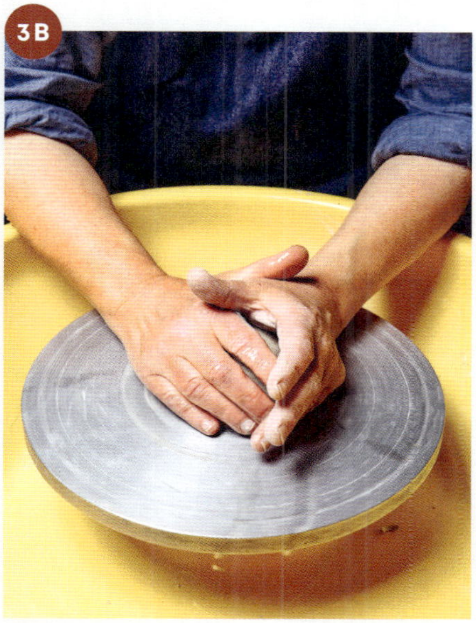
3B

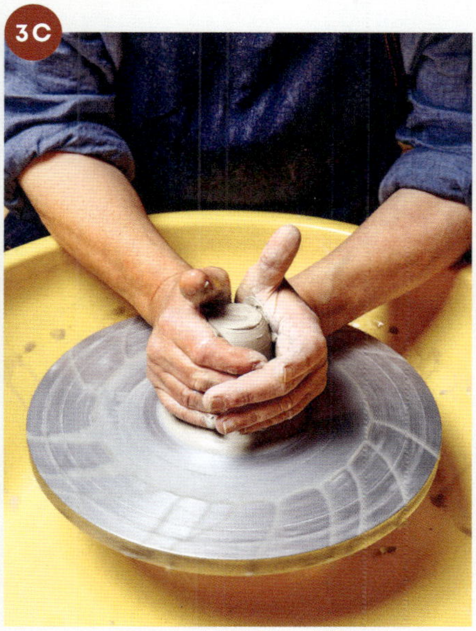
3C

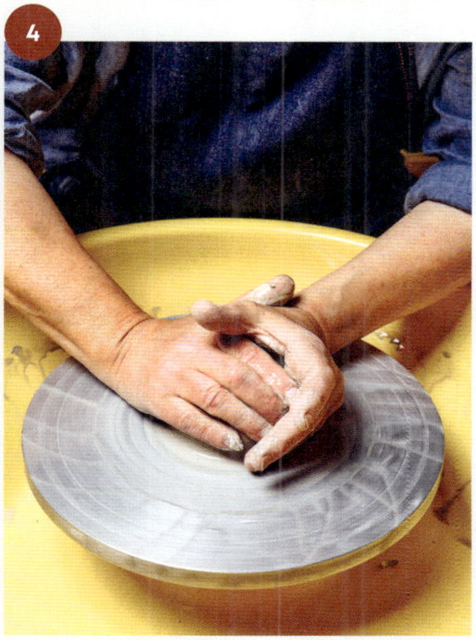
4

5

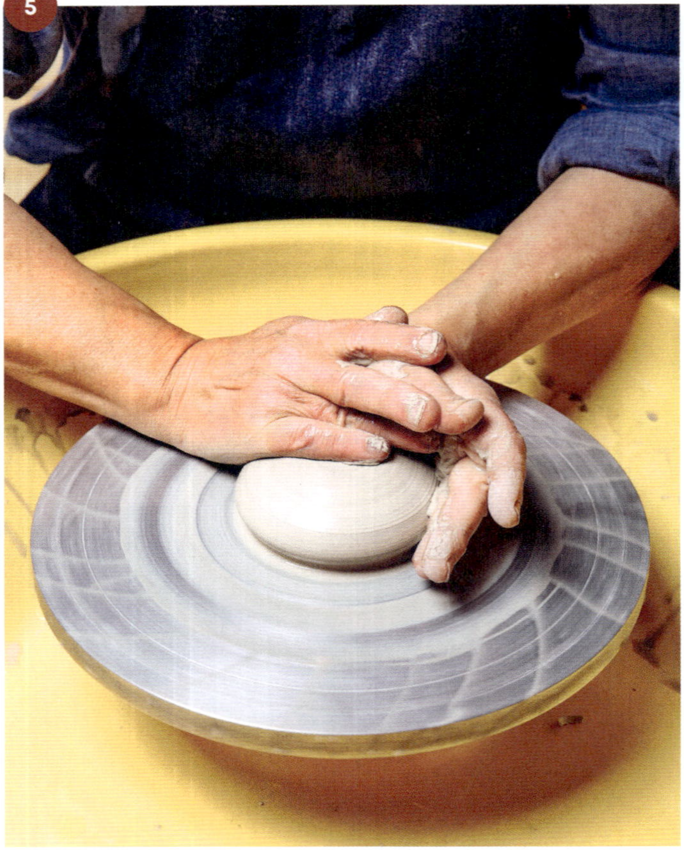

6A

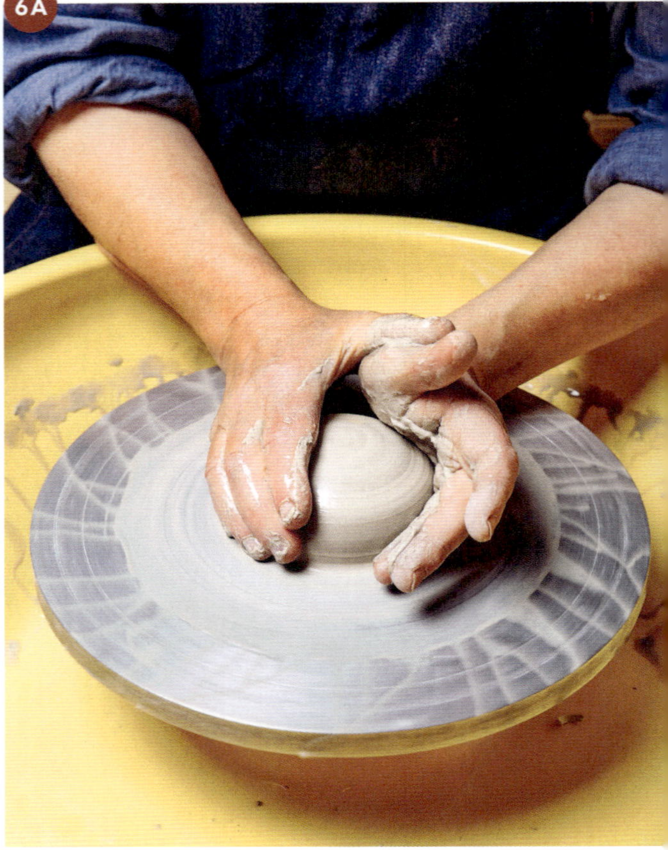

6B

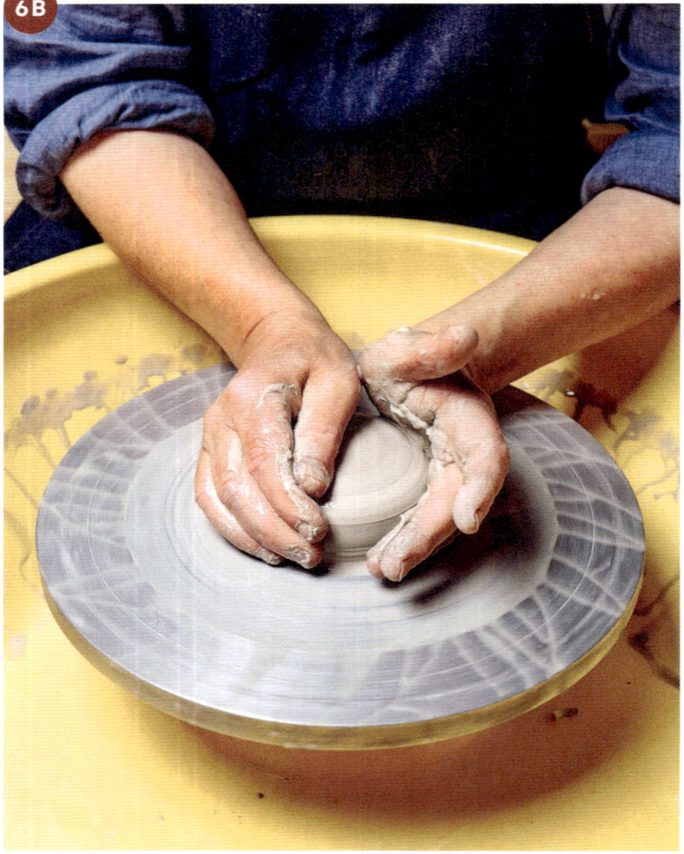

7

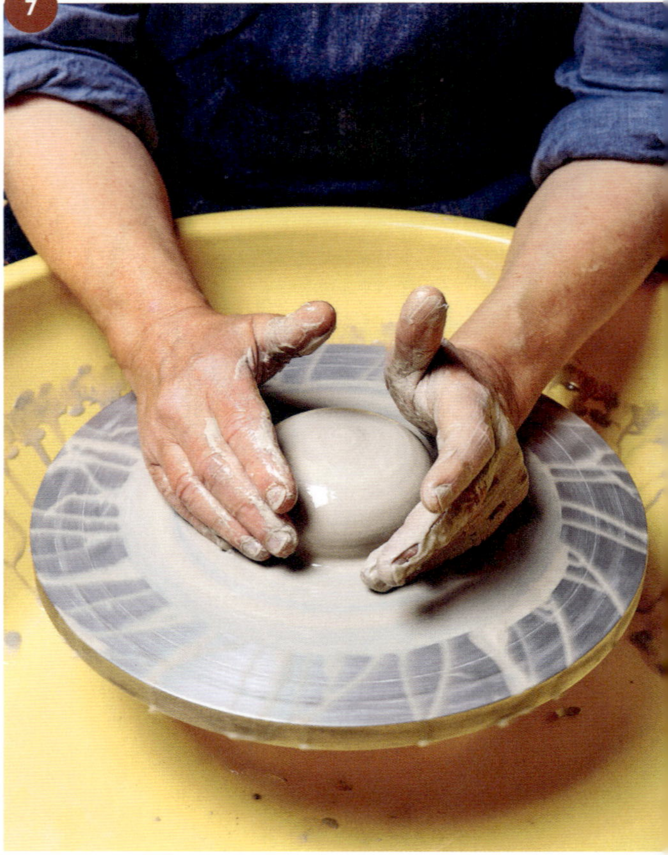

5. Maintaining the position of your left hand, apply pressure with the side of your right hand on top of the clay to flatten it off to a gently domed shape. It is this up-and-down movement and alternating pressure while the clay is rotating that gently eases it into the centre. You may need to repeat the process several times before you get it right.
6. Finally, level the top of the clay with the side of your right hand to prepare for the next stage of throwing (photo 6A). The clay is centred when it runs smoothly through your hands with no wobbles (photo 6B).
7. **It is vitally important** that you take your hands away from the centred clay gently, because it can easily be knocked off centre by jerky movement.

   You will have to practise many times before centring becomes second nature, but all of a sudden you will find that you have the knack and there will be no looking back.

TROUBLESHOOTING

Problem

The clay has not stuck to the wheel head.

Solution

Either the wheel head or the clay ball was too wet – both should just be damp.

Problem

The clay twists and tears away from the wheel.

Solution

You are not using enough water – there's a fine balance between using too much and too little.

Problem

The clay simply refuses to centre.

Solution

It could be that the clay is too hard. Try wedging some softer clay into the ball. Alternatively, try tucking your elbow into your stomach so that you can use your body weight to help push your left hand against the clay. Sometimes it helps to close your eyes so that you are feeling rather than seeing the clay.

Throwing a cylinder

Many shapes start from a cylinder, so it's important to learn to lift the clay wall properly so it is the correct thickness and even throughout its height. Once you have mastered this, you will be well on your way to becoming a thrower.

Opening up

Don't panic! This is not a call to confess all, simply the next stage in the throwing process! 'Opening up' is the term used to describe the technique of opening the centred ball of clay to form the wall and base of the pot.

1. Centre your clay (see page 46), then with your left hand at the side, position the first two fingers of your right hand at the centre of the mass, with your thumb resting on your left hand to keep it steady (photo 1A). Holding your fingers at an angle rather than vertically, gently press down into the clay until you are approximately 5 mm (¼ in.) from the wheel head (photo 1B).

   Do not open up the clay by creating a vertical hole down through the centre – maintain the angled position of the fingers as you work.

   Remember to lubricate the clay from time to time.

2. Still maintaining your hand positions, draw your right-hand fingers back towards your body to open out the base to your required diameter.

   Compress the clay in the base of the pot three times with your fingers, working from the centre to the outside edge. You can use a sponge to do this if you prefer.

   The basic form should now look rather like the shape of a dog bowl.

   The height of the cylinder is related to the diameter of the dog bowl – the wider the base, the higher the wall.

3. The next stage is called 'pinch and lift'. The purpose of this action is not to make the wall thin but to position the clay.

   Using both hands on opposite sides of the wall, pinching like a crab's claw, gently squeeze and lift the wall up. The claw shape should be about the thickness of a finger.

Continued overleaf

COMPRESSING

Compressing is a key step in the throwing process that strengthens the clay and prevents it from cracking while drying and firing. The term is often used when referring to bases and rims, but the clay of the walls is compressed naturally by both hands in the process of lifting the wall.

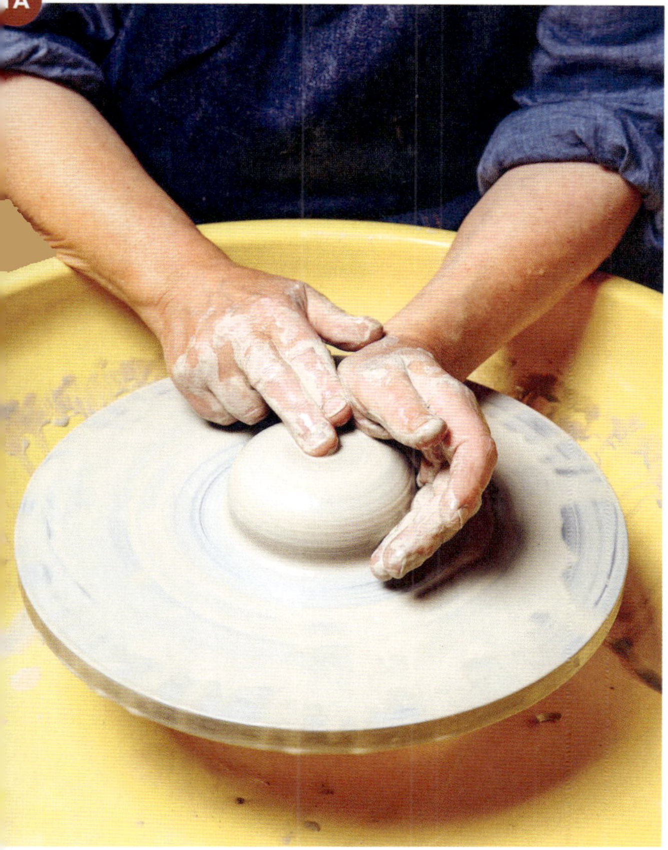
A

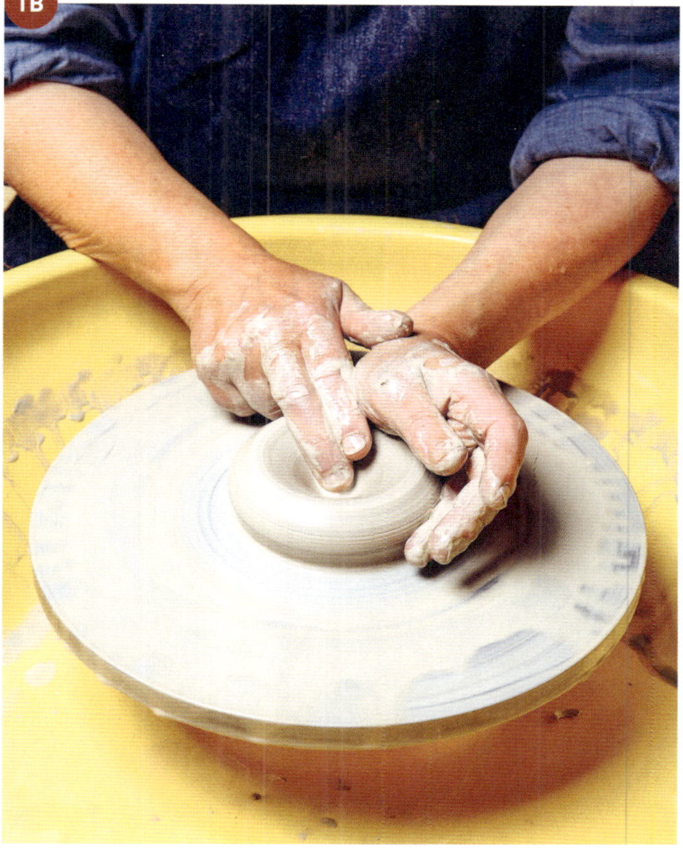
1B

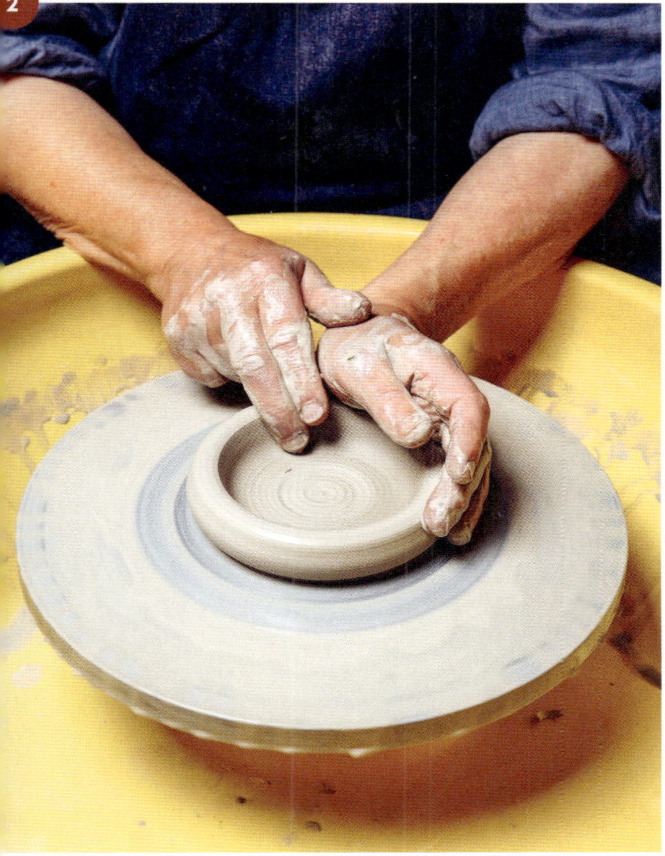
2

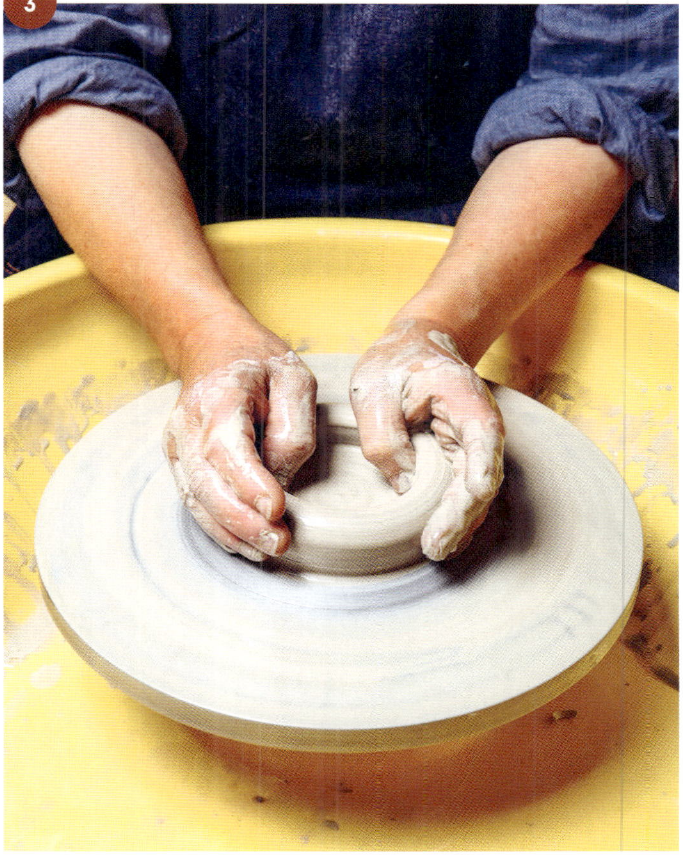
3

4A

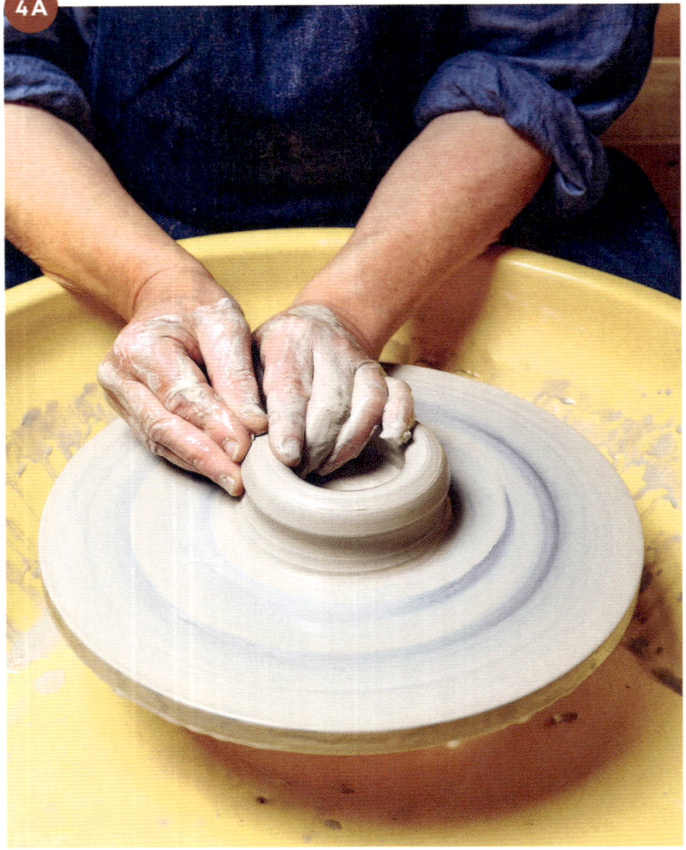

4B

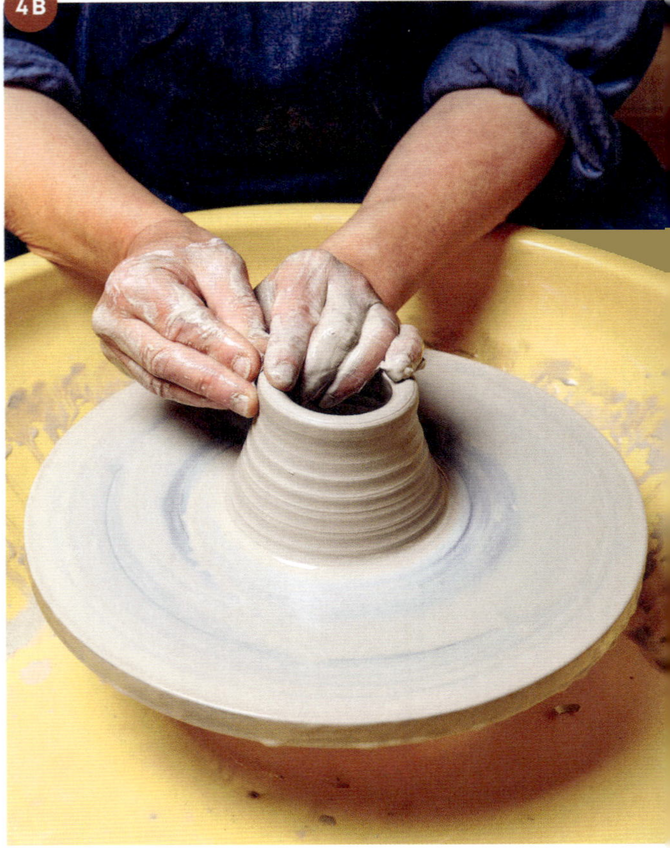

5

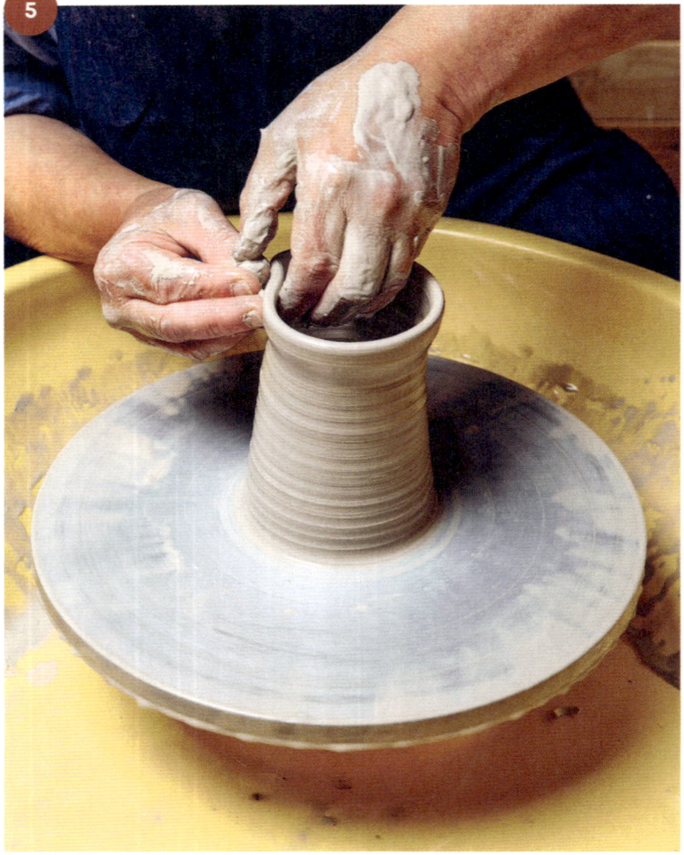

6

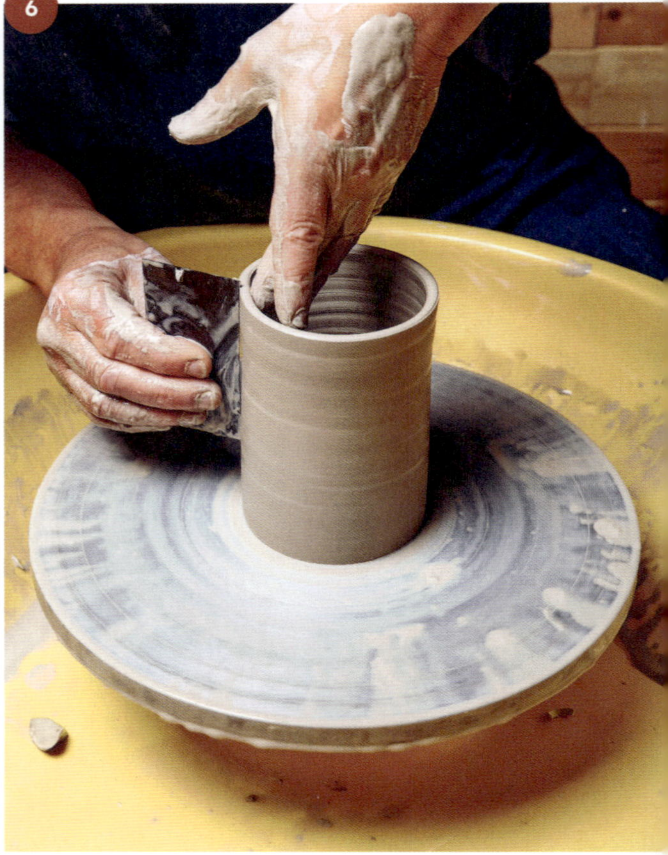

Continue to lift the form upwards and inwards. You should be aiming to keep the base broad and the top narrow.

When you have finished, check that the rim is running true by holding the position of your left hand at the top and resting the forefinger of your right hand on the rim. If you apply slight pressure with the finger, it will **compress** and level the clay slightly. **You should do this after each lift of the clay wall.**

4. Now place the fingers of your left hand on the inside of the wall, with your right-hand fingers opposite on the outside (photo 4A). Making sure you begin right from the base and maintaining an equal distance between your fingers, raise the wall, narrowing it as you reach the top (photo 4B).

MEASURING BASE THICKNESS

Foot rings (see page 66) are not generally turned on basic cylinder shapes, so the thickness at the base should be roughly equal to the thickness of the walls when the form is fully thrown.

Before lifting the walls of your cylinder, you can measure the thickness at the base by pushing a pin through the clay until it meets the wheel head and then running your finger down the pin until it meets the clay. Remove the pin with your finger still in place and you will be able to see the thickness of the clay. If it is too thick, repeat the opening-up process and measure again.

Smooth over the pin mark.

Note Many practised throwers use a knuckle to raise the wall from the outside rather than their fingers – this is a matter of preference and whatever you find easiest.

5. Repeat the lift again to raise the height further, remembering to begin from the base to maximize use of the clay.

   Once you have finished lifting the clay and have compressed the rim, it is most important that you relax and allow the shape of the top to come back to round before you remove your hands. If you remove your hands too quickly, the cylinder will be knocked off centre and have a wobble.

   It should be possible to complete the cylinder in two lifts, but beginners may need one or two more attempts to get the pot to the required height.

6. If you need a smooth surface on your cylinder in order to apply a particular surface decoration later, support the wall from the inside with your left hand, then work over the exterior surface with a rib to remove the throwing lines. This also acts to straighten the wall to vertical, widening the rim to match the base.

7. Clean away excess water and clay from the wheel head surrounding the cylinder and then, using the rib at a 45° angle, cut a bevel at the base of the pot to allow a clean transit of the wire.

8. Mop out excess water from the interior of the cylinder, using a sponge on a stick if you can't reach inside with your hand.

Continued overleaf

9. Holding your cutting wire taut, pass it under the base of the pot once only (photo 9A). Cupping the cylinder in both hands as close to the base as possible, gently tilt it back towards your body as you lift it off the wheel (photo 9B). This allows air to pass underneath, thus releasing suction as the pot is lifted, and makes the procedure much easier. Transfer the pot to a board as quickly as possible.

   Another method for removing a finished pot from the wheel, is to flood the wheel head with water before sliding the pot off the surface onto a waiting batt, this is appropriate if the form will be substantially trimmed later.

   Equally, don't delay in lifting the pot once you have wired it through.

JUDGES' TIPS TO AID LIFTING A FORM OFF THE WHEEL

› Lay a sheet of uncreased newspaper over the rim of the pot, then turning the wheel slowly, run a finger over the rim to fix it in place. The resulting airtight seal will hold the shape as you lift, thus minimizing distortion.

› Use a hot air gun or blow lamp to dry off the surface of the pot and firm up the clay a little before you lift it off the wheel head. This will help prevent the pot from distorting when you lift it.

› Avoid touching up or correcting the shape of a pot once you have lifted it off the wheel head. Glaze will cover slight handprints, but other corrections should be made at the leather-hard stage.

TROUBLESHOOTING

Problem

The rim seems to be centred but the body of the form is not.

Solution

You are not applying enough pressure from the hand that controls the side of the clay – it needs to be held more rigidly. Make sure both hands are braced correctly against one another.

7

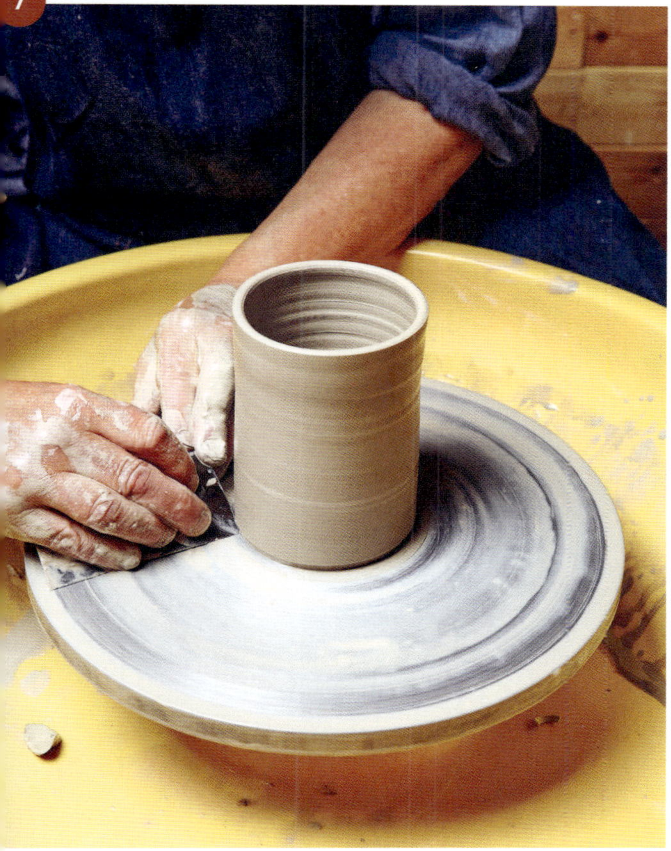

8

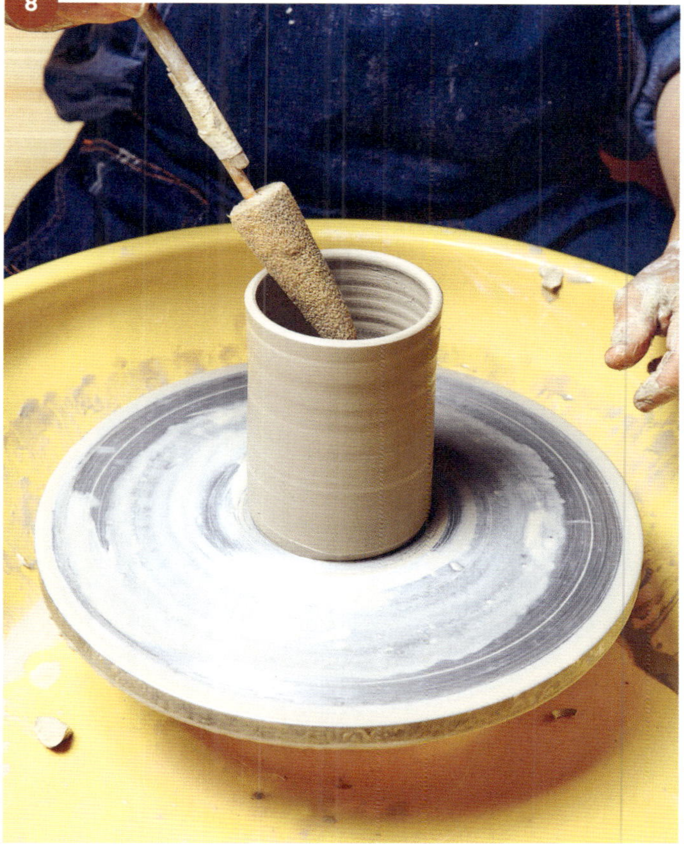

9A

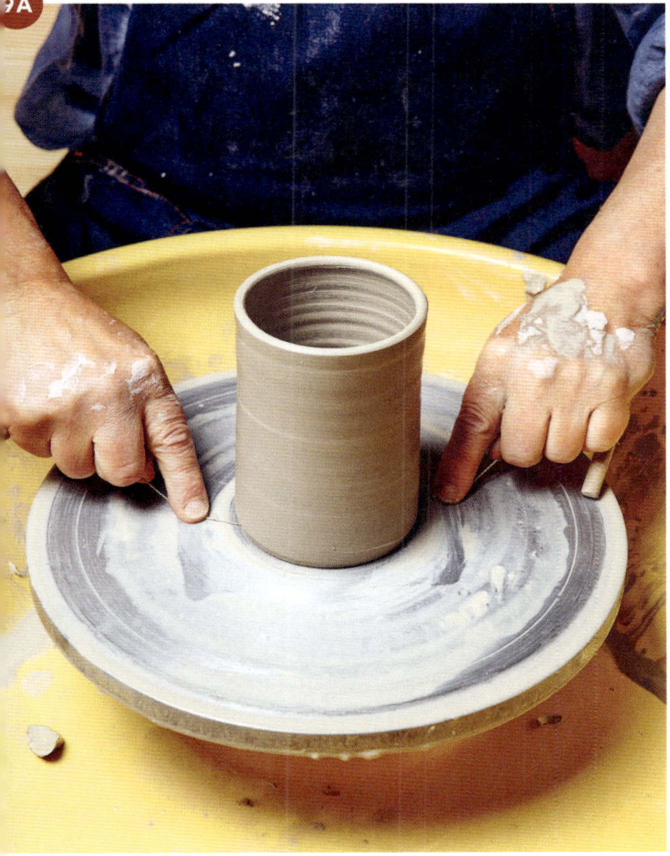

9B

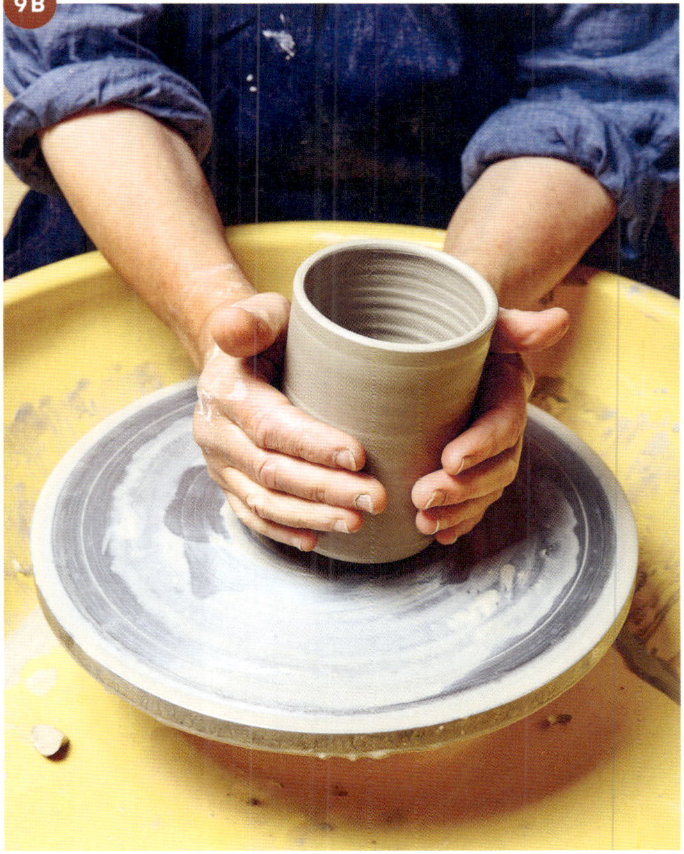

Throwing a bowl

There is something fundamentally satisfying about throwing bowls and they make great surfaces to decorate. They can be thrown directly on the wheel head but are generally thrown on batts (see page 46) to minimize handling – the choice is down to the skill level of the maker.

The key to throwing a successful bowl is to allow enough weight at the base to support the wall as it is thrown outwards and also to form the foot ring later if the base is going to be turned.

Unlike with cylinders, the focus when throwing a bowl is on the interior rather than the outer space, which is generally (but not always) developed later when trimming and turning a foot.

1. To make a small bowl, centre (see page 46) 500 g (1 lb) of clay to a doorknob shape by tucking the sides of your hands in at the base of the clay. This will allow your fingers underneath to lift the wall so that there is enough clay to support it without being excessive.
2. With the wheel turning at medium speed, open the centre of the clay to approximately 10 cm (4 in.) in diameter, with a slightly rounded base, as opposed to the flat one needed for a cylinder (photo 2A).

   In this case, the thickness of the clay at the base should be slightly deeper (10 mm/⅜ in.) to allow a foot ring to be turned later.

   If you want a flat-bottomed bowl without a foot, the base can be reduced to 5 mm (¼ in.) thick.

   When the diameter is established, compress the clay in the base by running your fingers over the surface from the centre to the outer edge three times (photo 2B).

Continued overleaf

Weights and measures for bowls

BOWL WIDTH	**AMOUNT OF CLAY REQUIRED**	**SUITABLE FOR**
15 cm (6 in.)	500 g (approx. 1 lb 1 oz)	Small servings of cereals, desserts
25 cm (10 in.)	1.5 kg (approx. 3 lb 4 oz)	Soup, pasta etc.
30 cm (12 in.)	2.5 kg (approx. 5 lb 8 oz)	Large salad, serving bowl, cooking bowl

1

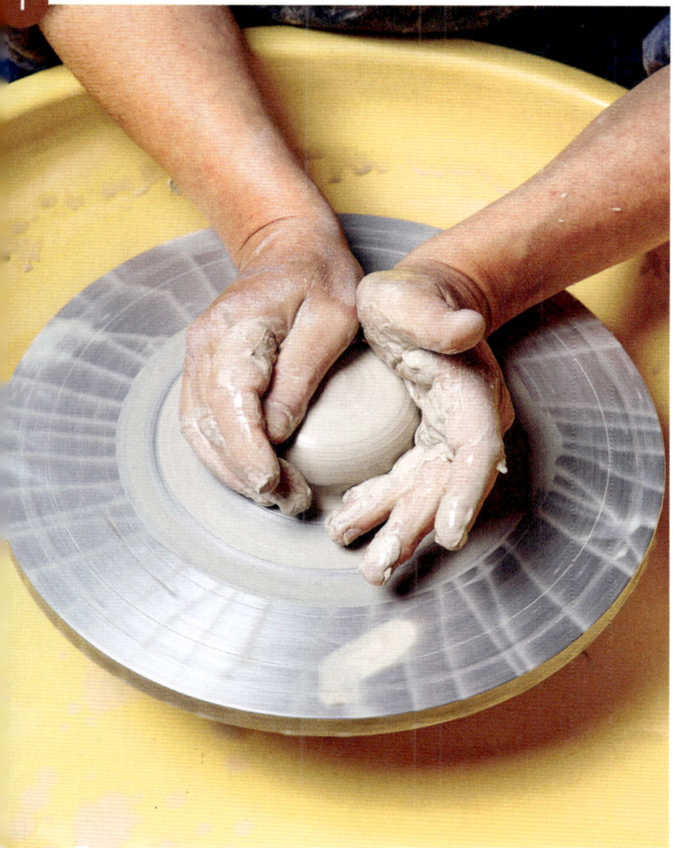

2A

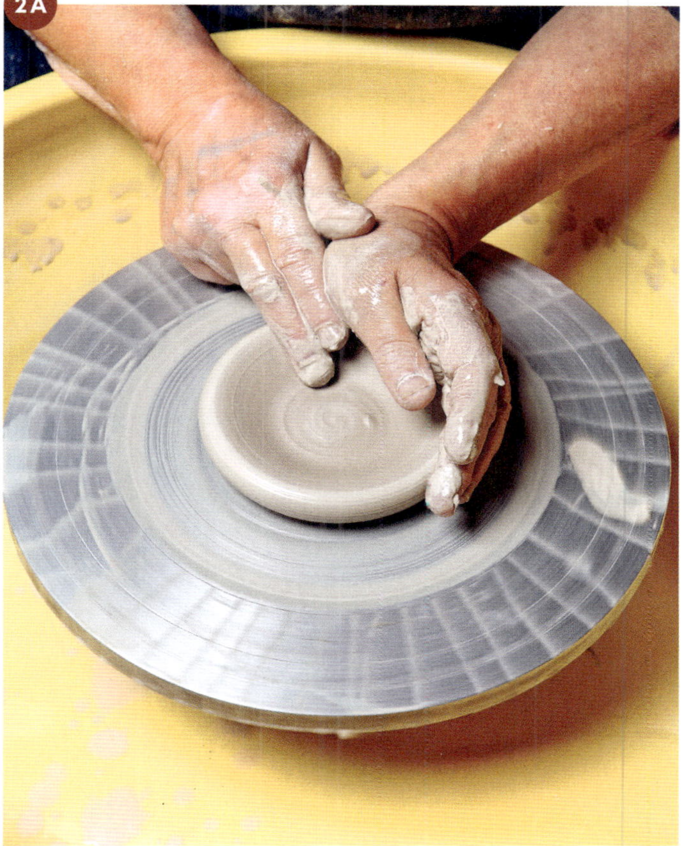

2B

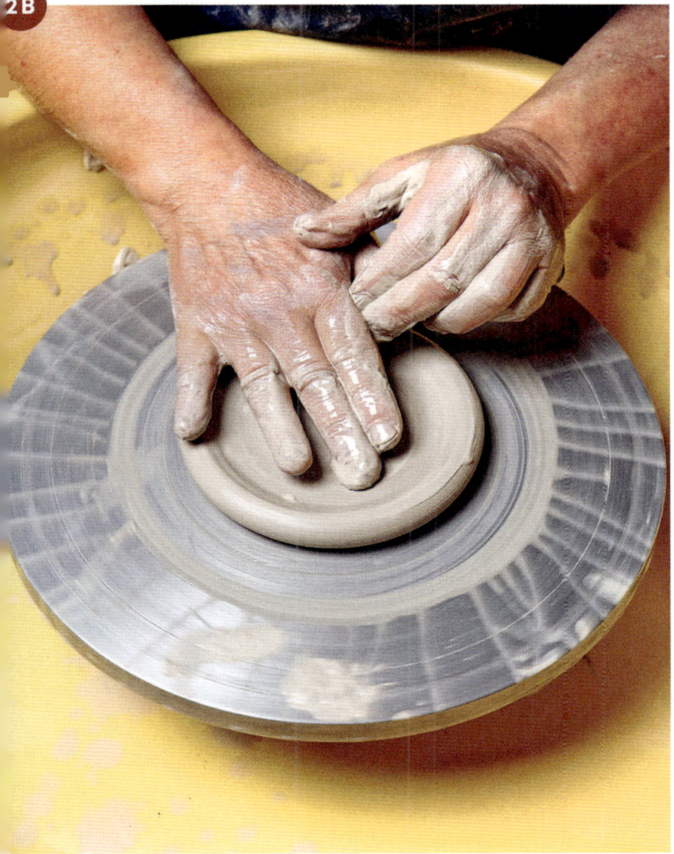

3A

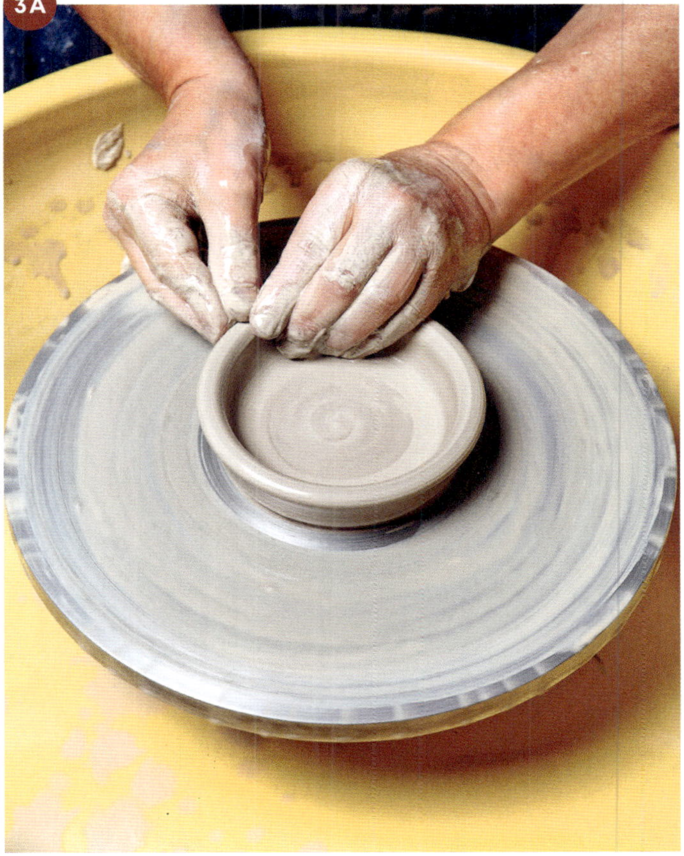

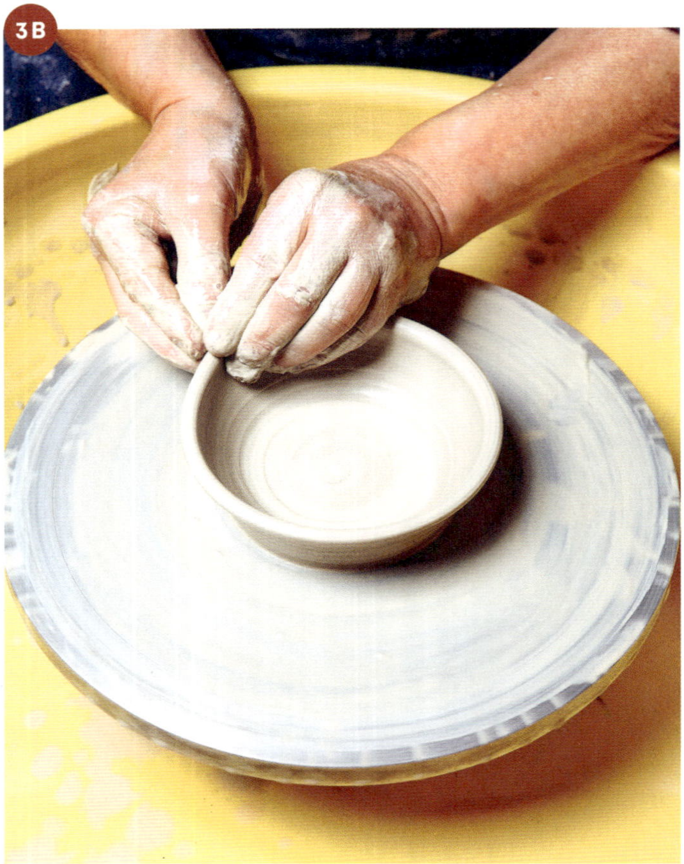
3B

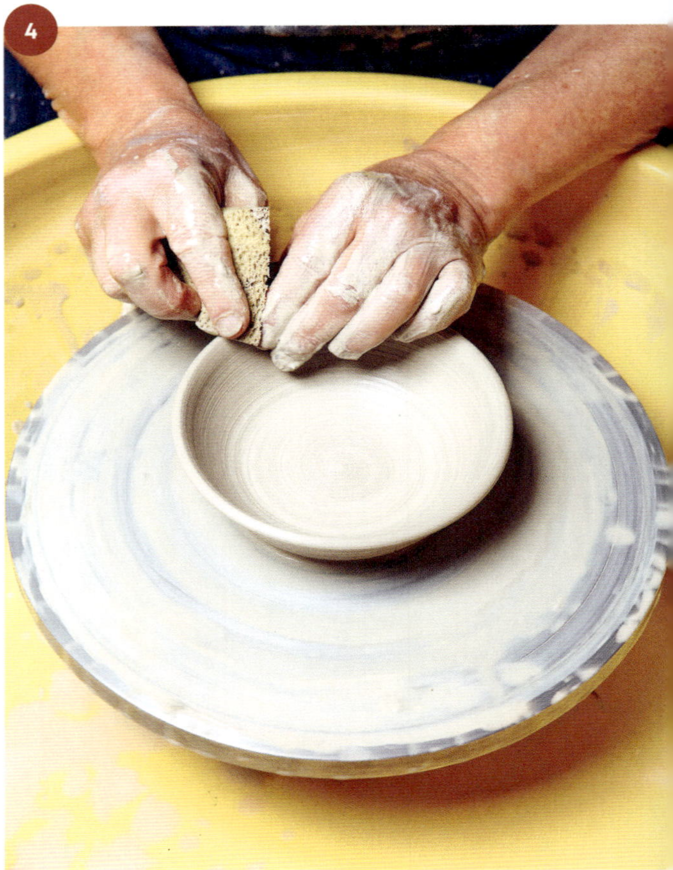
4

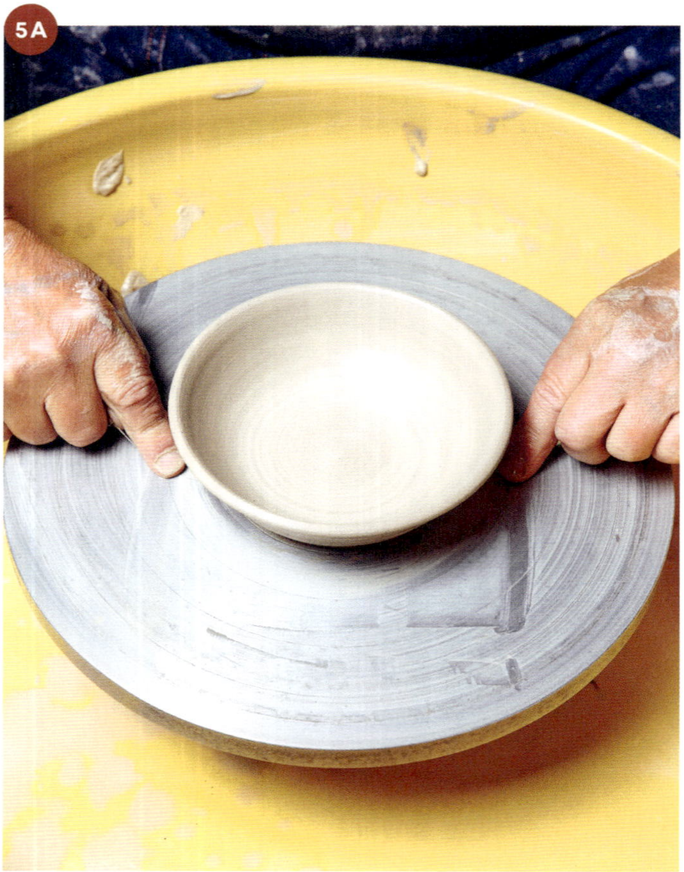
5A

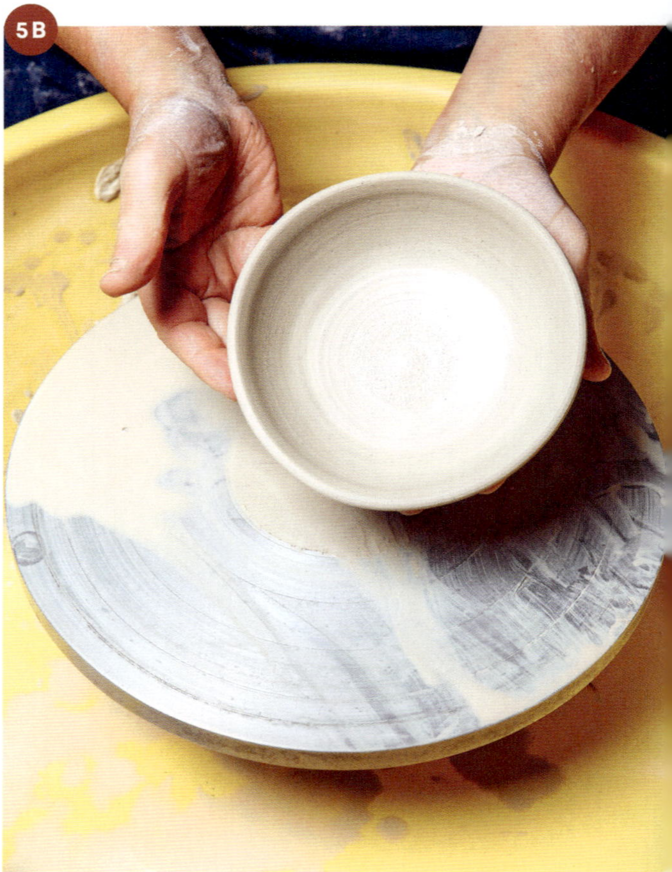
5B

3. Lift the wall in the same way as for the cylinder (page 50), but this time gently flare it outward to 15 cm (6 in.) in diameter (photo 3A). It is important to establish the width at the top of the bowl quickly, but to keep the shape rounded and not allow it to flare too wide.

   Remember to compress the rim regularly by pinching it gently between the finger and thumb of one hand while compressing the edge with the finger of the other hand (photo 3B).

   As a general guide for this weight of clay, the bowl should be approximately 5 cm (2 in.) high when finished.

4. Taking great care, sponge out excess water from the interior of the bowl, being mindful that it can easily be knocked off centre by sudden movement. Sponge excess water from the wheel head.

   Using a rib, remove the excess clay around the base on the outside of the bowl. Make sure you leave enough width to turn a foot ring when the piece is leather hard.

5. Wire the underside of the bowl (photo 5A), then quickly but carefully lift it off the wheel by holding it at the base on two sides (photo 5B). Transfer it to a batt and allow it to firm to leather hard.

JUDGES' NOTE

The small bowl demonstrated here is thrown directly on the wheel head, but I recommend you use a batt (see page 64) if you are not confident about lifting off the wheel successfully.

The best way to do this is to underwire the base and then carefully lift the batt off the wheel. Allow the bowl to firm to leather hard before handling it again.

Throwing a plate

There are many different shapes of plate, each requiring different levels of skill to make successfully. Here we demonstrate a simple, basic method that nonetheless has a very contemporary look.

1. Attach a batt to the wheel (see page 64), then run a barely damp sponge over the surface to moisten it. Take care not to drown it with water.
2. Centre (see page 46) 1.5 kg (3 lb) of well-prepared clay on the batt (photo 2A), reducing it down to be wide and flat following the instructions on page XX (photo 2B).
3. Supporting your right hand with your left and holding your fingers in the flattened position, open out the centre of the clay, pressing it down to within 6–8 mm (about ¼–⅜ in.) of the batt.

   Draw your fingers back towards your body in a steady action until the clay covers at least three-quarters of the batt, leaving a fat rim at the edge.

TIPS BEFORE YOU BEGIN

› Plates are not difficult items to throw but are notoriously inclined to cracking because of their large, flat, central expanse, so follow the instructions carefully to avoid this – don't leave any steps out.

› The key to success lies in good compression of the base, slow drying and equally slow firing.

› Plates should always be thrown on a batt.

› A dinner plate thrown in this style requires 1.5 kg (3 lb) of clay – smaller plates obviously require a smaller amount if thrown in the same way. This method does not include a foot ring, therefore the weight is relatively low.

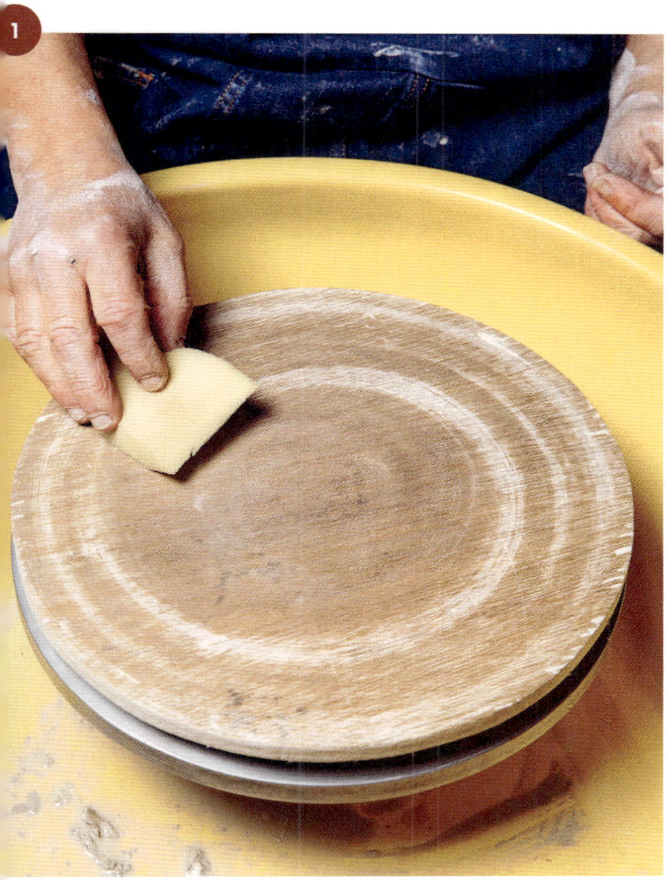
1

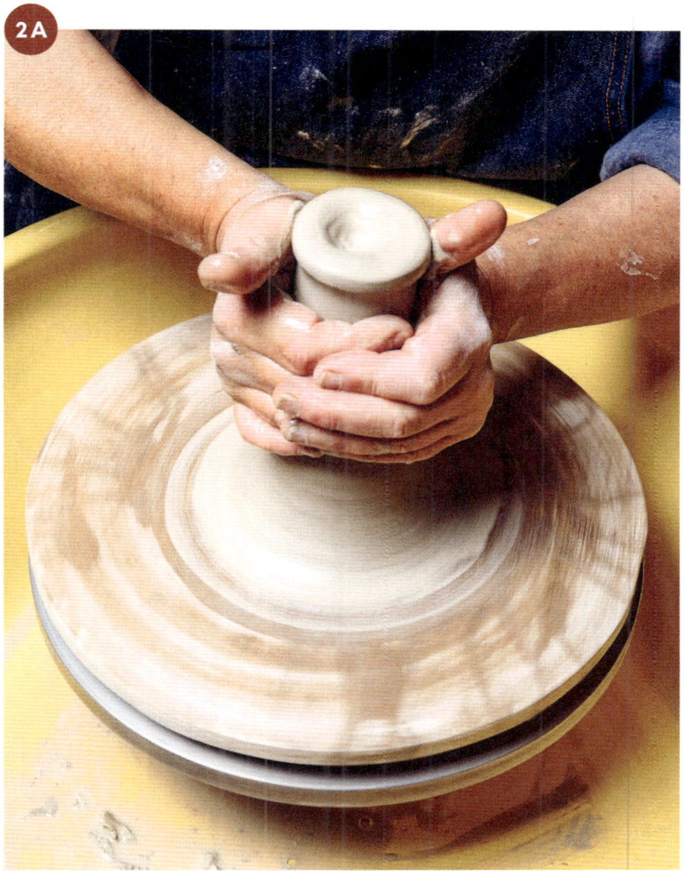
2A

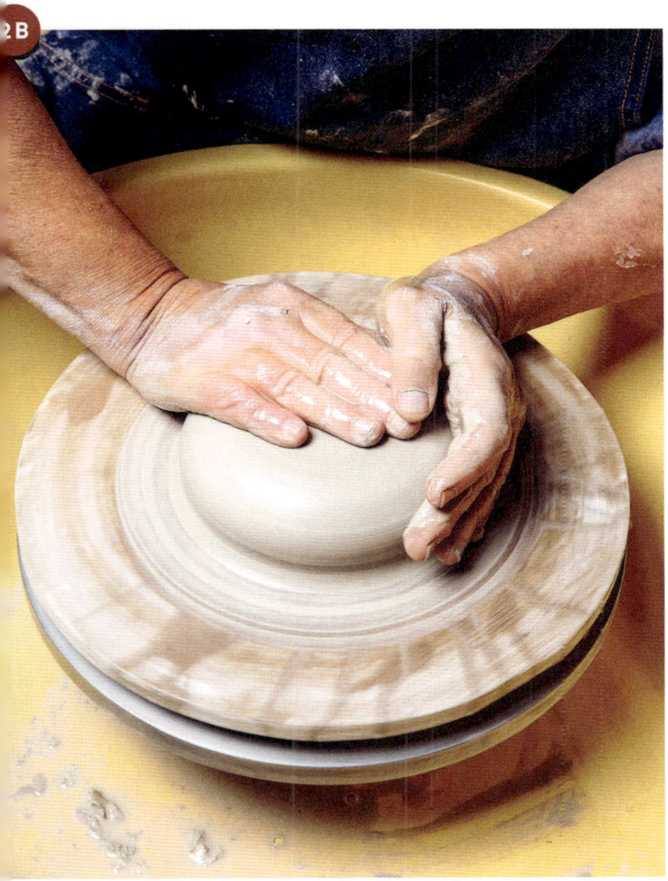
2B

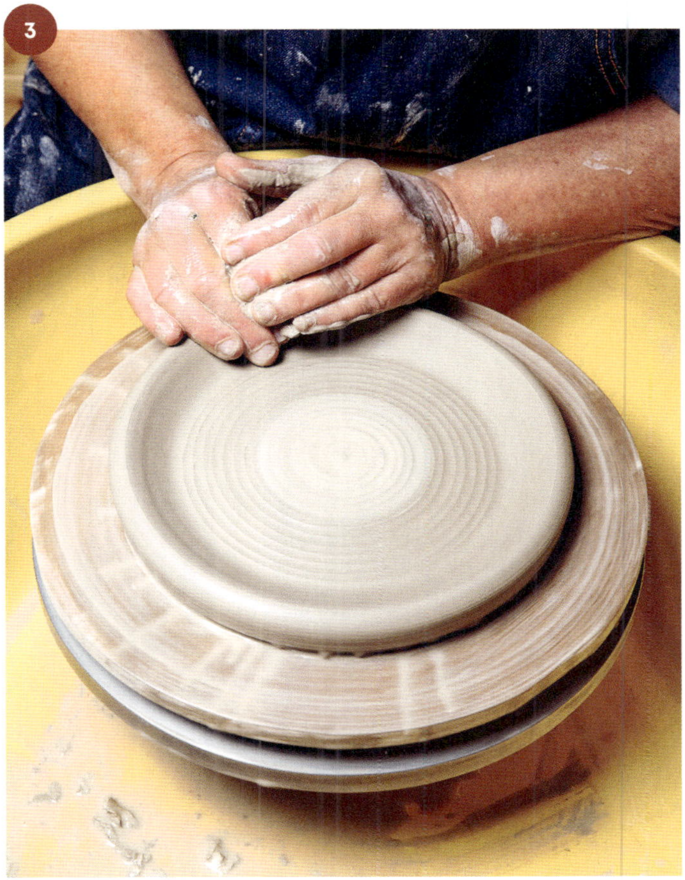
3

4

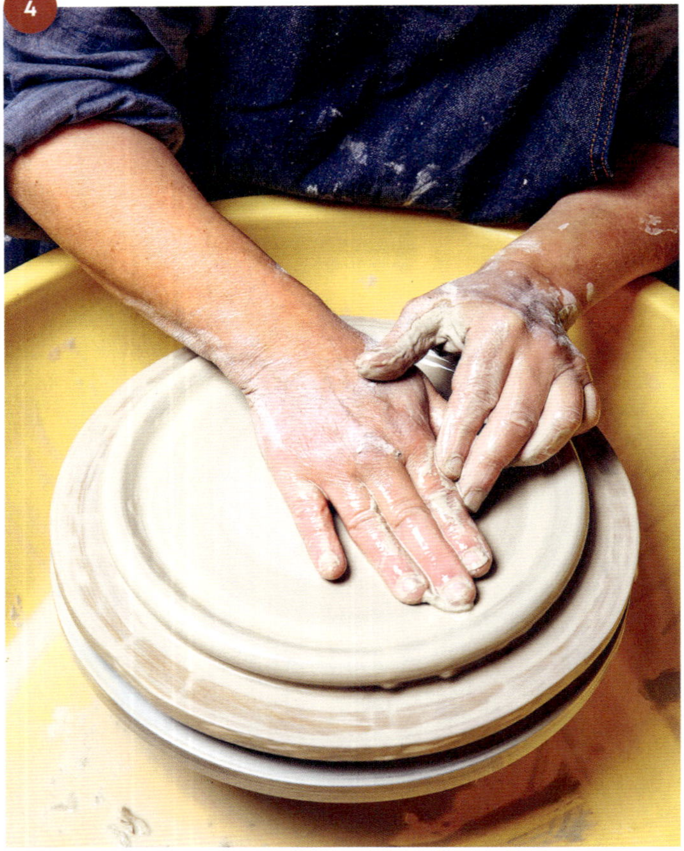

5

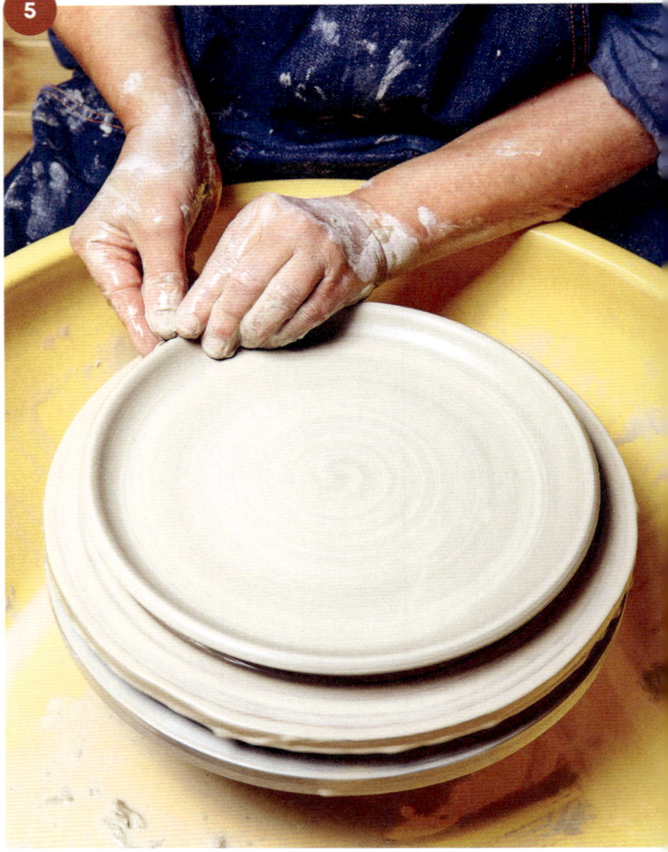

6

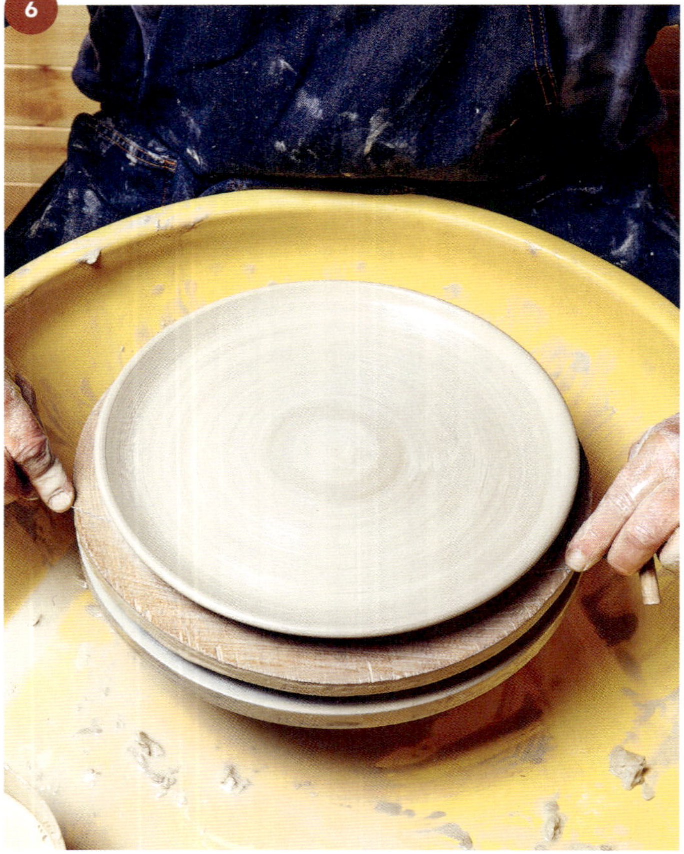

7

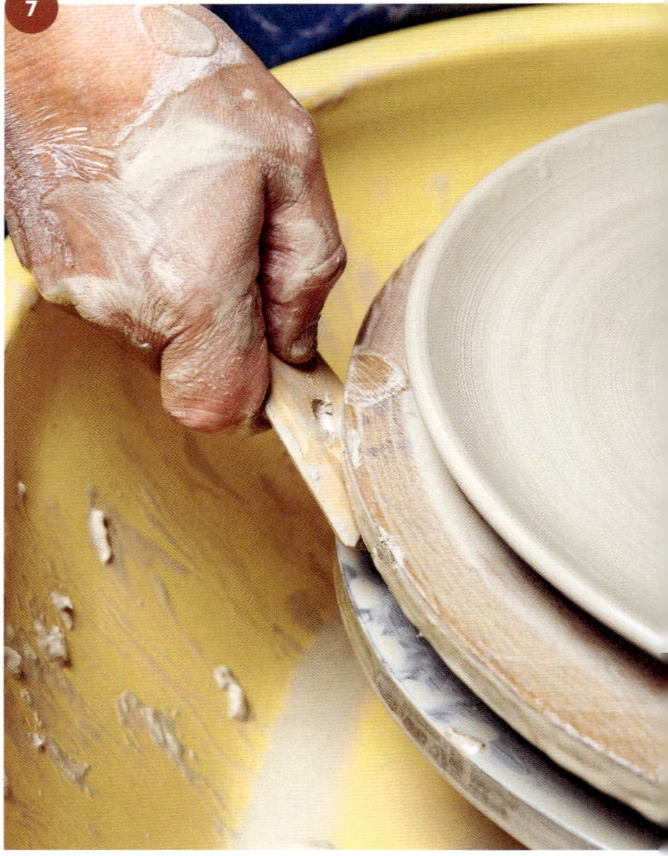

4. Compress the clay in the base by running your fingers over the surface from the centre to the outside edge several times.

   It is critical that you do not omit this step, because it goes a long way to preventing the base from cracking later.

5. Position the fingers of your left hand inside the fat rim, with your right-hand fingers opposite on the outside, and carefully lift the plate edge upwards and slightly outwards.

   This is a tricky manoeuvre because there is not much space for the fingers on the outside, but try to use all the clay available and remember to compress the clay at the rim when finished.

6. Sponge away excess water and slurry from the surface of the plate, then holding your wire really taut, underwire the base of the plate once.

7. Ease the batt off the wheel carefully, using a sturdy tool at several positions around the edge. It is important to remove the batt smoothly in order to avoid distorting the plate.

   Allow the plate to firm to soft leather hard *in situ* on the batt before handling it, then turn it over to allow it to dry to full leather hard ready for trimming if required.

Using a batt

Many forms are best thrown on a batt to avoid distorting their shape when you lift them off the wheel. Modern wheels come with a quick-fit mechanism for batts, and other devices are available that can be attached to an existing wheel. However, these come at considerable cost, so when you're first learning to throw, it is best to learn how to attach a batt in the time-honoured, traditional way, on a clay pad.

1. Centre (see page 46) a minimum weight of about 1.5 kg (3 lb) of clay (photo 1A). Don't be mean with the amount, because it needs to cover the wheel head and will flatten out with use. Also, you need a little bit of height between the batt and the wheel to allow for an easy release once the form has been thrown and you won't have this if you don't use enough clay.

   Open out the clay to cover the greater part of the wheel head, leaving a thick, doughnut-like ring at the outer edge (photo 1B).

2. Clean away all excess water from the surface of the clay pad using a sponge.

3. Place a wooden batt over the pad (photo 3A), making sure it is central before thumping it down at the centre with your fist to secure it in place (photo 3B).

   You are now ready to go.

1A

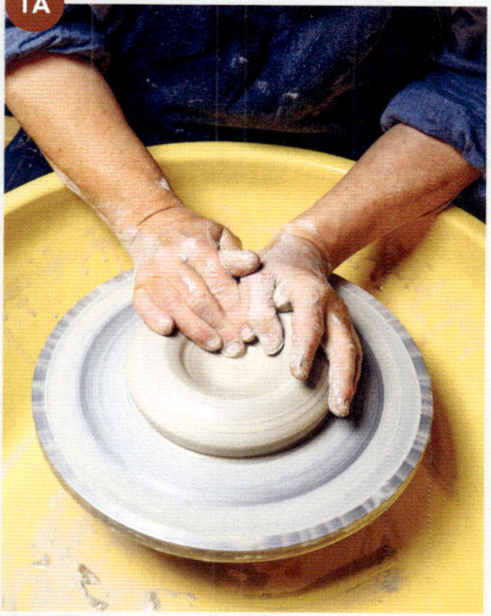

1B

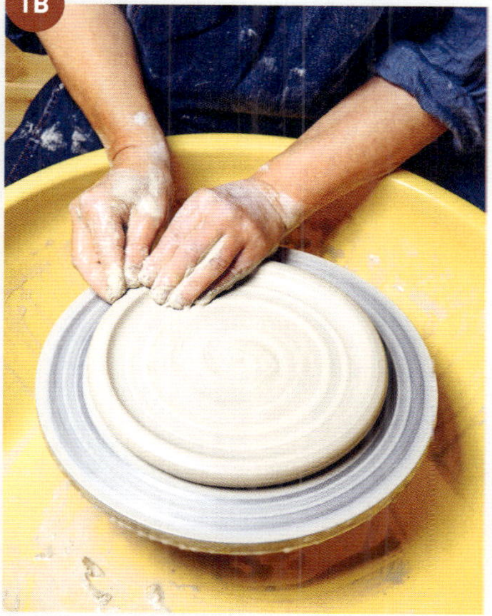

2

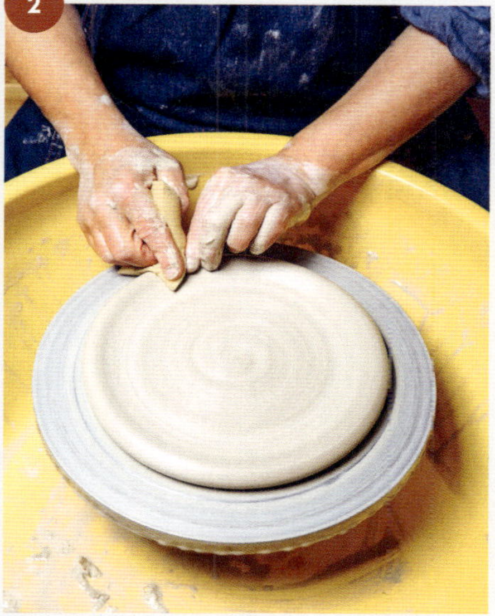

3A

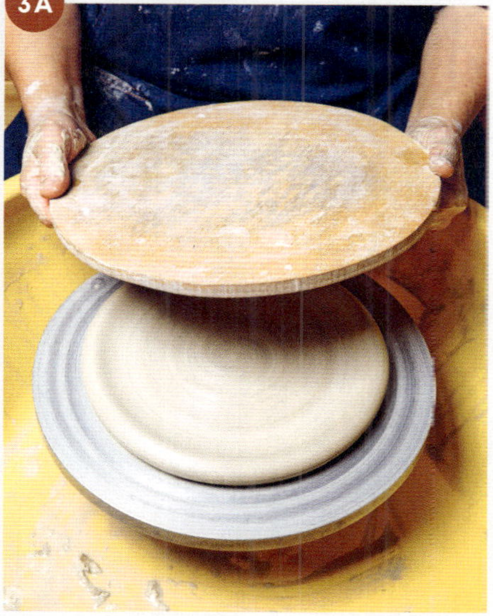

3B

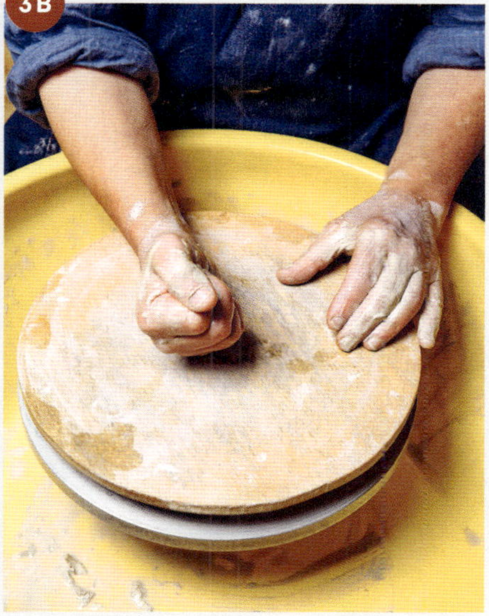

Turning and trimming

Many thrown forms need some kind of refinement after the initial making process. Whether it be trimming away the excess clay needed to hold the shape as it firms up or turning a foot ring into the clay to improve the shape.

A foot ring serves more than one purpose. From an aesthetic point of view it can refine the shape of a form; from a practical perspective, it minimizes contact with a surface helping to prevent burns if the piece contains hot food.

Making a foot ring

1. Dampen the surface of the wheel head minimally, then run a damp finger around the rim of the thrown form.

   Position your form rim down at the centre of the wheel, using the concentric lines as a guide.

   Test that the form is centred by holding a finger rigid against its side as the wheel turns slowly. If your finger misses in places the form is not centred, so re-position it and repeat until it runs true.

   Apply a little pressure to the form to secure it or, if you prefer, secure it with wads of soft clay.

2. Using your turning tool of choice (see page 16), begin by flattening the raised base of the form, working from the centre to the outside edge with the wheel turning at a slow to medium speed. Then, holding the form in position with your thumb, cut down vertically to establish the side of the foot.

   You can also take the opportunity to remove clay from the wall below the foot at this stage if you feel it is too thick.

3. Bevel the outside edge of the foot slightly to neaten it, so that you can develop the final shape more clearly later.

4. Now mark the thickness of the foot with the tip of the turning tool, measuring it from the outside edge of the base.

5. Hollow the inner section of the base of the form from the centre to the established inner edge of the foot. The depth will depend on the amount of clay you have at the base for turning, but practically it should be at least the depth of the foot on the outside. If you are turning a larger form such as a bowl, it should follow the gentle curve of the interior space so that the wall remains the same thickness throughout.

   When you are happy with the depth of the foot and the surface you have trimmed, cut a shallow bevel on the inside of the foot to match the outer one.

6. Using your trimming tool or a kidney-type rib, trim the wall of the form down from the foot until the thickness is the same throughout, the shape pleases you and the surface is smooth and even.

FOOT SIZE

The dimensions of the foot relate directly to the size and shape of the form and must be balanced and practical.

A tea cup requires a relatively small foot for delicacy, but it must still be a balanced size for the form itself; if it is too small and unstable, it will be dangerous to fill with hot liquid. Conversely, kitchen and table-type bowls require a wide foot for practicality.

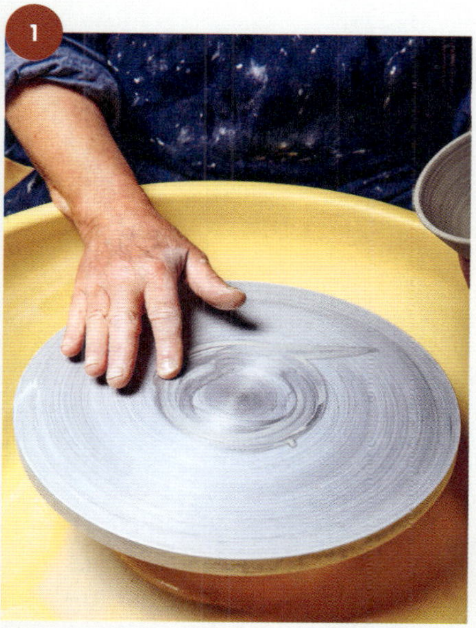
1

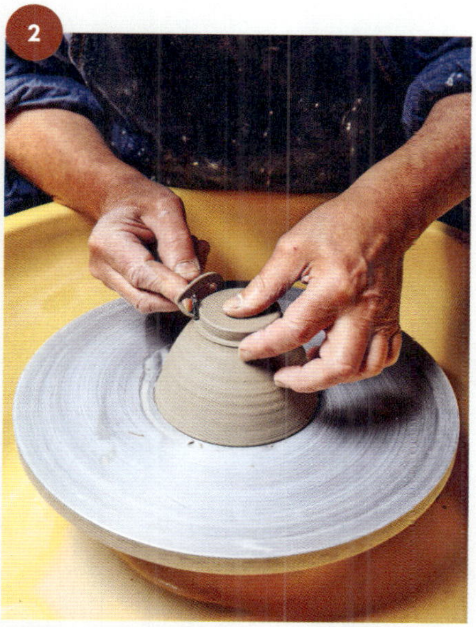
2

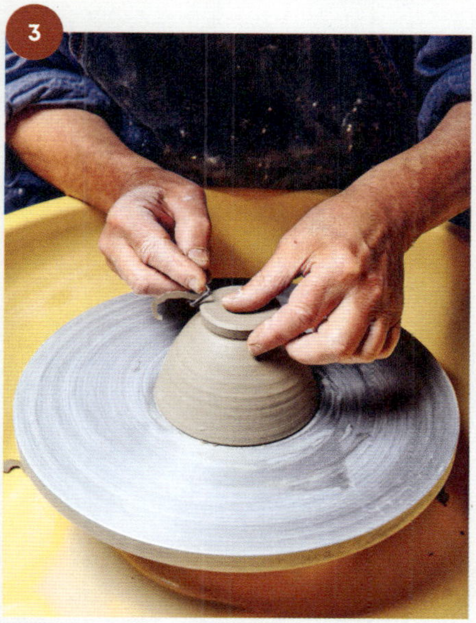
3

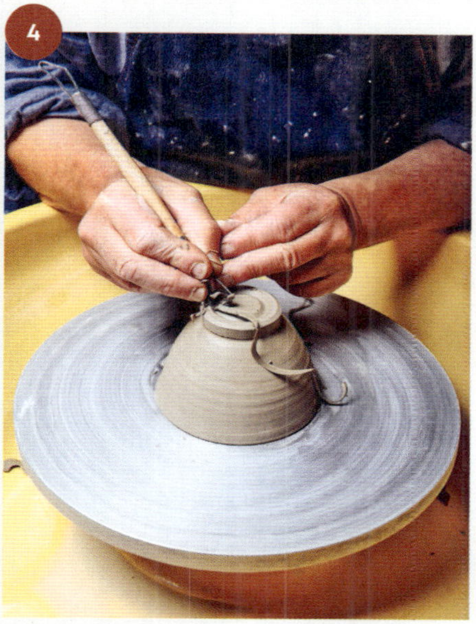
4

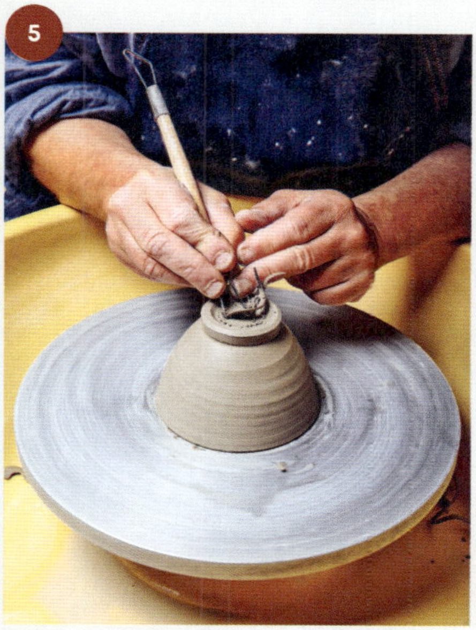
5

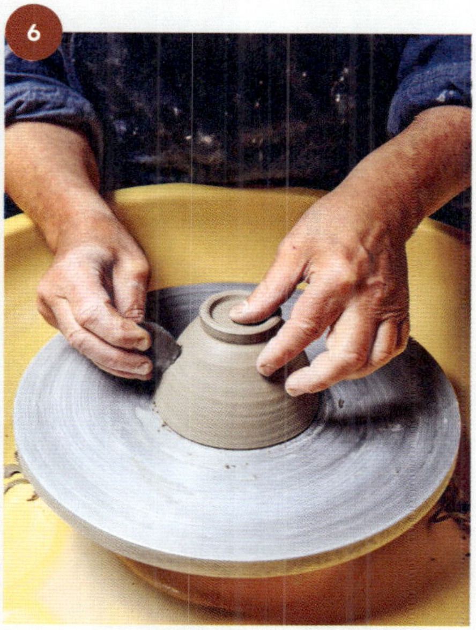
6

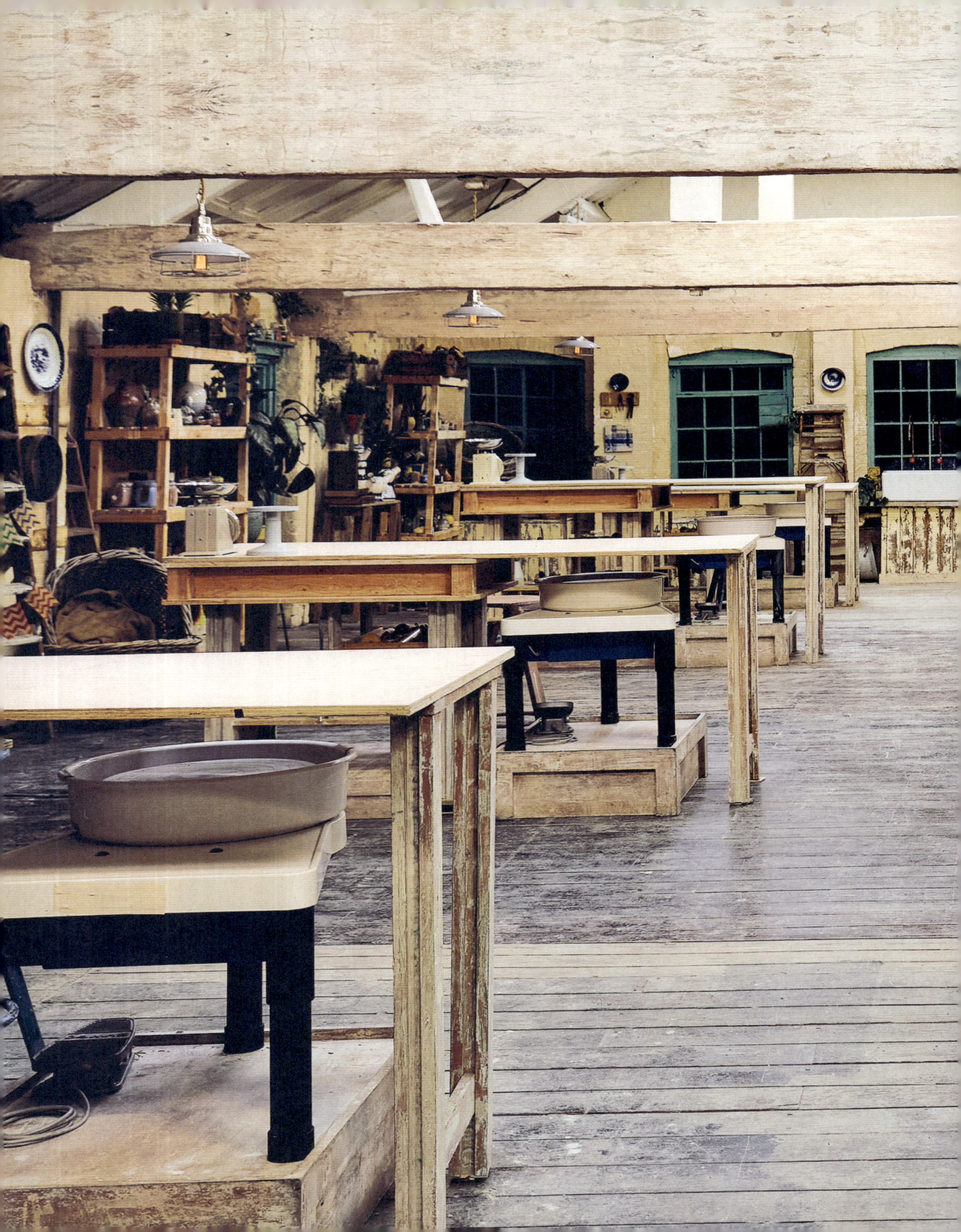

Main makes

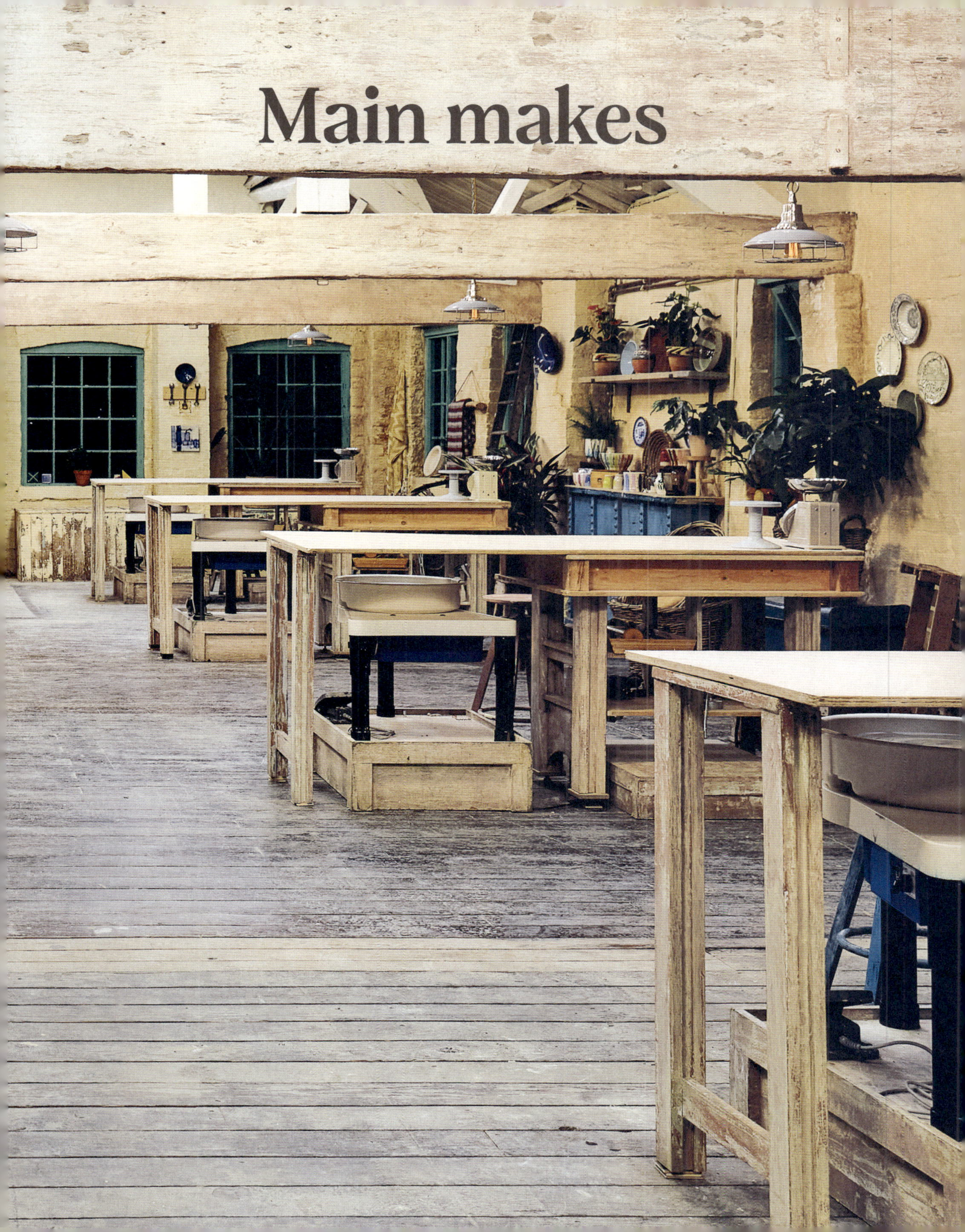

Egg cup

This easy project combines the basic techniques of slabbing and pinching to make a composite form. It is quick to make, so you could easily create a whole set in no time at all.

YOU WILL NEED

Clay of choice (earthenware or stoneware): approx. 225 g (8 oz) for a set of four

Card to make a template for the base of the egg cup

Tools: Plastic sheet, roller guides (no thicker than 5 mm/¼ in.), rolling pin, basic tool kit

Glaze(s) of choice to decorate

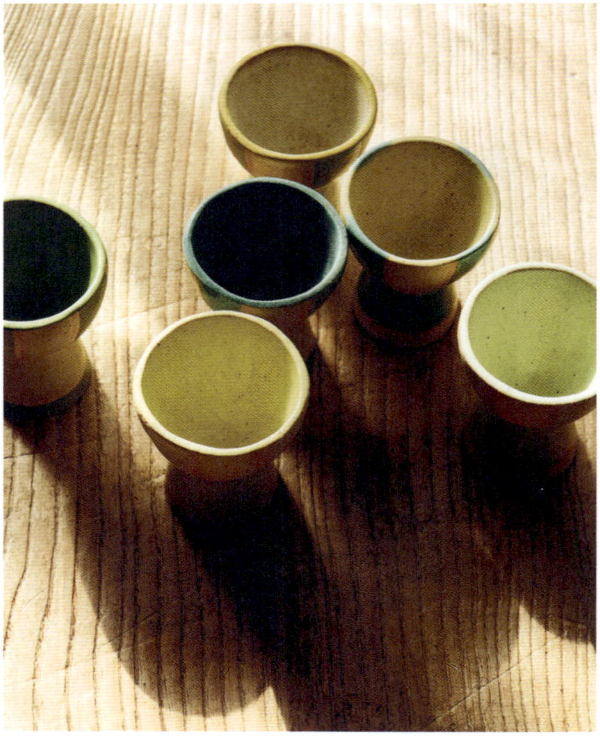

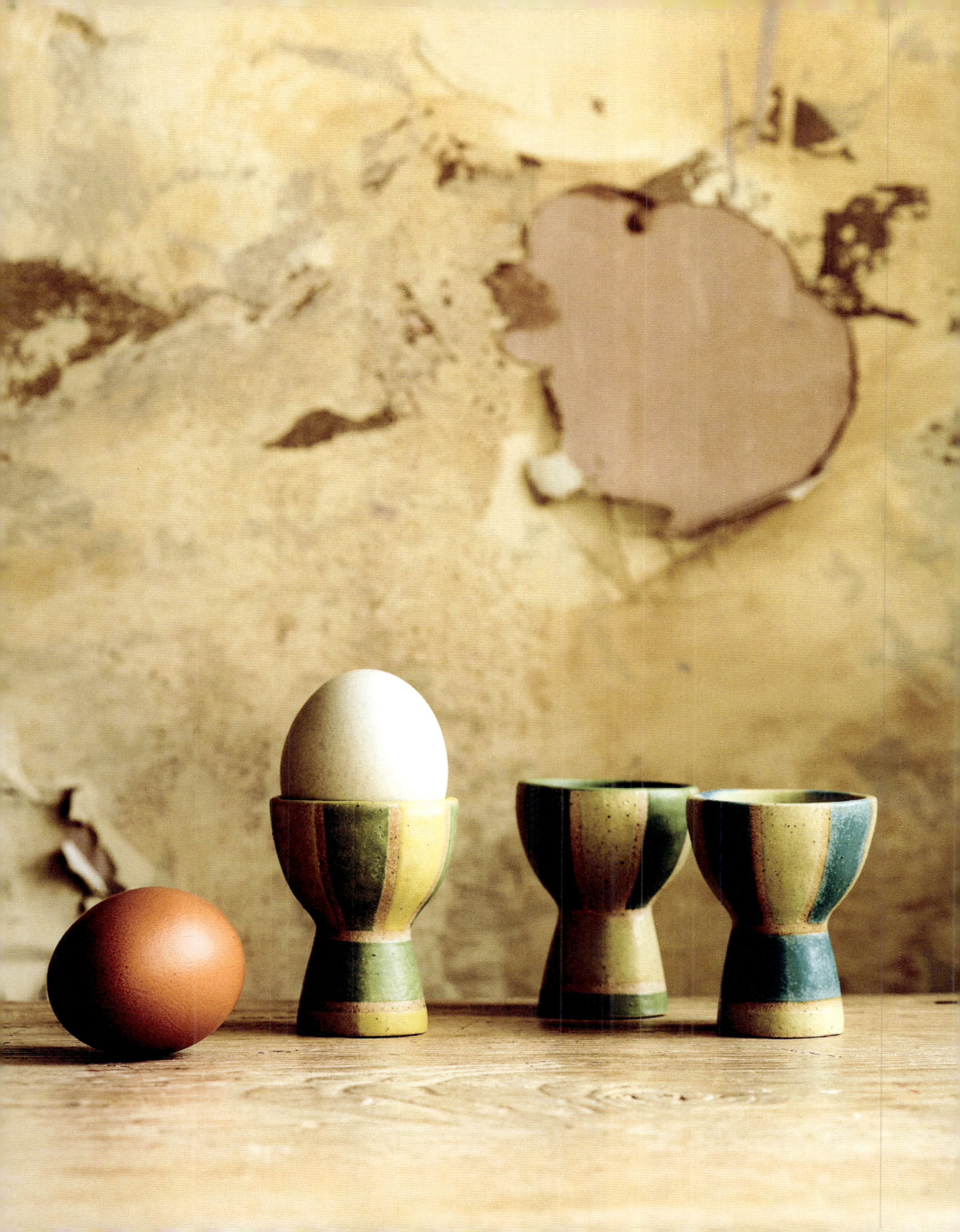

1

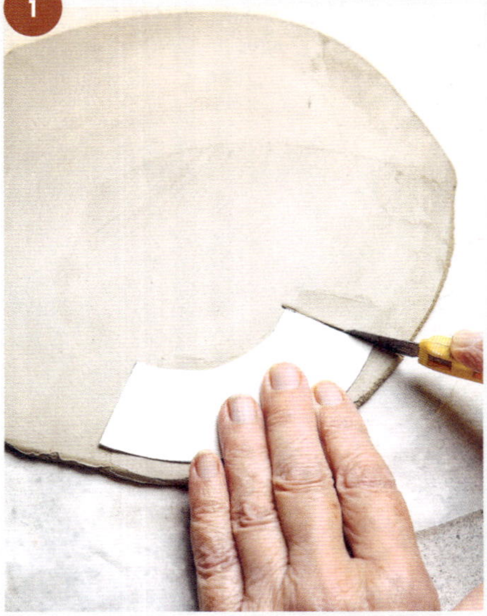

2

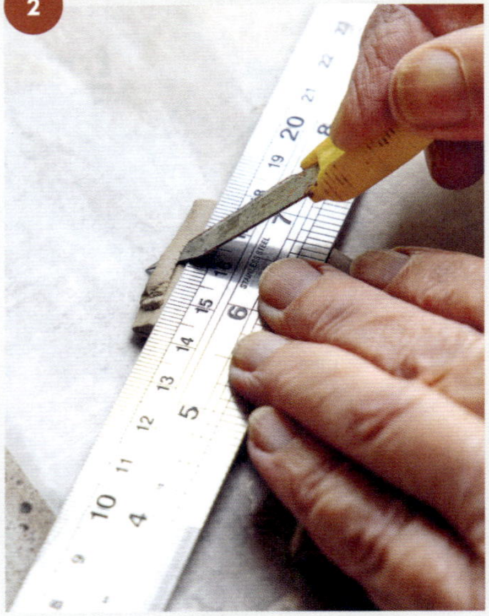

3

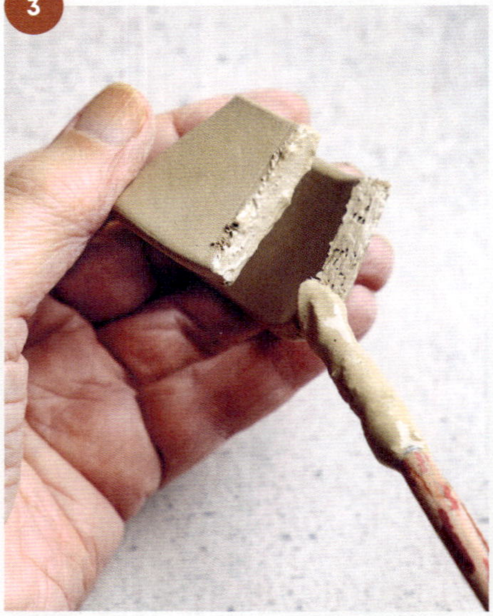

4

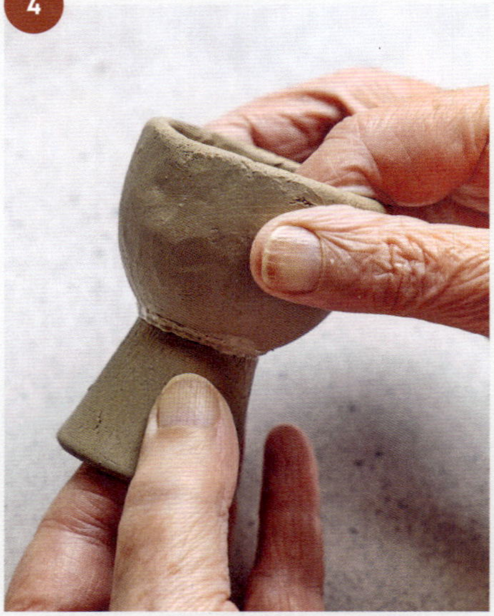

5

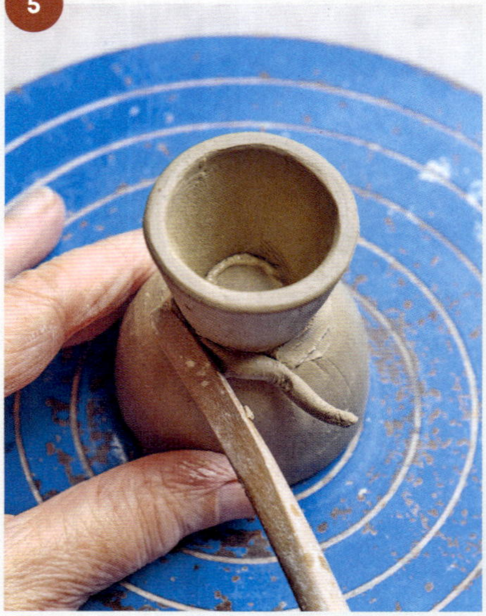

6

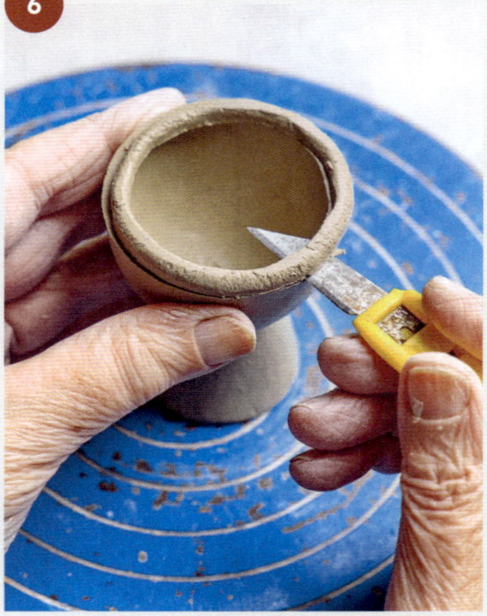

1. Make a card template for the base by cutting out a circle roughly 20 cm (8 in.) in diameter, then cut out and remove a 15.3 cm (6 in.) circle from the middle so that the remaining ring is 5 cm (2 in.) deep

   Cut the circle into four equal parts and use one of the sections as your template.

   Roll a small slab of clay (see page 40), then place the template on the surface and cut out the shape.

2. Bevel the first end of the cut-out slab section by placing a ruler 5 mm (¼ in.) in from the edge, then cutting through the clay at an angle, with the tip of the knife on the board and the blade resting on the ruler.

   Before removing the ruler, score the bevelled edge with a serrated kidney, then turn the slab over and bevel the opposite end in the same way.

3. Apply some joining slip to the scored edges, then curve the slab into a circle and join them together securely.

   Work over the join with a rib to tidy up inside and out.

4. Beginning with 20 g (approx. 1 oz) of clay, pinch a small cup (see page 37) of a sufficient size to hold an egg, allowing a little extra for clay shrinkage.

   Place the cup on the base and draw a pin lightly around the cup where the base meets the surface to mark the position for the parts to fit together. Score and slip adjoining positions on the base and cup and fix the sections together.

5. Reinforce around the join with a thin coil of soft clay and blend it in with a wooden tool. Smooth over the area using the rounded end of a small rib.

6. Sit the egg cup at the centre of a whirler, then holding a knife rigid, carefully level the top.

   Work around the cut edge with a rib to gently round and smooth it off

Mug

We all tend to have a favourite mug, so what better than to make your own? This might sound like quite a daunting prospect: if you're a regular *Great Pottery Throw Down* viewer, you've probably immediately conjured up visions of Keith's 'bucket of doom', into which mugs are thrown when they're not all uniform. However, our version could not be simpler: all you need is a suitably sized tube former to form the slabs around and you'll have a whole range of identical mugs in no time. This can be made from cardboard but bear in mind that, to allow for clay shrinkage, it does need to be a little larger than the mugs you want to make, so don't opt for one that is too narrow.

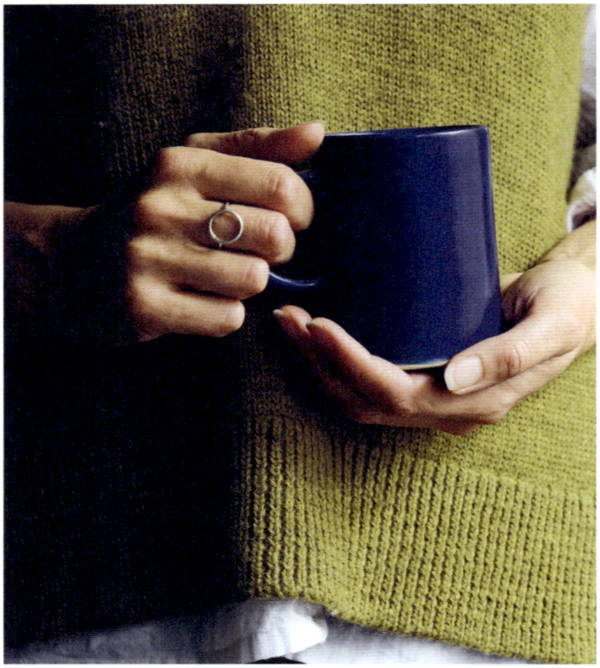

YOU WILL NEED

Clay of choice (earthenware or stoneware): approx. 225 g (8 oz) for each mug, plus extra for handles

Tube former and newspaper

Tools: Plastic sheet, roller guides (no thicker than 5 mm/¼ in and preferably thinner), rolling pin, basic tool kit, cookie cutter with a diameter larger than tube former, hair dryer (optional).

Glaze(s) of choice to decorate

BEFORE YOU BEGIN

Wrap the tube former in a sheet of newspaper and secure it in place by stuffing the excess newspaper in at each end of the former.

Cut a card or paper template to fit around the former with at least a 5-cm (2-in) overlap. This overlap is to accommodate the difference in thickness between clay and paper.

Roll a slab of your clay of choice using guides no thicker than 5 mm/¼ in (see page 40). Aim to roll a long rectangle if possible but it must be large enough to accommodate the template with some extra for the base and handle.

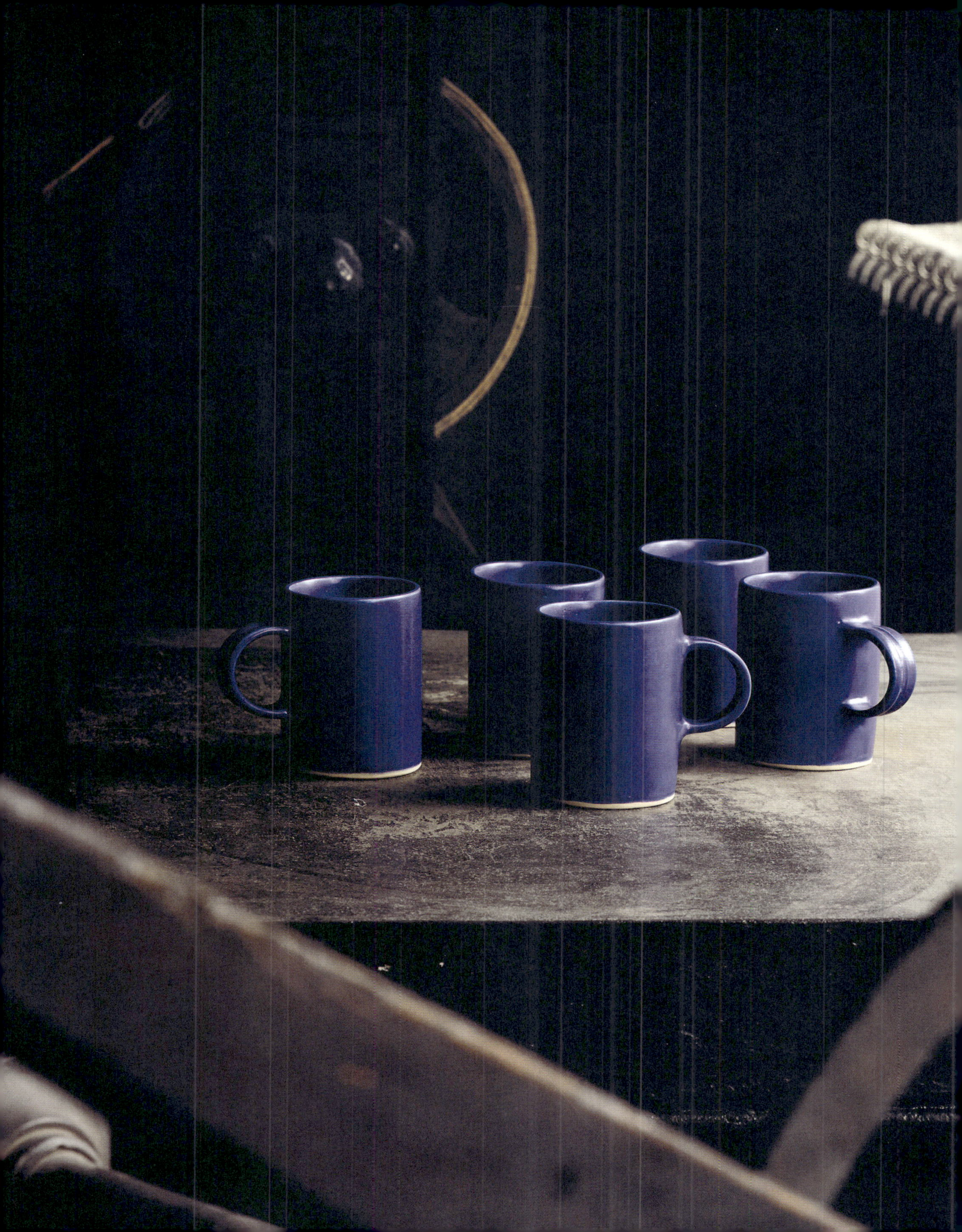

1

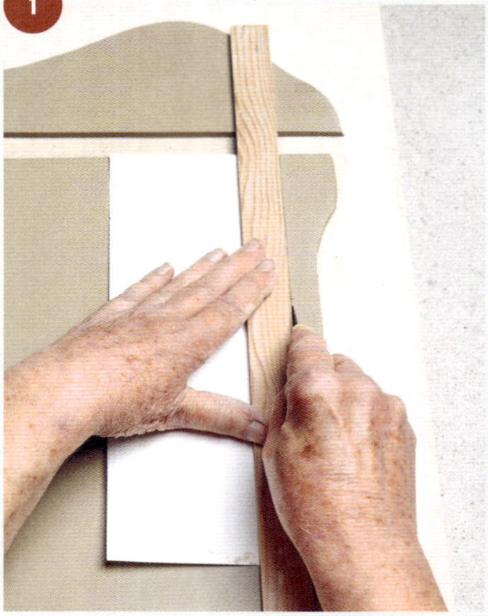

2

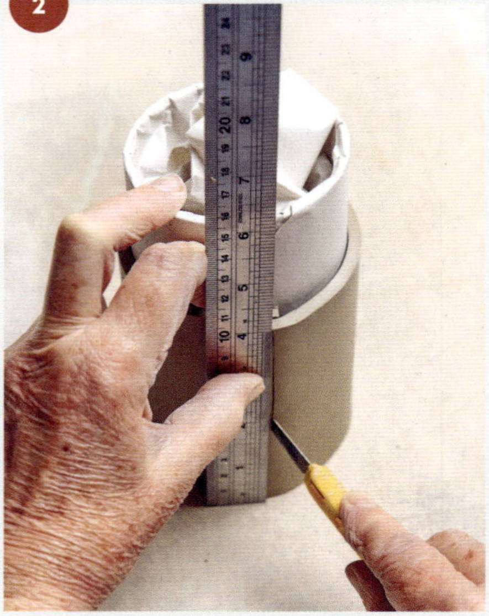

3

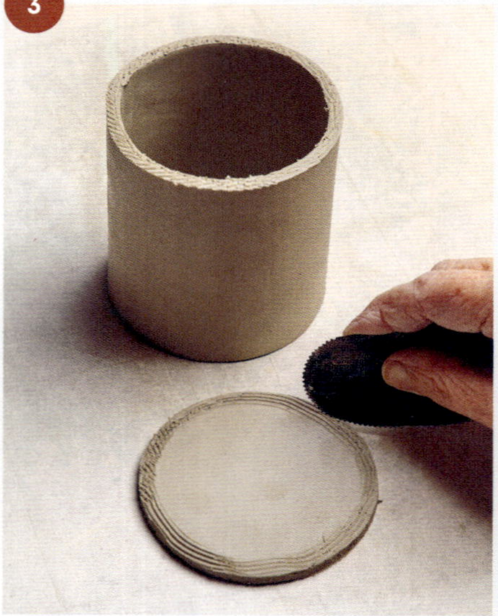

4

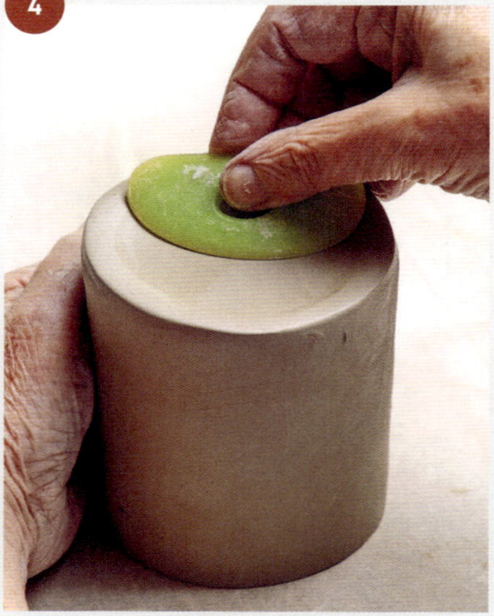

5

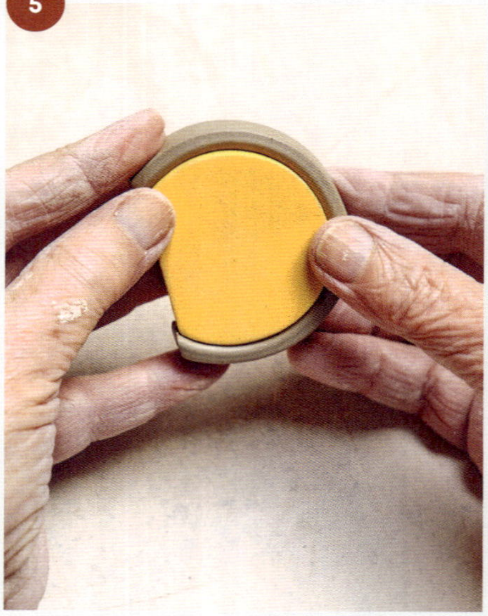

6

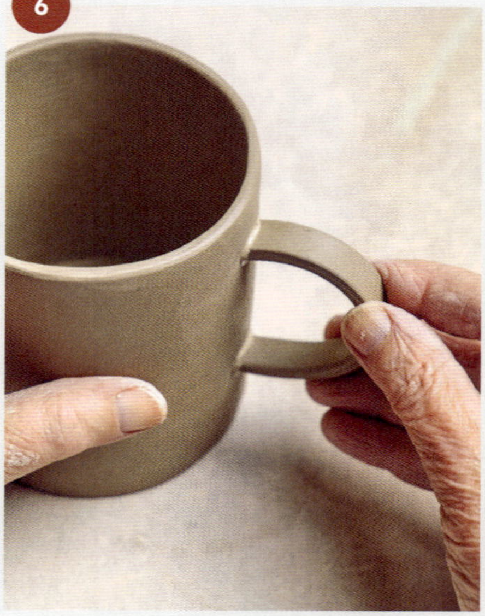

1. Place the template on the slab in a corner so as to maximize its use and carefully cut around it, using a batten as a guide to cut the edges straight.

   Keep the remaining part of the slab under plastic wrap for use later.

2. Wrap the slab around the tube former so that the ends overlap. Stand a ruler upright against the overlap and cut through both layers of clay at an angle, using a sharp knife.

   Score and slip the cut edges, then join them together securely. Work over the join with a rib to remove excess slip and tidy up.

3. Remove the tube former from the cylinder by first releasing the newspaper from the top interior, then gently sliding the tube out. Remove the paper last, taking care not to distort the shape in the process.

   Next, cut out a circle for the base, using a cookie cutter slightly larger than the diameter of the body.

   The cookie cutter must be larger than the diameter of the tube for the same reason as above – clay is thicker so the diameter is extended by the thickness of the slab once the body has been made.

   Score and slip the lower edge of the mug body and the outer edge of the base circle, then fit the parts together. Tap the base on the work surface a couple of times to ensure the sections seal fully together.

4. Work around the outer edge of the base to tidy up, then using the rounded side of a small rib, gently indent the base of the mug a little.

   Turn the mug upright and work around the rim with a rib to gently thin and round it off so that it will be pleasant to drink from.

5. From your remaining slab, cut a short strap to form the handle, then manipulate it to a shape of your choosing. Use a handle former for this if you wish (see note below). Firm it up in this position using a hair dryer until the shape will hold.

6. Score and slip the ends of the handle and the corresponding positions on the side of the mug and carefully fix it in place. As a precaution, reinforce around the joins with thin coils of soft clay and blend them in using a wooden tool.

   Allow the mug to dry out really slowly, ready for bisque firing.

JUDGES' NOTE

You can shape the handle over a handle former, as shown here (photo 5); these are widely available from craft outlets and ceramic suppliers, but are not an essential piece of equipment. If you're not using a handle former make a card template, just as you did for the body of the mug, so that all your handles are the same size.

Candle holder

Candle holders were once essential household items, but these days they are generally only used for decorative purposes – especially for special occasions such as Christmas, when they look lovely as a table centrepiece with floral wreaths around them. The style of our candle holder hails from a time before electricity, when light had to be carried from room to room and candle holders required a handle and dish at the base to contain hot dripping wax. It is quick and easy to make and combines the pinching method with an unusual technique for making tubes.

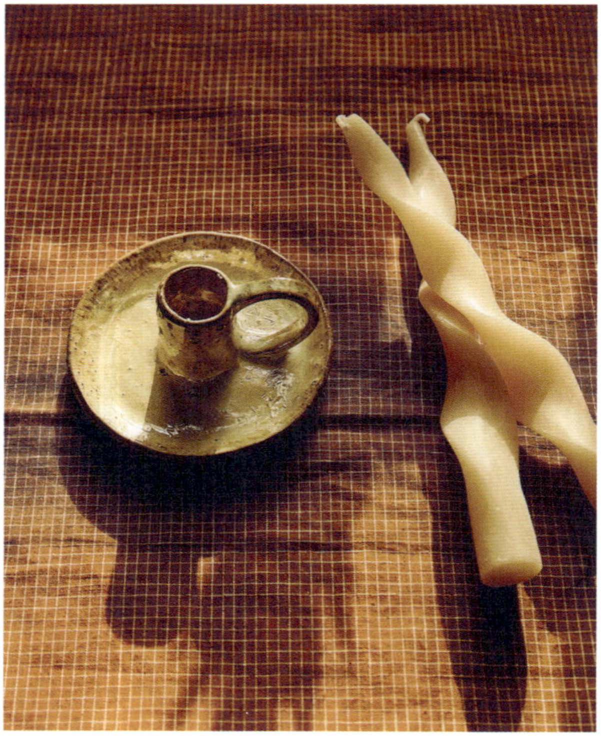

YOU WILL NEED

Clay of choice (earthenware or stoneware): approx. 170 g (6 oz) for a candle holder 5 cm (2 in.) high

Tools: Basic tool kit

A short length of 5-mm (¼-in) dowel or similar (a pencil would work)

Glaze(s) of choice to decorate

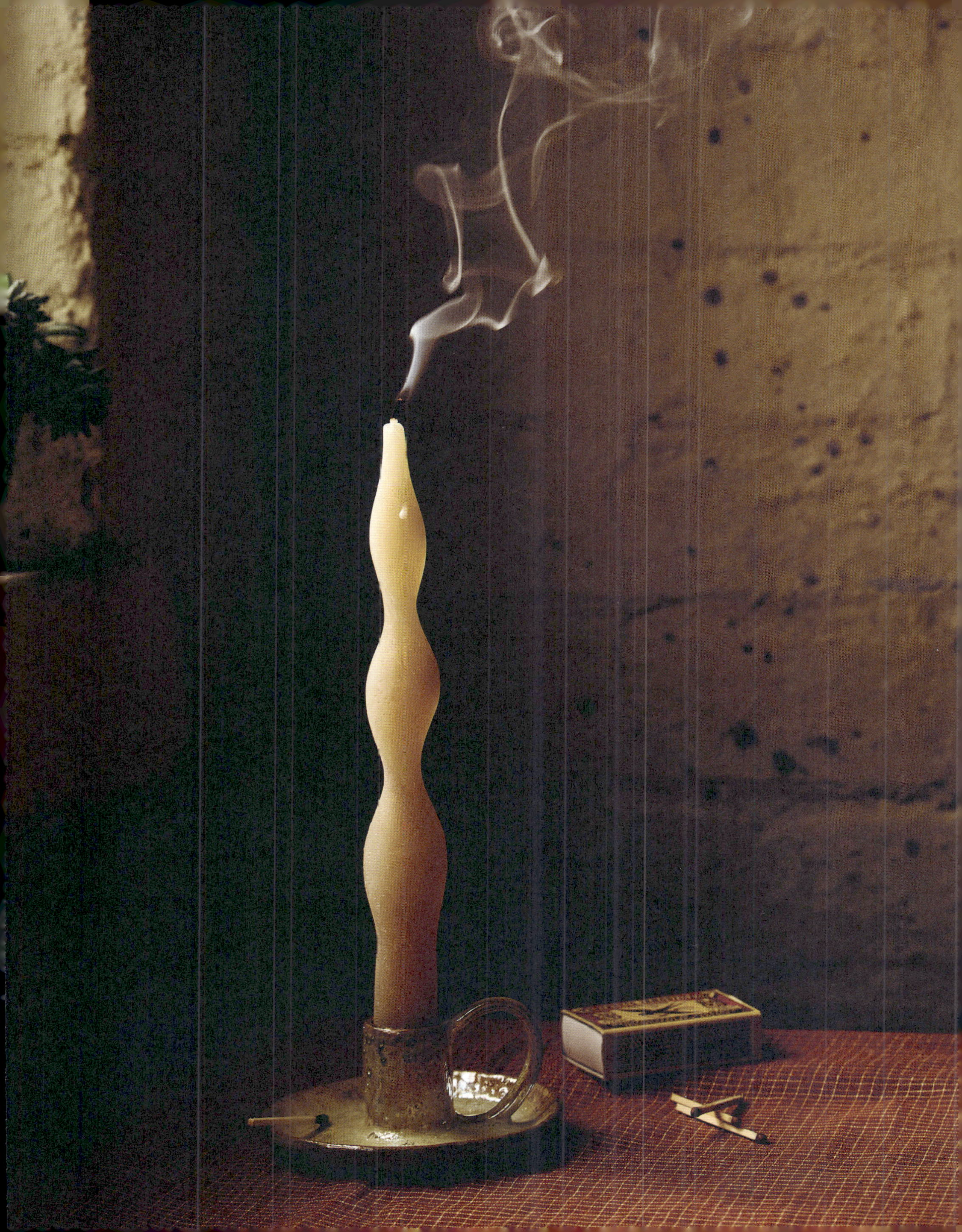

1

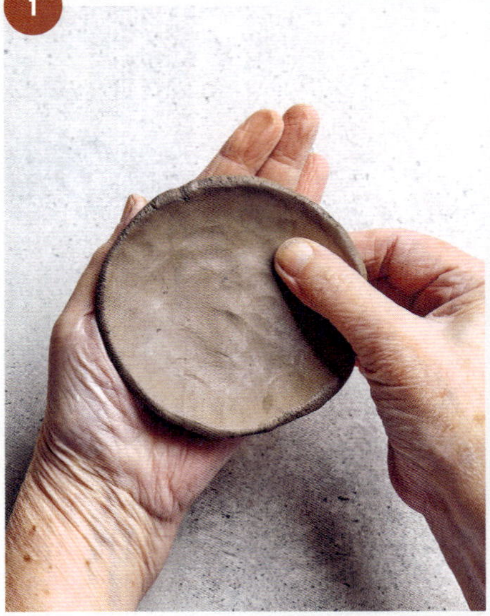

2

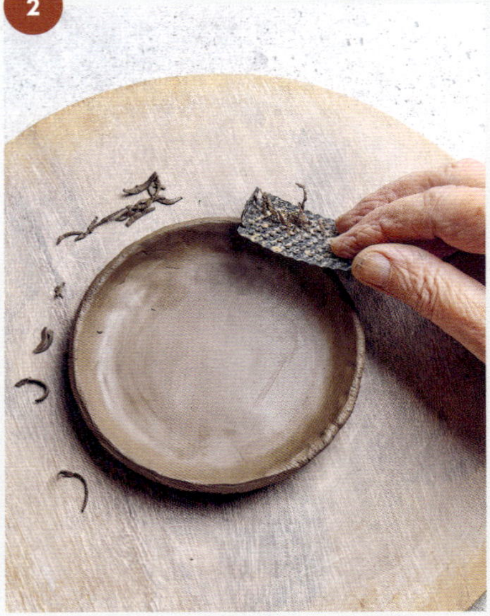

3

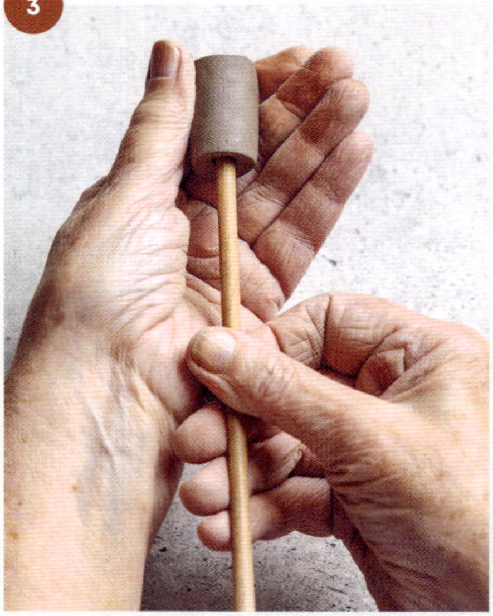

4

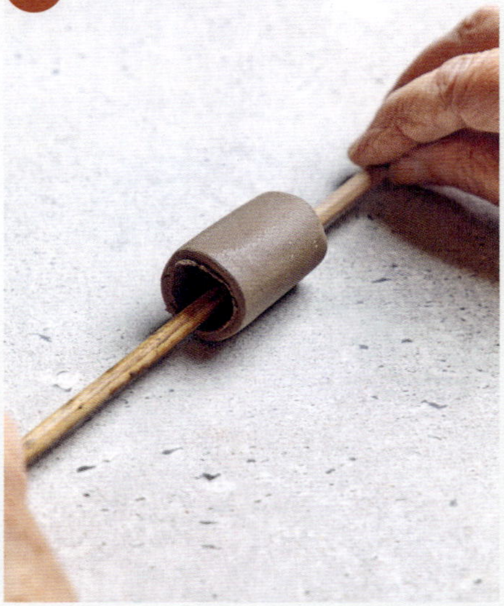

5

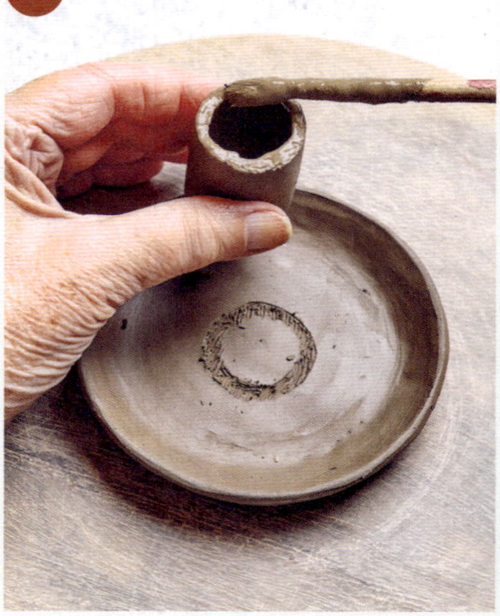

6

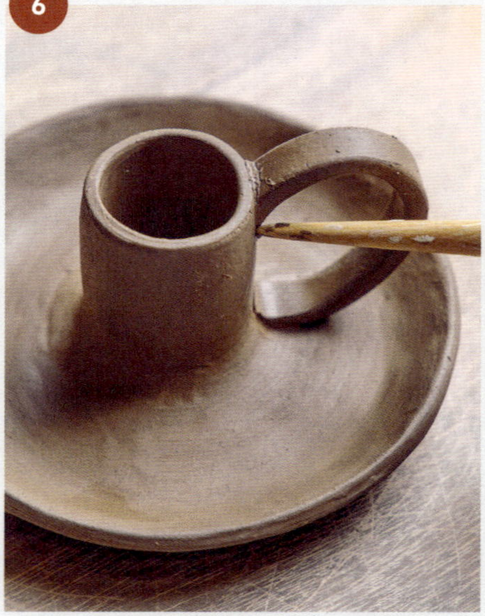

1. Following the method outlined on page 37, pinch a small ball of clay out to a flat dish with a raised edge.
2. Place the dish on a board and carefully work over the surface with a rib to refine and smooth it. Using a surform rasp, level the rim. Gently round off the levelled rim with a rib to finish.
3. Roll a short, thick coil of clay and cut a length no greater than 3 cm (1¼ in.). Carefully push the dowel through the centre length of the coil until it comes out at the opposite end.
4. Holding the dowel at each end, roll the coil over the work surface. As you do this it will open out to form a tube. Continue to roll until the tube is large enough to accommodate a candle, allowing a little extra for clay shrinkage (see page 166).
5. Score and slip a position for the tube at the centre of the dish and at the base of the tube itself, then fix the tube in place.

   Reinforce around the join with a thin coil of soft clay and blend it in until seamless.
6. Roll and flatten a thin, short coil of clay to form a simple handle and cut it to an appropriate size to fit the candle holder. Fix the handle in place, attached to the tube, after scoring and slipping all adjoining areas.

   Work around the joins with a wooden tool to remove excess slip and tidy up.

   Allow the candle holder to dry out slowly before bisque firing.

Spoon rest

Despite years of debate about the usefulness of a spoon rest – some argue a plate does just as well – they are actually really handy (especially when you need the plate at the table).

YOU WILL NEED

Clay of choice (earthenware or stoneware): approx. 340 g (12 oz) for a spoon rest measuring 23 x 17 cm (9 x 6½ in.)

MDF or hardboard for former

Paper or card for template

Tools: Plastic sheet, roller guides (5 mm/¼ in thick, maximum), rolling pin, rib, basic tool kit, small cookie cutter

Foam block at least 8 cm (just over 3 in.) thick

Glaze(s) of choice to decorate

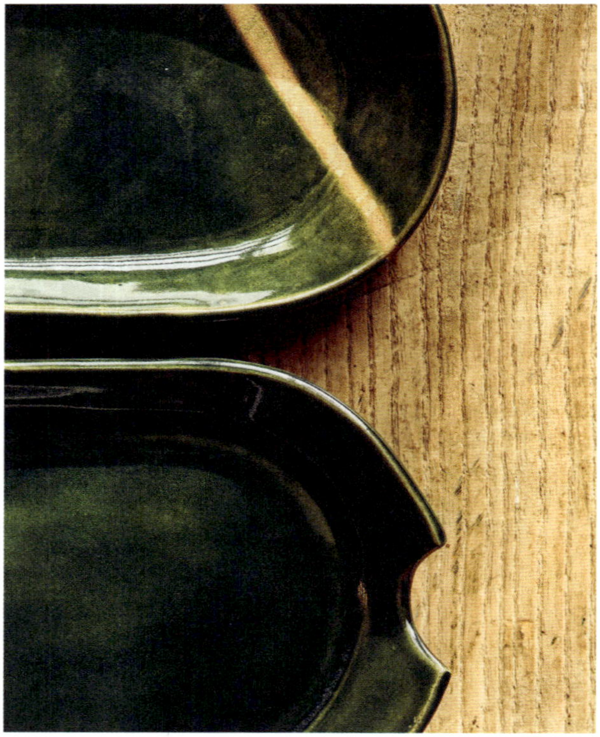

JUDGES' NOTE

Foam blocks are widely available from interiors stores and sewing and craft outlets. Choose one at least 8 cm (just over 3 in.) deep for best results.

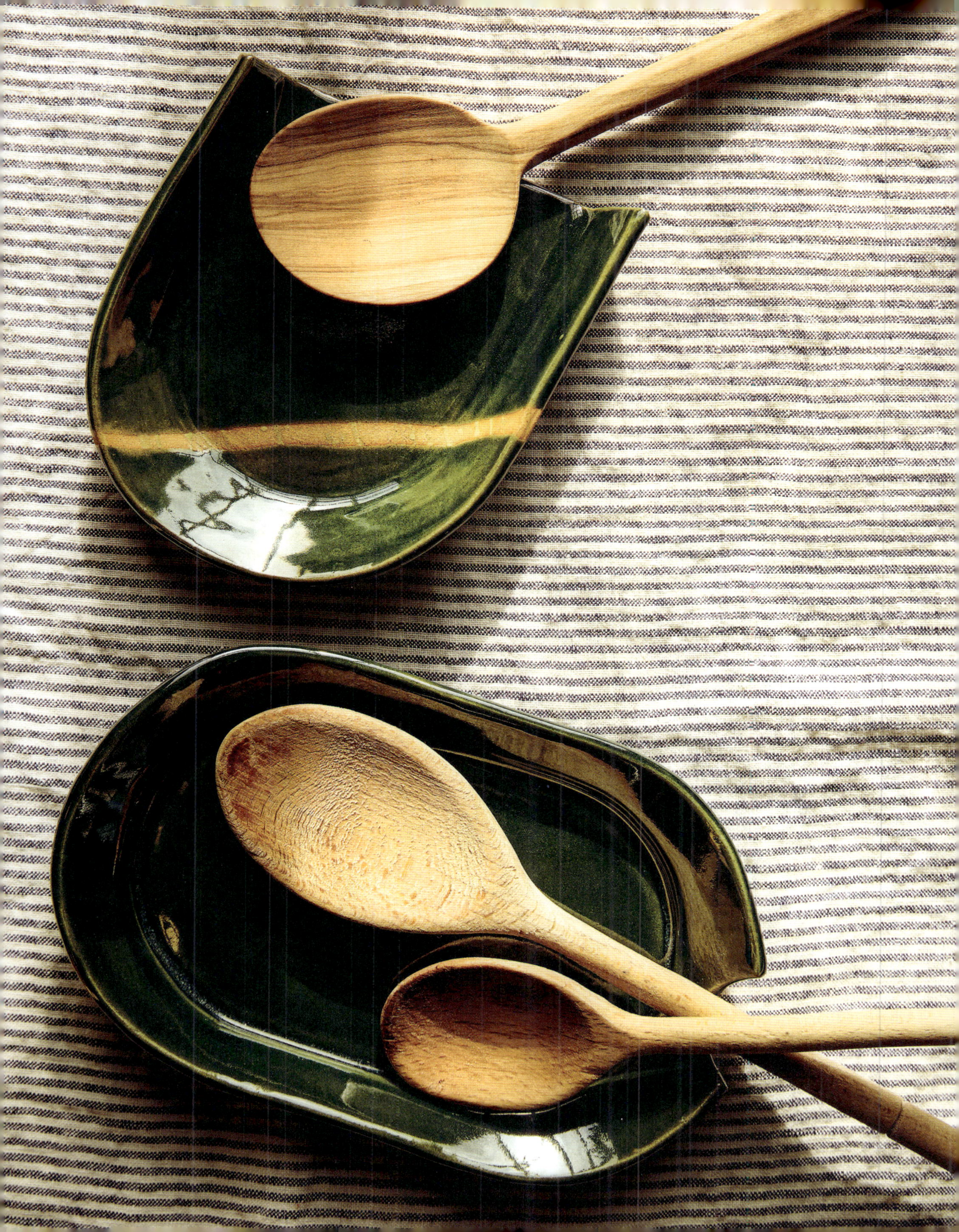

1

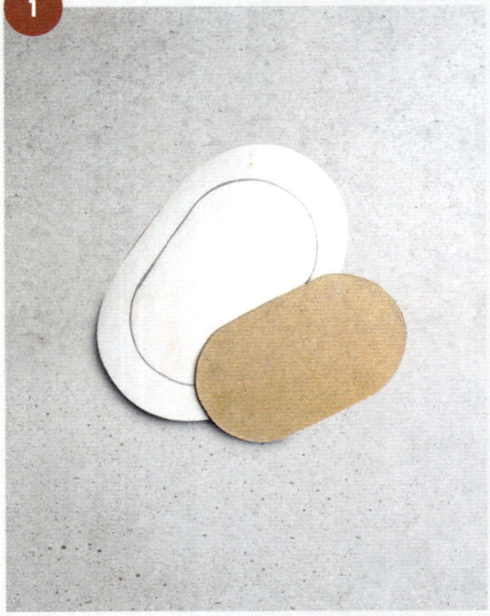

2

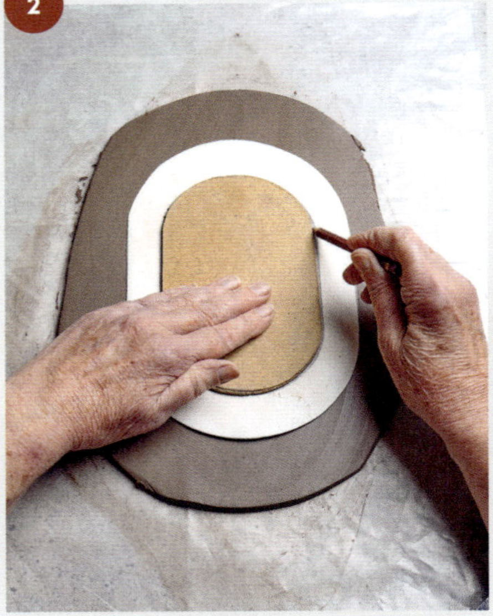

3

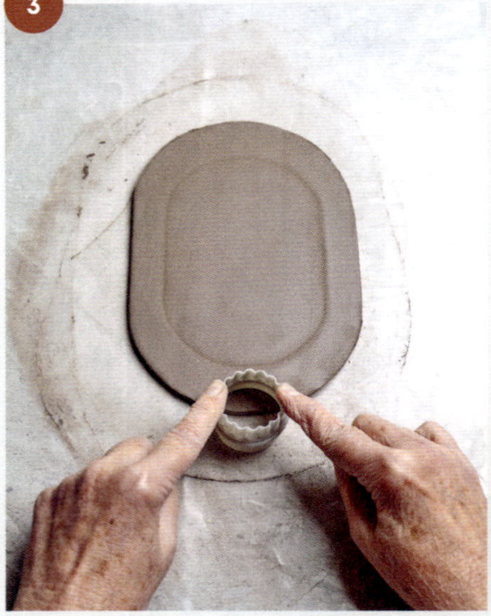

4

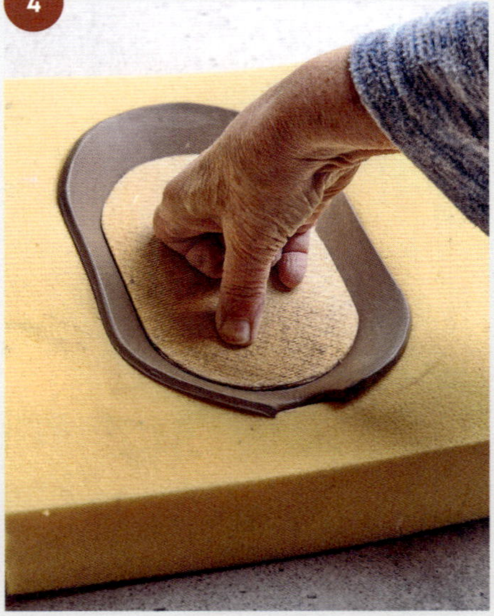

5

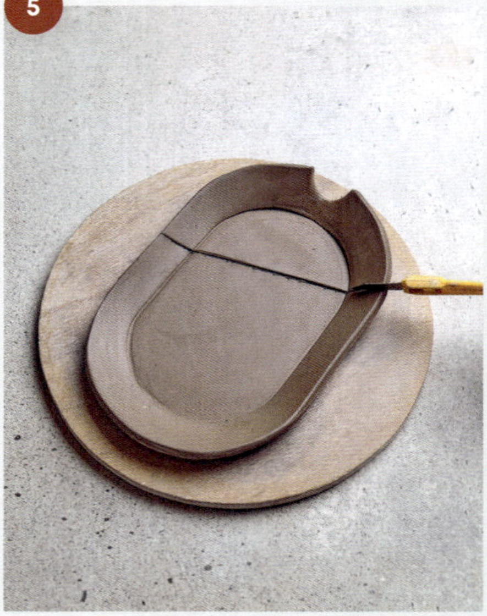

6

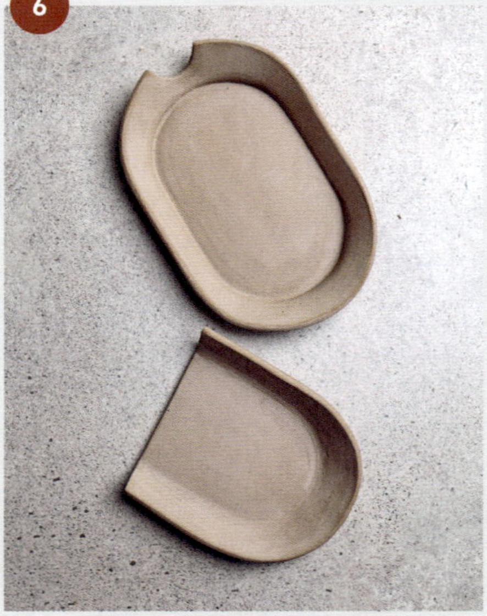

1. First draw and cut out the former. You can use thin MDF, hardboard or even stiff cardboard, but it must be a material that holds its shape. Cut out a rectangle to your required size. We used the following measurements for the example opposite, 17 x 11 cm (6½ x 4½ in.). Then using a protractor, round off the ends with a pencil line then cut the shape out carefully.

   Place the former on a large sheet of thick paper or card and draw around the shape, then draw another line 3 cm (1¼ in.) outside the outline of the former, all the way around. Cut out the shape then round off the corners to create an oval.

2. Roll out a slab of clay (see page 40) on your plastic sheet, using roller guides to achieve the thickness suggested for your chosen clay type.

   Place the paper or card template on the slab with the former at its centre aligned to the pencil outline. Carefully draw around the former again with a pencil to transfer an impressed outline to the clay beneath.

3. Remove the former and the paper template, then cut the shape out around the template. Discard the surplus clay.

   Next, using the cookie cutter, cut a notch or semi-circle out at one end of the slab to create a rest for the handle of the spoon.

4. With the impressed line of the former uppermost, carefully transfer the slab to the foam block, then place the former itself on the slab, aligned to the impression.

   Push down firmly on the former with one or two hands. As you do this, the wall of the spoon rest will rise up to form a dish shape.

5. To make a smaller version without a handle rest, cut through the dish at an angle three-quarters of the way along its length and discard the handle rest end. You could, of course, also cut it to this shape before forming it on the foam if you wanted to save clay.

   It is often a good idea to firm the dish up a little using a hair dryer before lifting it off the foam. When you have done this, carefully transfer it to a board, then remove the former.

   Work around the rim of the dish to soften and round it off to finish.

6. Both shapes of spoon rest work well, but the full version is the better option for keeping liquids contained.

   Allow your spoon rests to dry out slowly before bisque firing.

Decorative tile

Making tiles is relatively easy because they are basically formed from precision-cut slabs. When it comes to decoration, however, keep in mind Keith and Rich's oft-repeated mantra that 'less is more' – particularly with the paper resist technique shown here. Go for a bold, instantly recognizable outline, as anything small and fiddly will be difficult to handle. These stylized olive twigs and branches fit the bill perfectly.

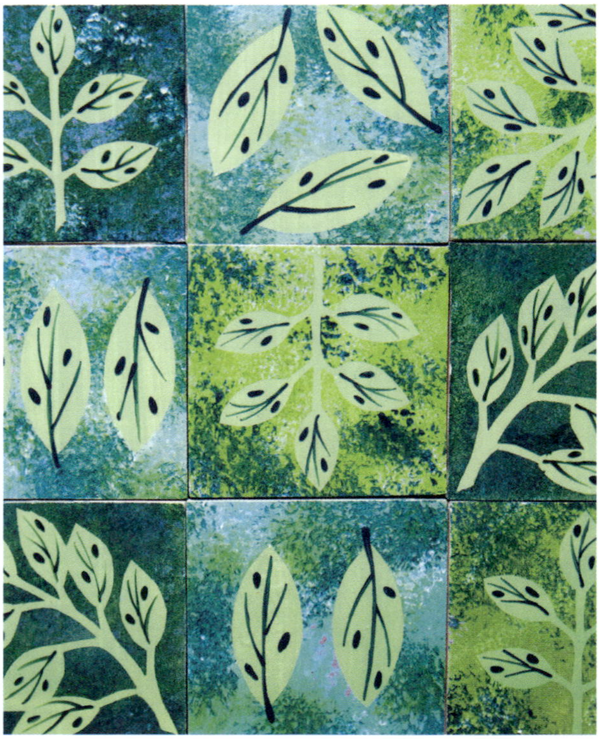

YOU WILL NEED

Clay of choice (earthenware or stoneware): approx. 1350 g (3 lb) for nine tiles, although this will depend on the thickness of the slab used

Tools: Plastic sheet, roller guides (thickness of choice for your tiles), rolling pin, basic tool kit

Tile cutter (available from ceramic suppliers) or a square card template, precisely cut to the size you want your tile to be

CLAY CHOICE

You can use earthenware or stoneware for your tiles, but for a wet area such as a bathroom, a higher-firing stoneware clay would be better.

Tips to keep your tiles flat

› Try drying the tiles on wire racks – the types used in the kitchen for baking are good, though you will need quite a few to accommodate all your tiles. If you are using this method, turn the tiles regularly so they dry equally from both sides.

› Wooden racks also work, but you will need to turn the tiles more regularly to ensure even drying.

› The best method is to dry the tiles between absorbent boards with a weight on top to ensure equal contact with the boards. Plaster board or fireboard work well; both are available from builder's merchants or DIY stores.

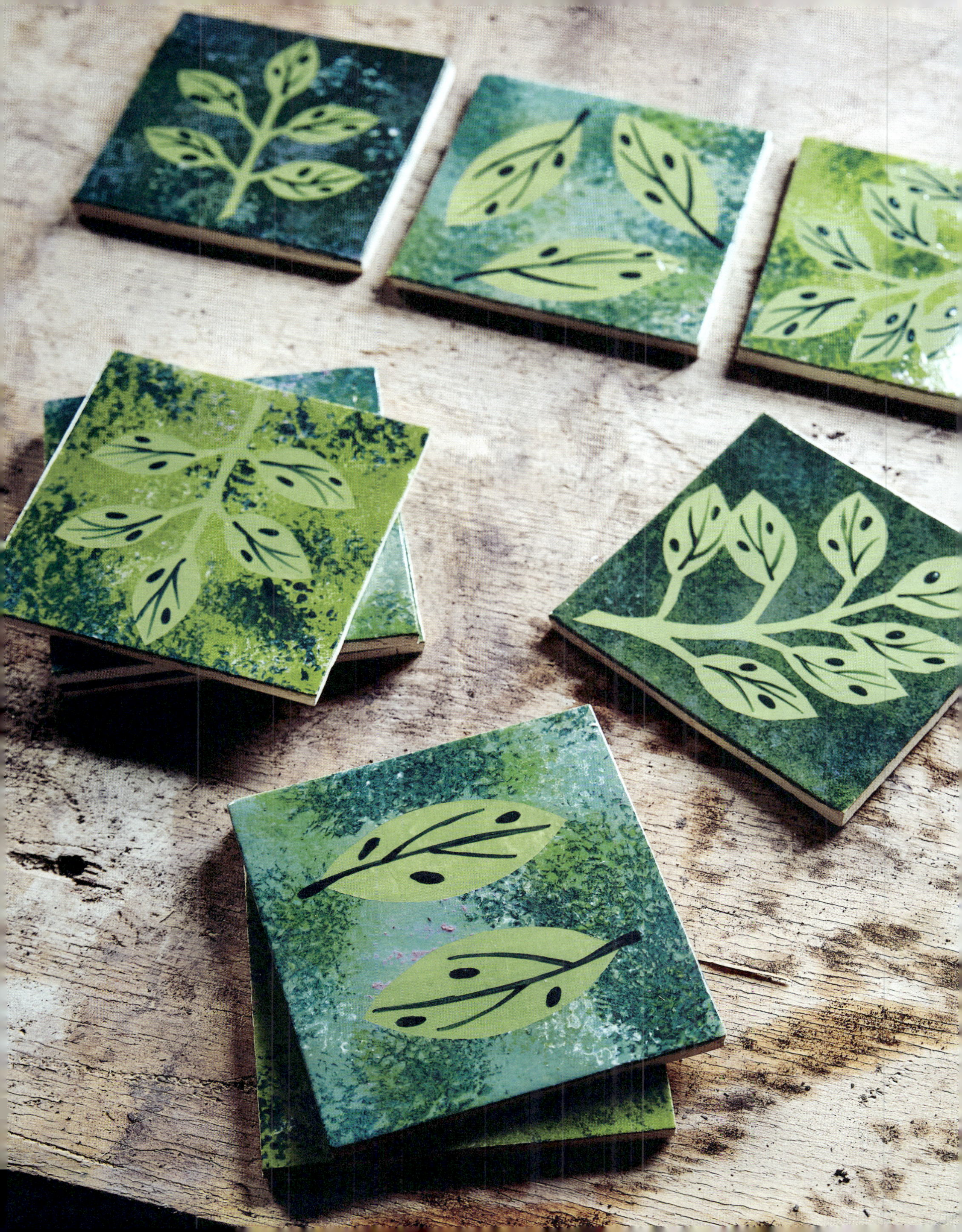

USING A TILE CUTTER

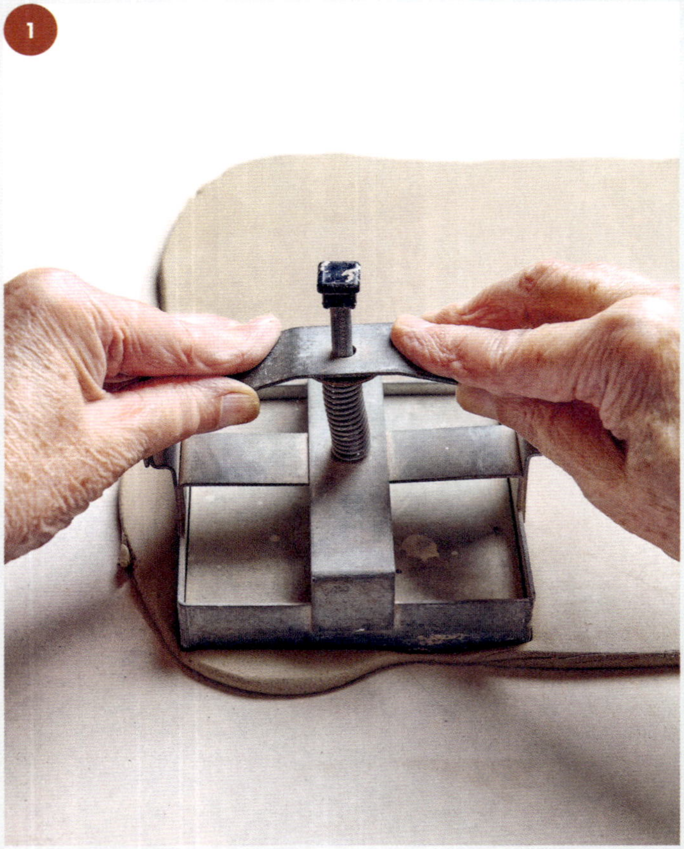

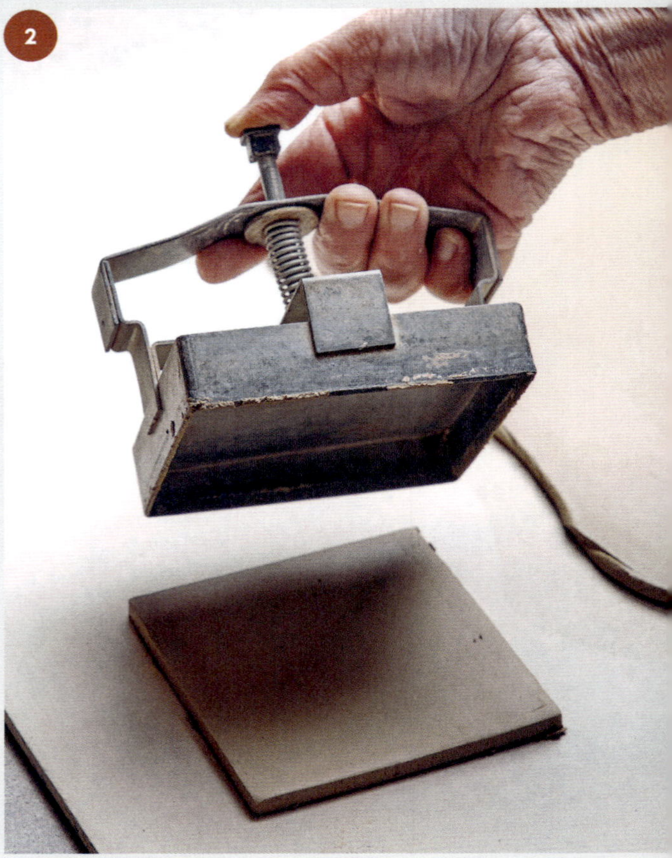

USING A CARD TEMPLATE

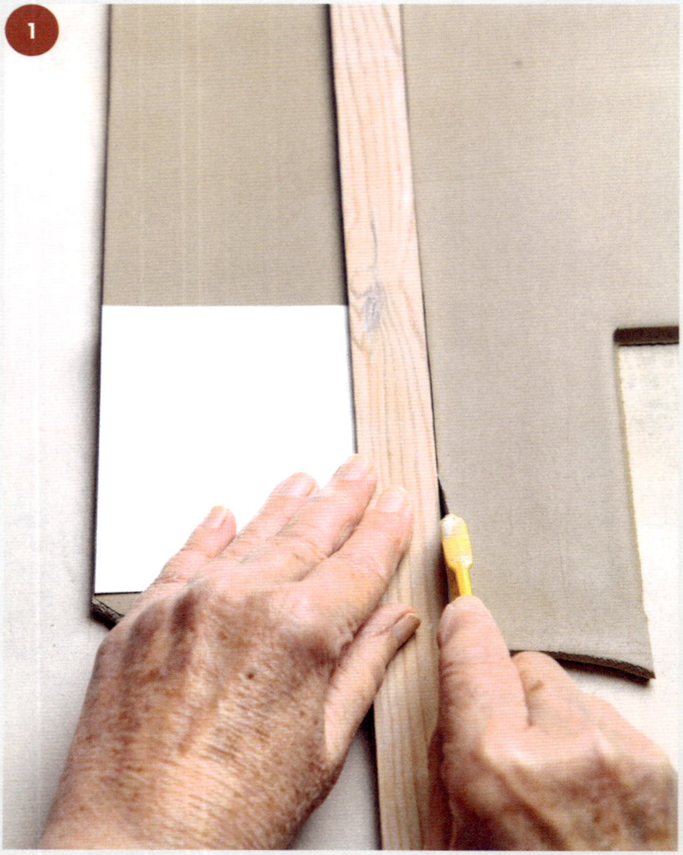

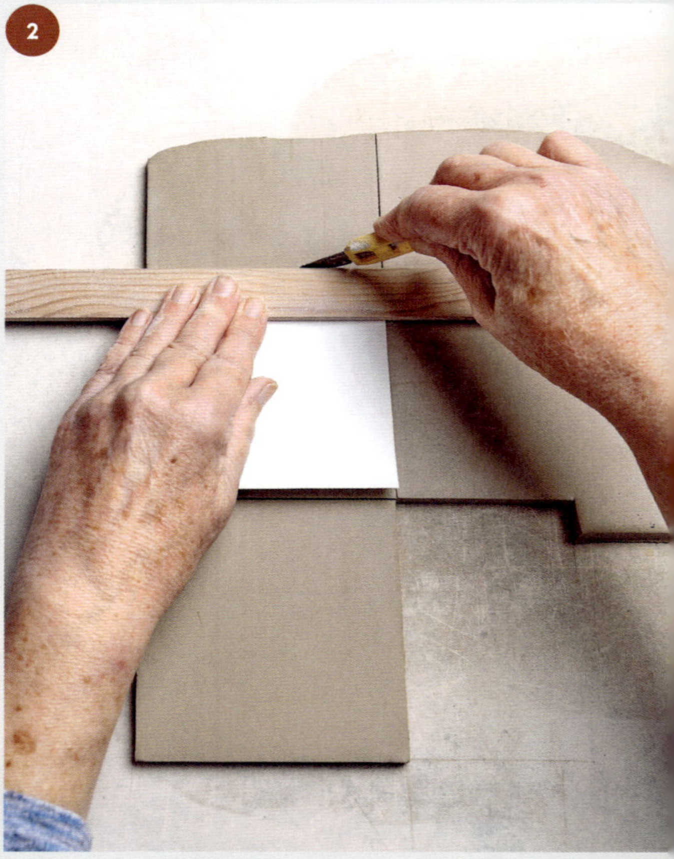

Using a tile cutter

1. Roll a large slab of clay following the method demonstrated on page 40. A good thickness of roller guide to use is 5 mm (¼ in.), but the tiles could be thinner or thicker if you prefer.

   Turn the slab onto an absorbent board and smooth over the surface with a rib. Positioning the tile cutter as close to the edge of the slab as possible to maximize its use, cut out the first tile.

2. Release the tile from the cutter onto another absorbent board, then cut out as many more as you can from the slab, working in the same way.

Using a card template

1. Place the card template as close to the edge of the slab as possible to maximize its use, then cut around it using a batten as an extra aid to cut the sides straight.

2. Repeat the process, placing the template against the last edge cut on the previous tile, until all the slab has been used up.

See page 160 for a method of decorating the tiles using paper resist.

JUDGES' TIP

If you intend to use the tiles on a wall, they will stick better if you texture the back. You can do this simply by scoring lines with a fork or similar implement before they dry out.

Animal figurine

Pinched animals make great projects for children because they don't feel the need to make them as lifelike, as adults often do, and so manage to add character without trying very hard. The animal we have chosen to make here is a koala but you can use the same method to make any kind of animal on a small scale. It's simply a matter of manipulating the parts to the rudimentary shape, then adding details to distinguish it. Then why not try your hand at making a collection for your own Noah's Ark.

YOU WILL NEED

Clay of choice (earthenware or stoneware): 60 g (about 2¼ oz) plus extra for added features

Tools: Basic tool kit

Underglaze colours to decorate, plus a small amount of transparent glaze

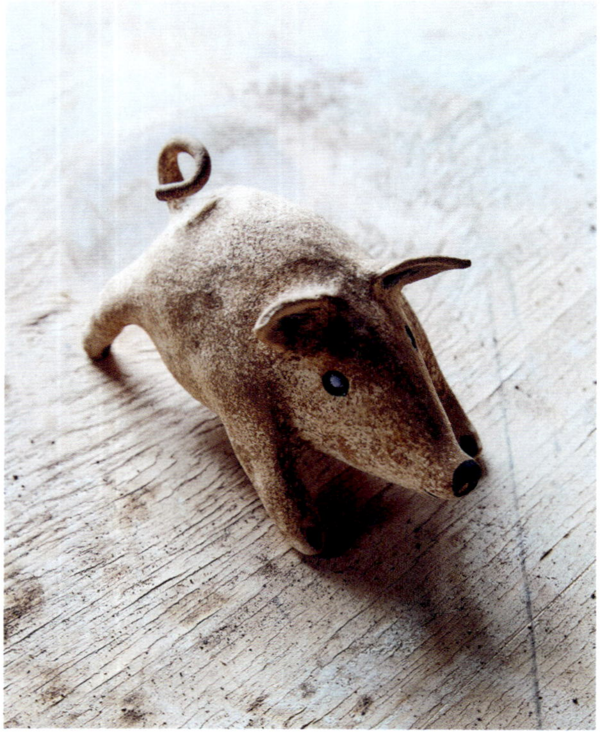

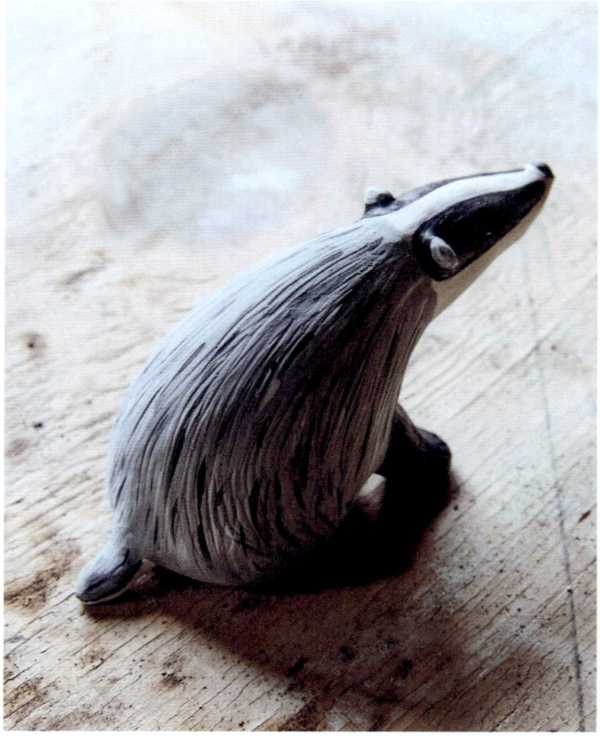

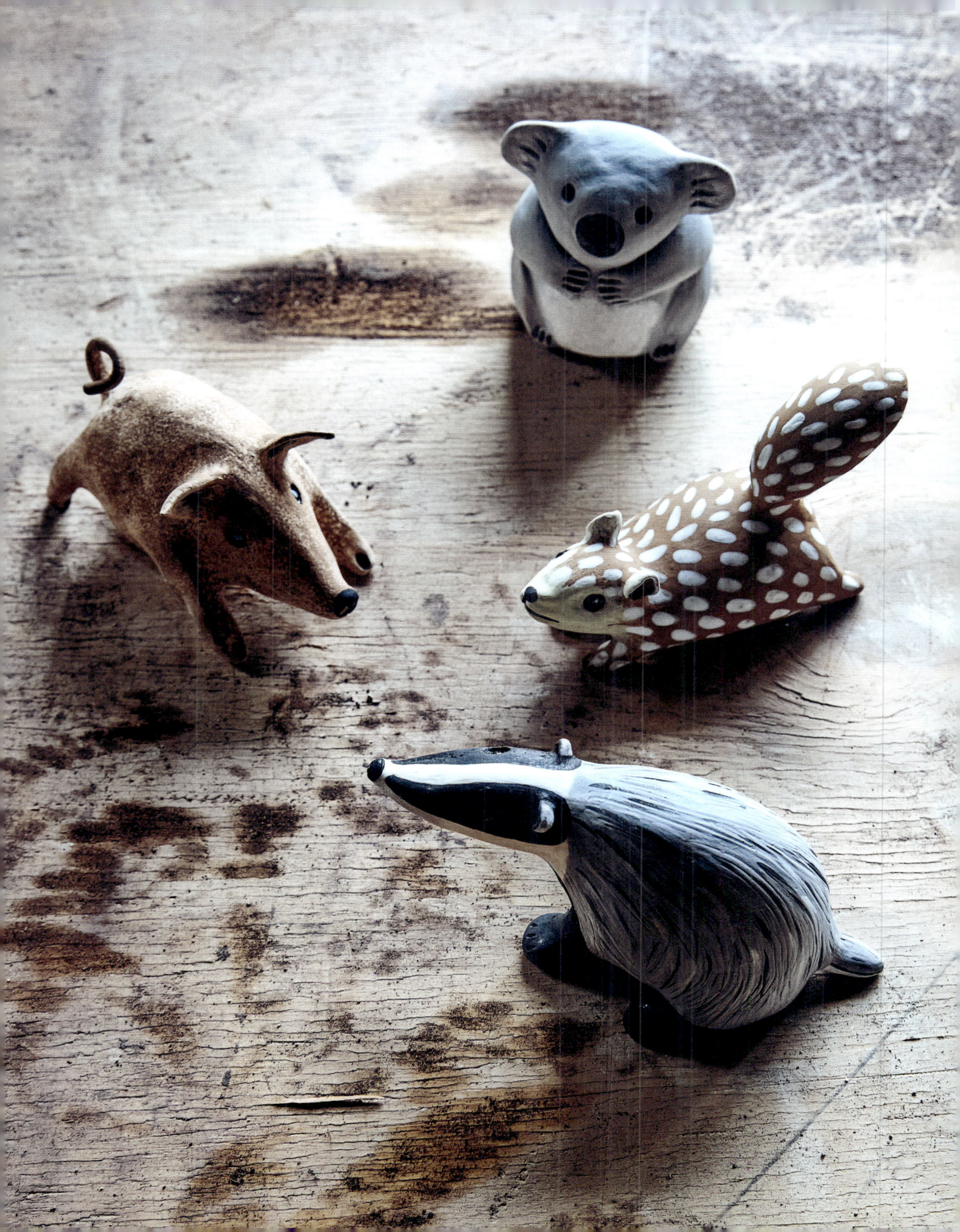

1

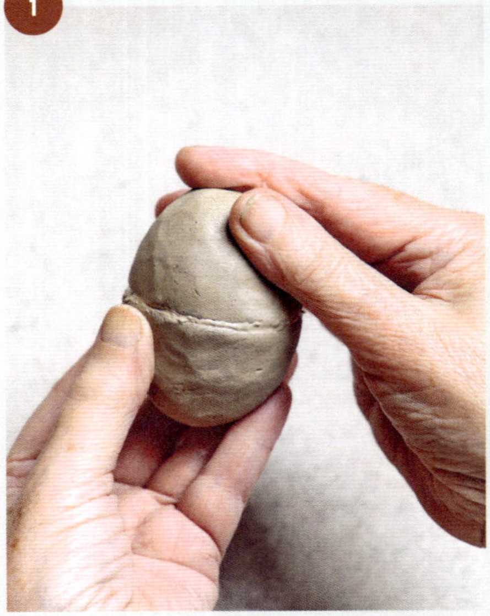

2

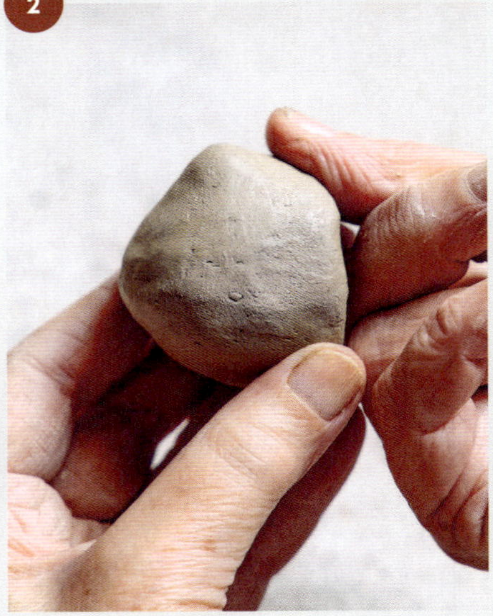

3

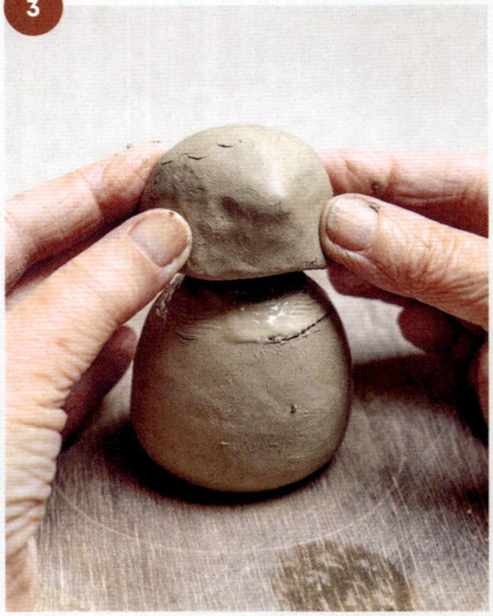

4

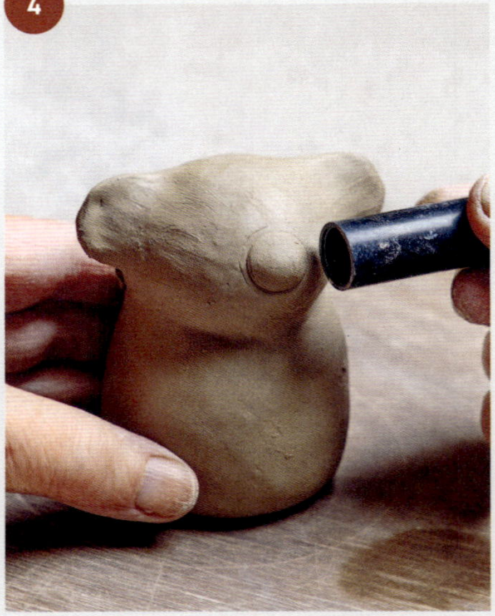

5

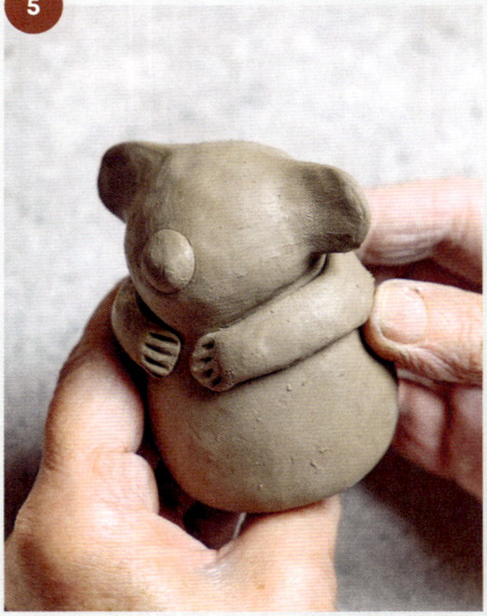

6

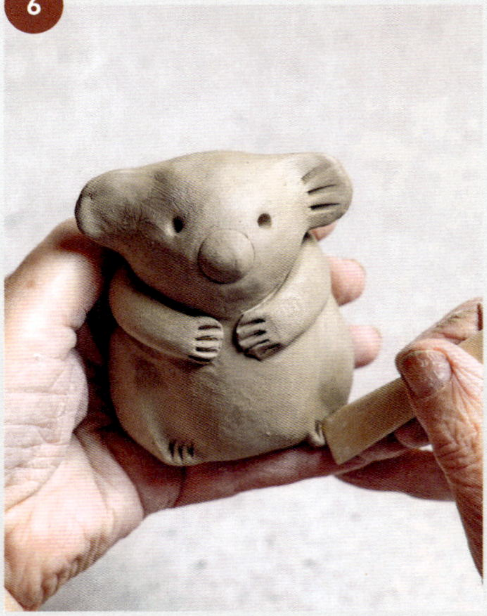

1. Begin by pinching two 20 g (¾ oz) balls of clay to two equally sized cup shapes. As you pinch the second ball, periodically check the dimensions of the rim against those of the first one until they match exactly.

   Score and slip the rims of both cups, then join them together, holding them in that position for a minute or two for the seal to set a little.

   Reinforce the join with a coil of soft clay and blend it in with a finger, then work over the area with a rib, removing excess clay for a tidy, smooth finish.

2. Now weigh out a third 20 g (¾ oz) ball of clay and pinch it to a rudimentary cup shape as before – but this time manipulate the shape using a finger to form the basic features of the koala's head.

3. Score and slip the rim of the head and the corresponding position on the body, then fix the head in place. Blend the clay from the head onto the body until the join is seamless.

4. Pinch two small balls of clay to form the ears, then attach them to the head, spaced quite wide apart. Reinforce the ears with tiny coils of soft clay and blend them in seamlessly.

   Make the nose by impressing something small and round, such as an old pen top, into the clay.

5. Roll two small, thickish coils to form the arms of the koala, then impress the fingers at one end using a wooden tool.

   Score and slip the relevant areas, then attach the arms to the body, wrapping them around to almost meet at the front.

   Tidy around the arms with a wooden tool to remove any excess slip.

6. Use a pin to impress the eyes above the nose. Push the pin fully into the head cavity to allow the release of moisture when drying and firing.

   Finally, impress any further details you want to add, such as marks in the ears to suggest furriness or marks similar to the fingers for the toes.

   When you have finished, make a discreet hole in the body to allow for the release of moisture when drying and firing. Warning: failure to do this could result in the animal exploding in the firing process, especially if the clay wall is uneven or the kiln is fired too quickly.

   Give the animal lots of time to thoroughly dry out before firing.

JUDGES' NOTE

The key to success is weighing the clay before you begin so you can pinch the parts to roughly the same dimensions.

Wine cooler

Many wines, especially those of a white or fizzy variety, are best consumed chilled and a cooler is the perfect way to keep them at the correct temperature for every celebration. There is a school of thought that says a wine cooler is best made from unglazed earthenware, which, when dipped in cold water, is sufficient to keep the wine at the right temperature. Here, though, we have opted for a decorative glazed stoneware form designed to contain ice.

YOU WILL NEED

Clay of choice (earthenware or stoneware): approx. 1.5 kg (3 lb)

Tools: Plastic sheet, roller guides (at least 5 mm/ ¼ in. thick), rolling pin, basic tool kit

Glaze(s) of choice to decorate

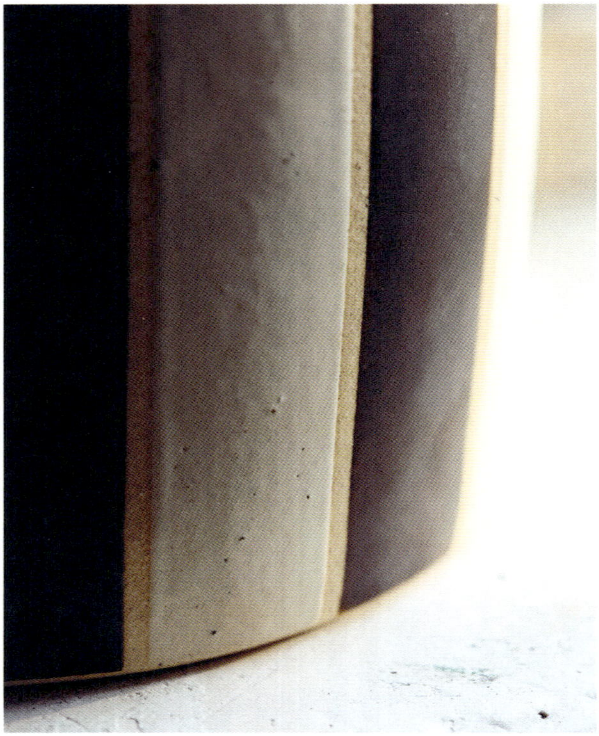

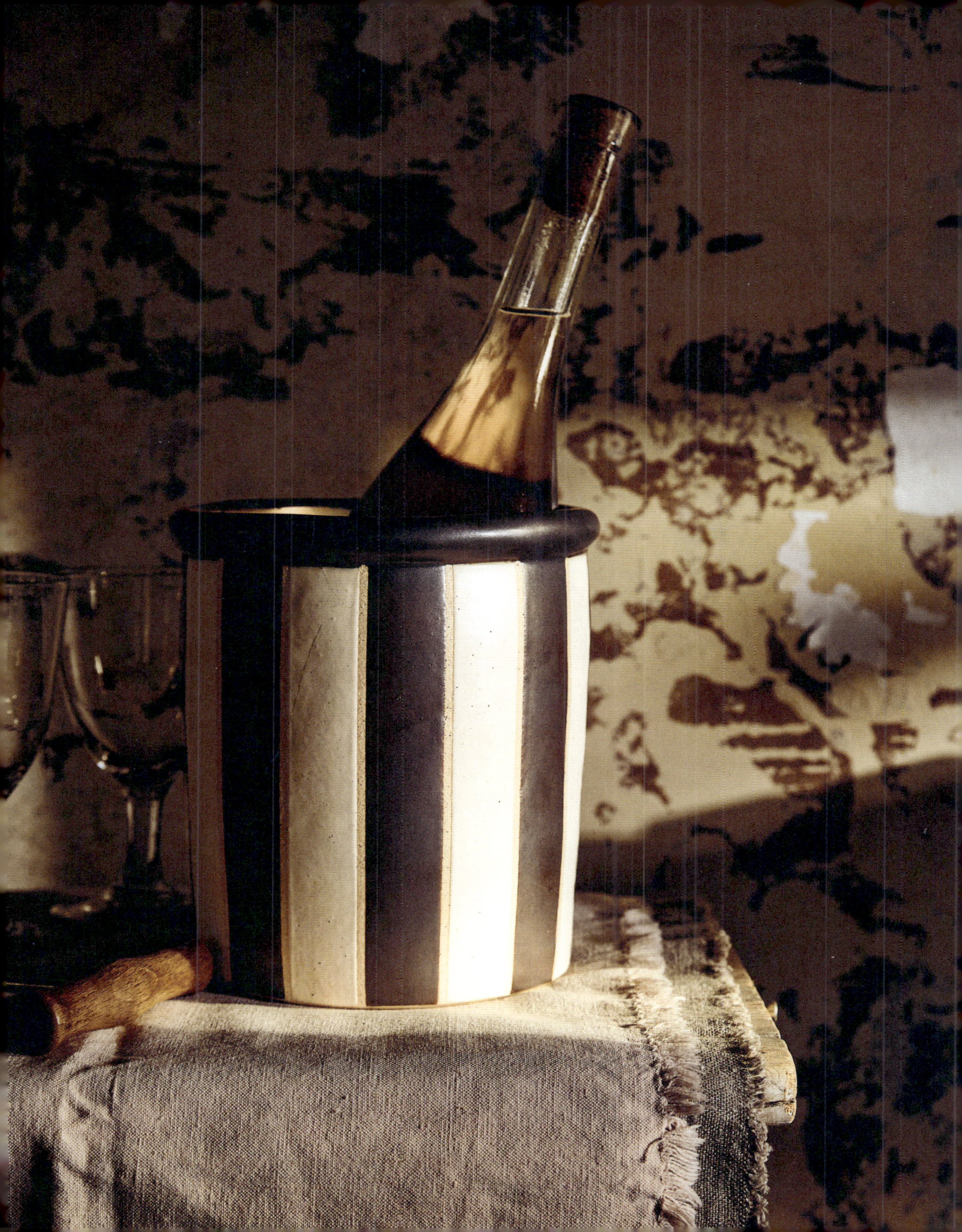

1

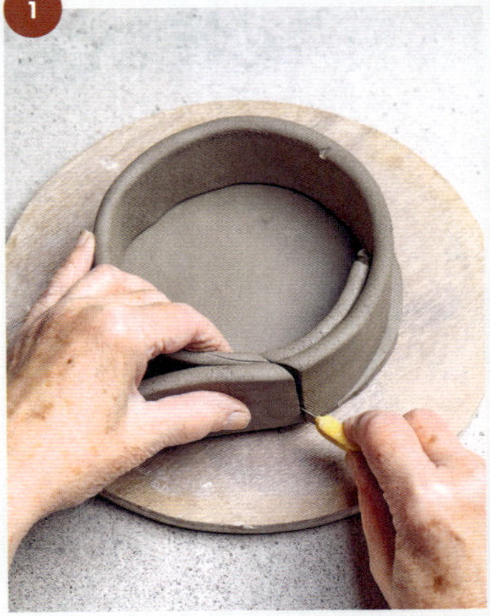

2

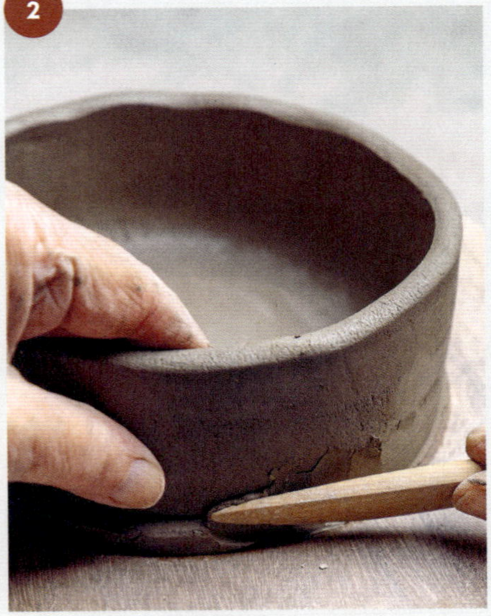

3

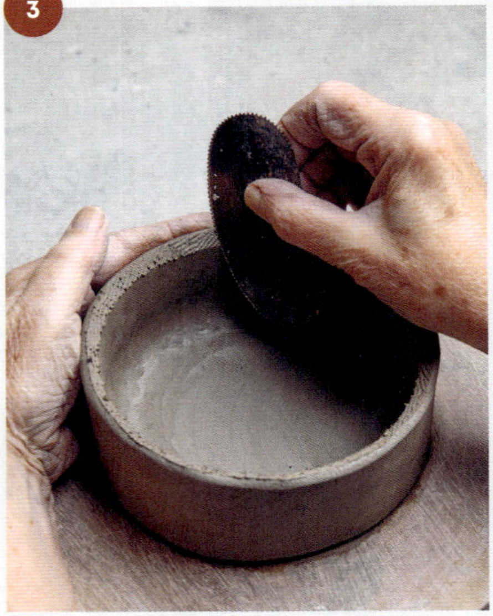

4

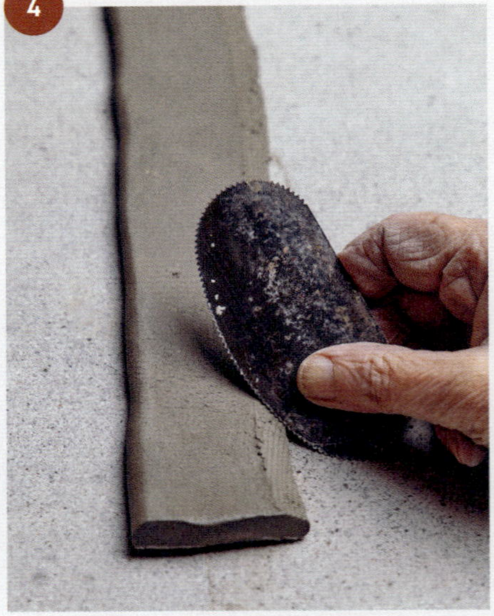

5

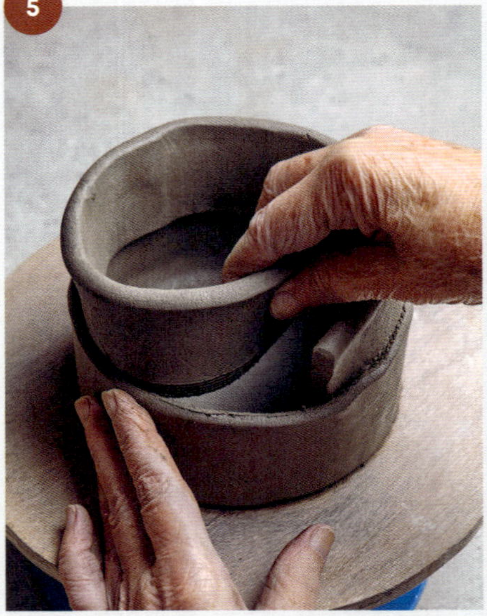

6

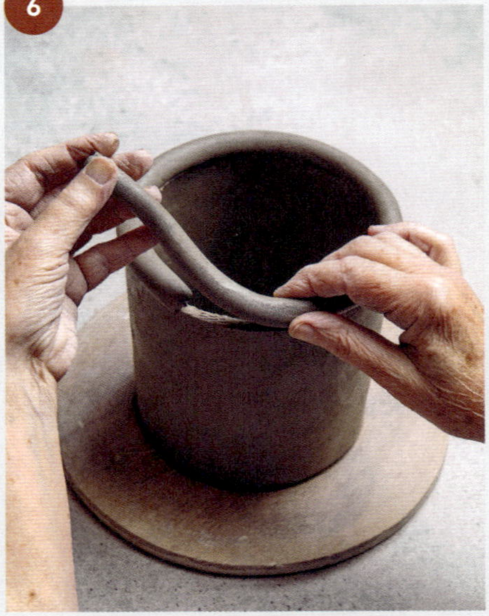

1. Following the method on page 40, roll out a slab large enough to cut out a 15-cm (6-in.) circle. Place the circle on a wooden board, then roll and flatten a coil (see page 42) long enough to fit the circumference of the base and approximately 3–4 cm (1¼–1½ in.) deep.

   After scoring and slipping the adjoining areas, fix the coil onto the base 3–5 mm (⅛–¼ in.) in from the edge. Overlap the ends.

   Cut through the overlap at an angle and discard the surplus, then join the ends together securely, using a little slip if required.

2. Reinforce the inside of the join with a coil of soft clay. Blend the coil in well, then neaten up with the rounded end of a rib.

   Next, holding the coil with one hand, blend the clay from the base slab up onto the wall on the outside, using a wooden tool. Work around the area with a rib to smooth and neaten the surface.

3. Use a serrated kidney to both bevel and score the rim of the wall at a downward and inward angle from the outside edge.

4. Roll and flatten a second coil long enough to fit the circumference again, then bevel and score along the length of one edge.

5. Fitting the bevelled edges together, fix the second coil onto the first one and cut through the overlap at the ends as you did on the first coil. Join the coil ends together, then blend the clay from the first coil up onto the second one on the outside, using a finger or tool as preferred.

   On the inside, blend the clay from the second coil down onto the first one.

   Work over the join, inside and out, with a rib until the seam is no longer visible and the wall is an even thickness and straight.

6. Continue to build the wall up in this way until the cooler is the height you require – it might help to have a wine bottle handy to measure it.

   As a finishing detail, roll an even, round coil, then attach it to the rim after scoring and slipping all adjoining areas. Tidy around the join with a wooden tool.

   Allow the cooler to dry out slowly before bisque firing.

Vase

This is another project that utilizes the coiling method but this time in a traditional way, with rounded, rather than flattened, coils. Although *The Great Pottery Throw Down* draws on time-honoured pottery techniques, we like to give them a contemporary twist: here, the round shape of the vase is gently altered to an oval during the final stage of building and sections of the rim are cut out to create a modern, slightly edgy profile.

GLAZING

Red earthenware or terracotta clay is quite porous even after firing, so it is imperative to at least glaze the interior of the vase if you want it to hold water.

YOU WILL NEED

Red earthenware clay: 1–1.5 kg (2–3 lb), depending on the size you want to make

An outline former of the shape you want to make – cut from thin MDF or similar

Tools: Basic tool kit, including a surform rasp; small cookie cutter

Glaze(s) of choice to decorate

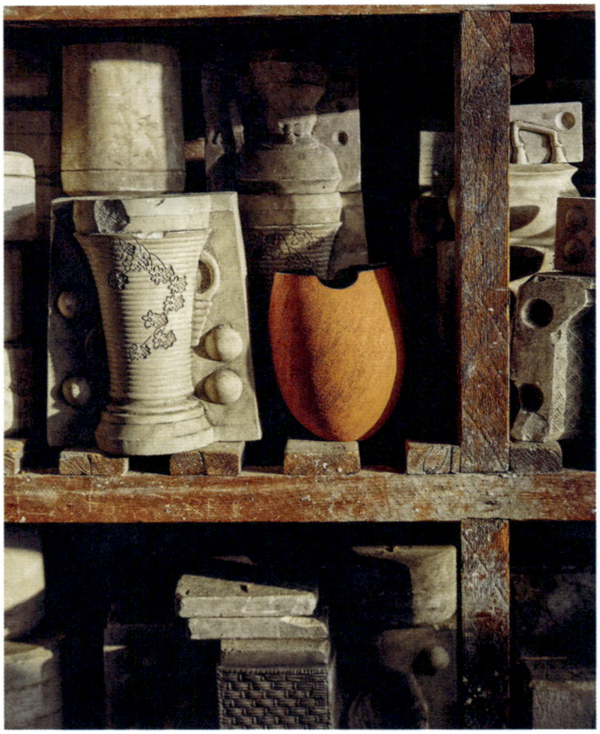

A NOTE OF WARNING

If you regularly use white clay and decide to work with red on this occasion, be aware that it is very contaminating; you will need to clean up meticulously when finished, otherwise flecks of red clay will appear in all your work.

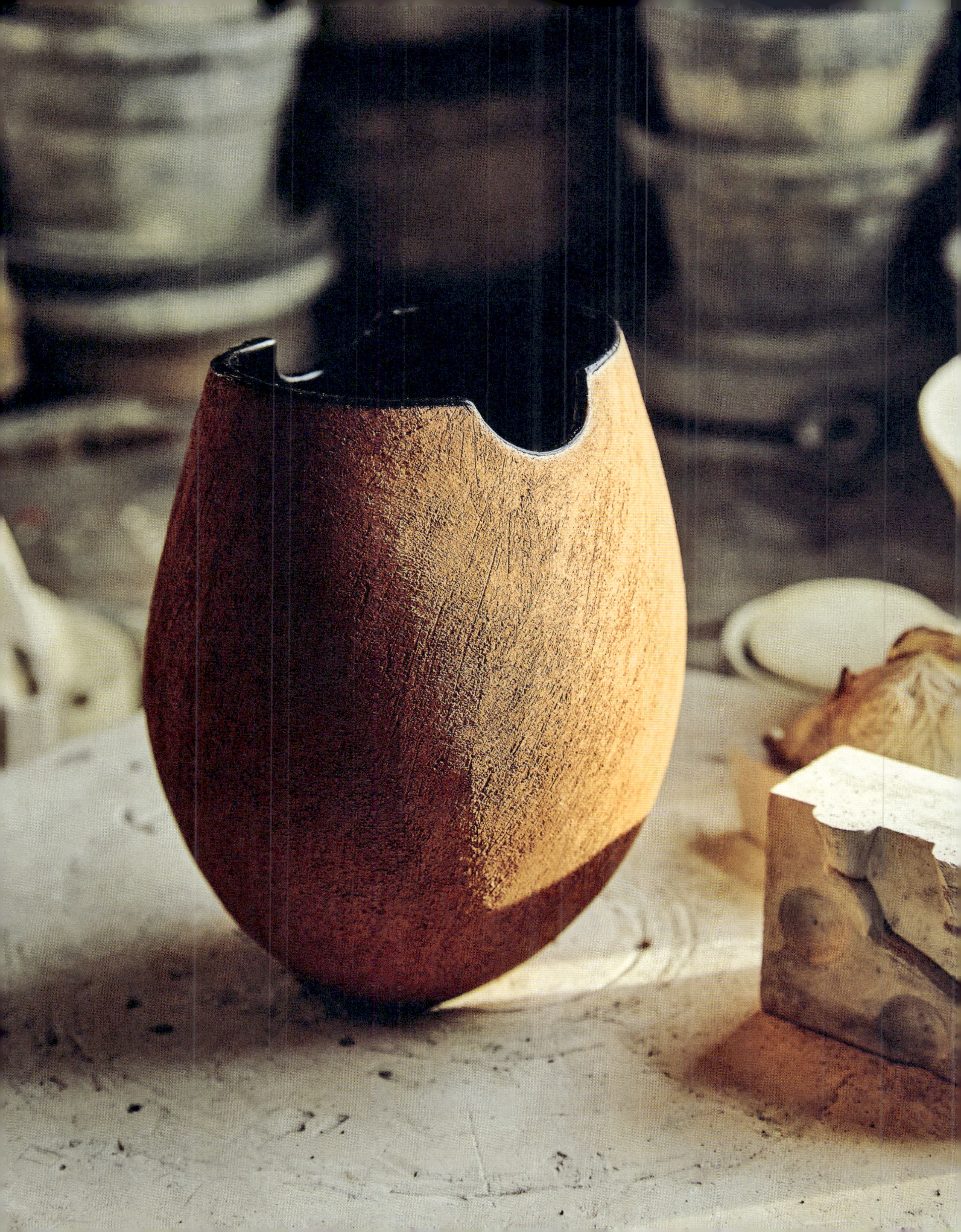

1

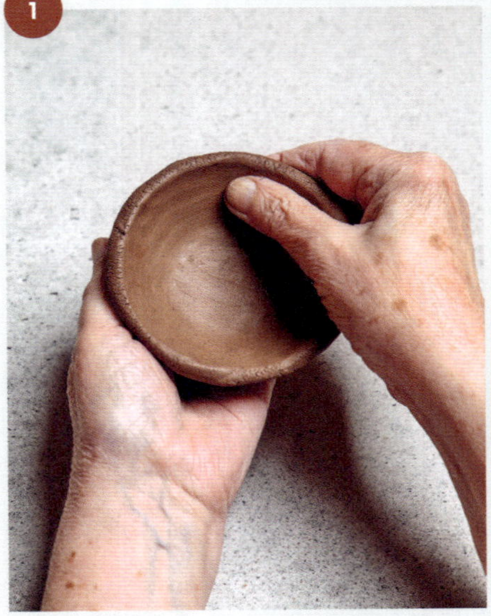

2

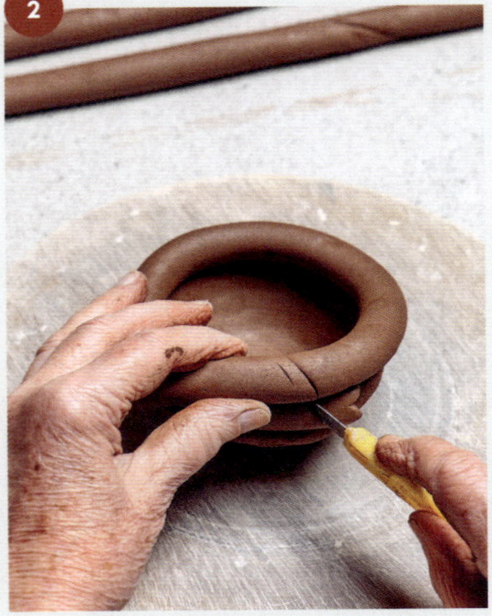

3

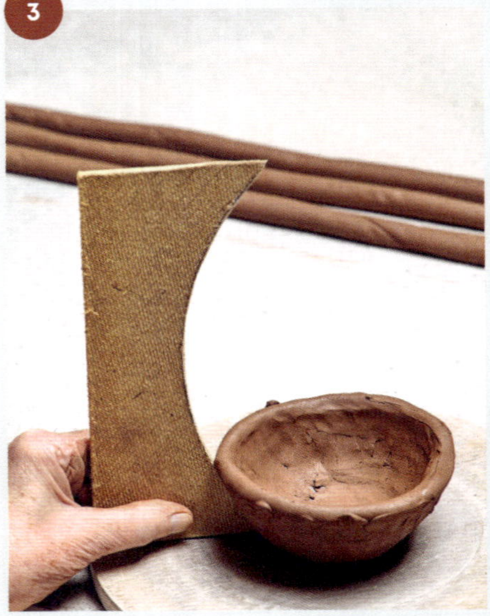

4

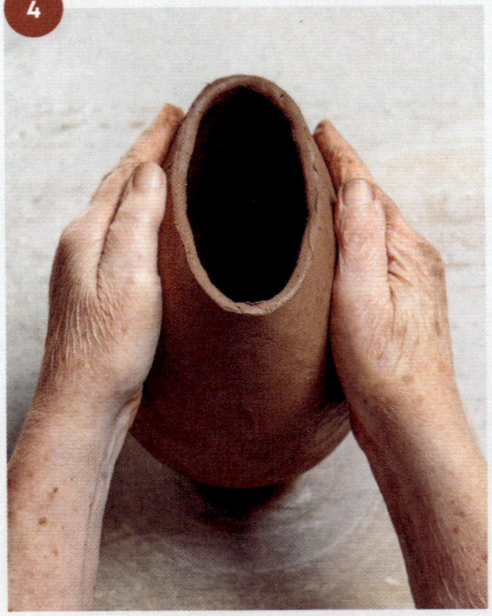

5

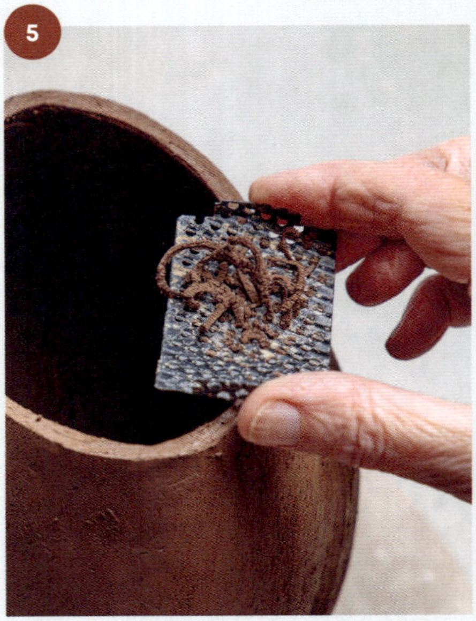

6

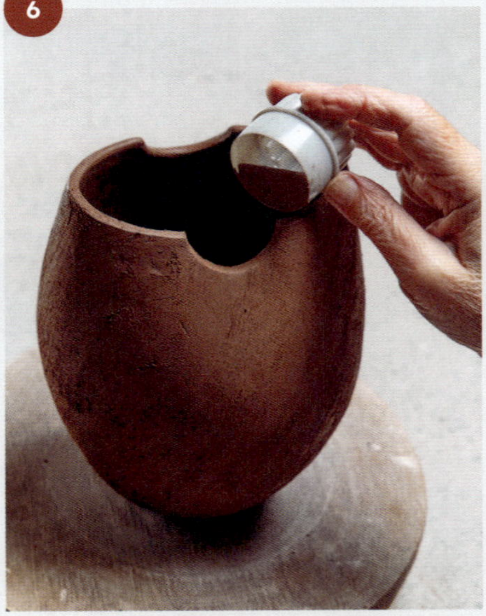

1. Begin by pinching (see page 37) a small ball of clay into a bowl with a flat base and gently outward-curved wall.
2. Roll a good few, evenly thick coils of a suitable length to fit around the circumference of the bowl, then sit the first one around the rim and overlap the ends. Cut through the overlap at an angle.

   If the clay is soft enough, join the ends together; otherwise, use some slip to stick them together. Discard the surplus clay if it is not long enough to fit around again.

   Blend the coil onto the bowl inside and out with a finger.
3. Now use your outline former to check the shape is correct so far.

   If the base shape is not wide enough, simply pinch the wall until it fits to the former.

   If the base shape is already too wide, cut a couple of V-shaped sections out of the wall, then draw the clay back together securely. Repeat this until the former fits exactly.

   When you are happy with the fit, refine the surface inside and out with a rib. Do this after each coil is added.
4. Continue to build up the wall in this way, regularly checking the shape to fit the former and refining the surface until you have reach the height you require.

   Next, place your hands on opposite sides of the top section of the vase and gently squeeze it into an oval.
5. Carefully refine the shape of the rim using a surform rasp so that it has a slight curve.
6. Use a small cookie cutter to carefully cut out a semi-circle on opposite sides of the rim, then work around the whole rim with a rib to gently soften and round it off.

   Allow the vase to dry out slowly before bisque firing.

Olive bowl

This is the perfect dish for olives, divided in two for black and green varieties with a handy little container at the centre for cocktail sticks or stones. However, you could easily divide it into more sections to serve dips or other hors d'oeuvre. We have decorated ours using the glaze spattering technique (see page 159) for a contemporary, rustic finish.

YOU WILL NEED

Clay of choice (earthenware or stoneware): approx. 680 g (1½ lb) for a dish measuring 18 x 12 cm (7 x 4¾ in.)

Tools: Plastic sheet, roller guides (no thicker than 5 mm/¼ in.), rolling pin, basic tool kit

Absorbent board

Glaze(s) of choice to decorate

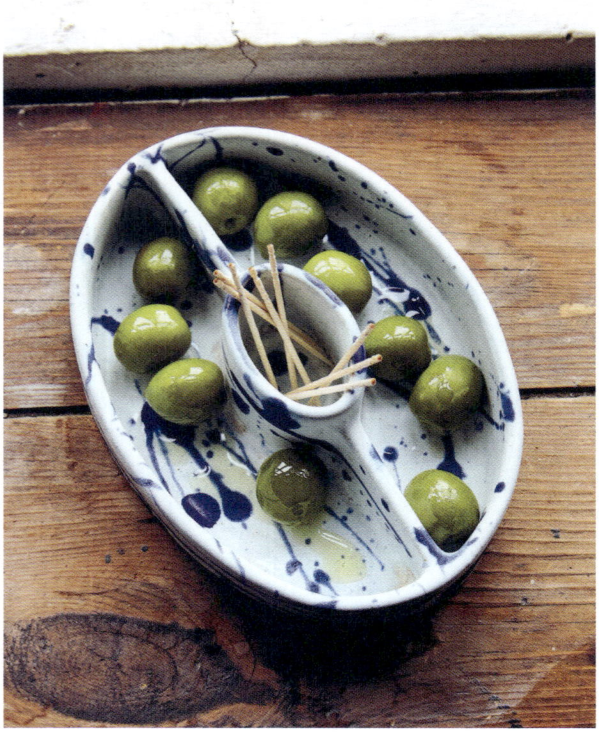

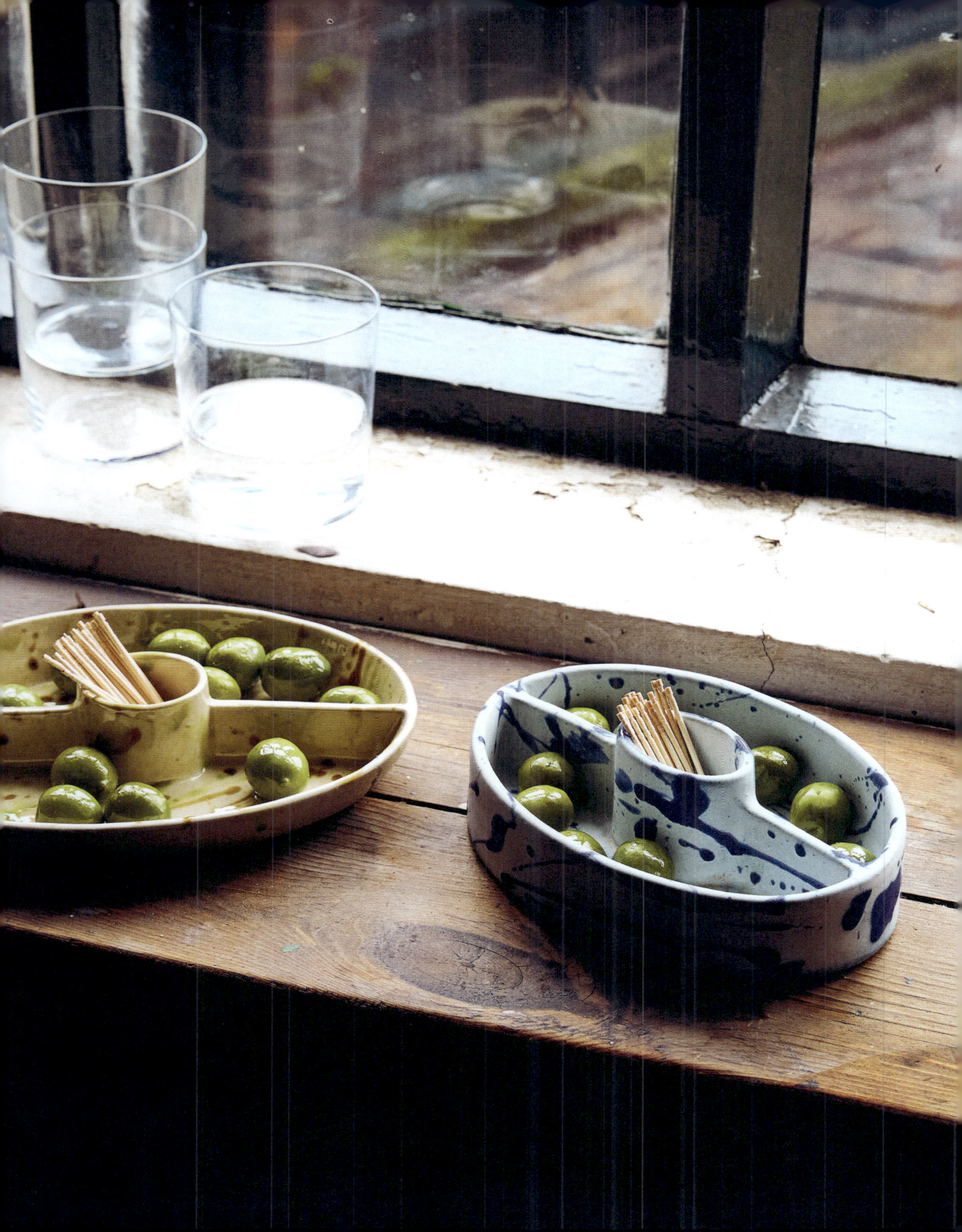

1

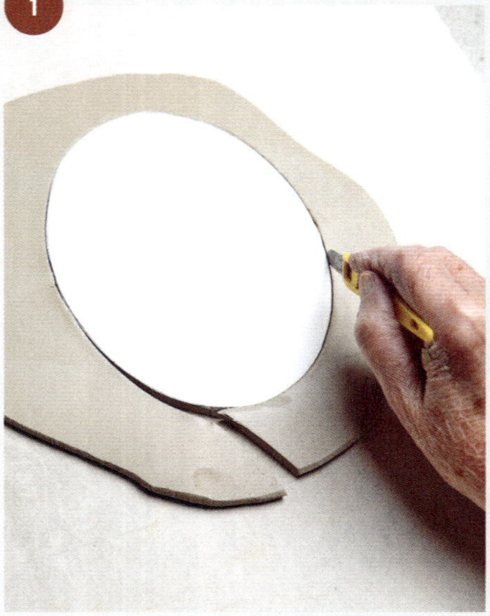

2

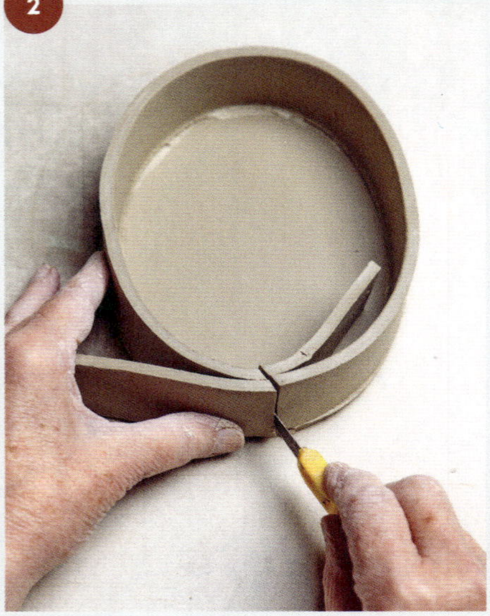

3

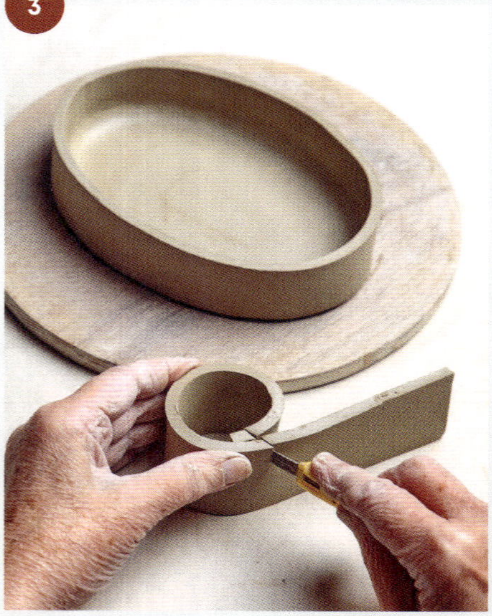

4

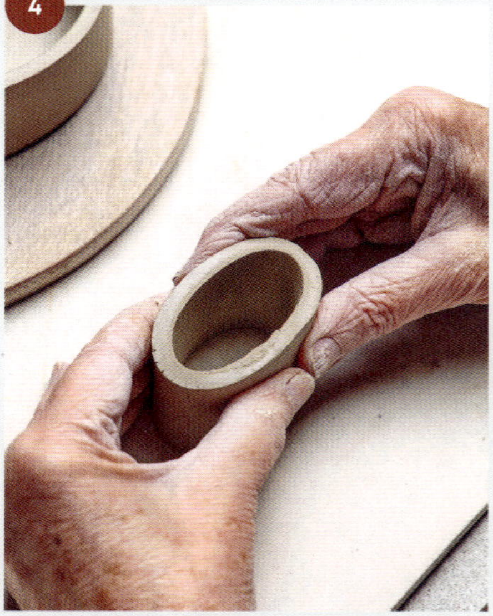

5

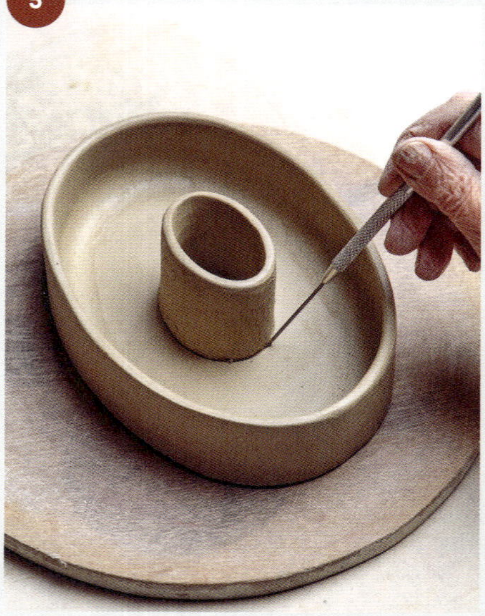

6

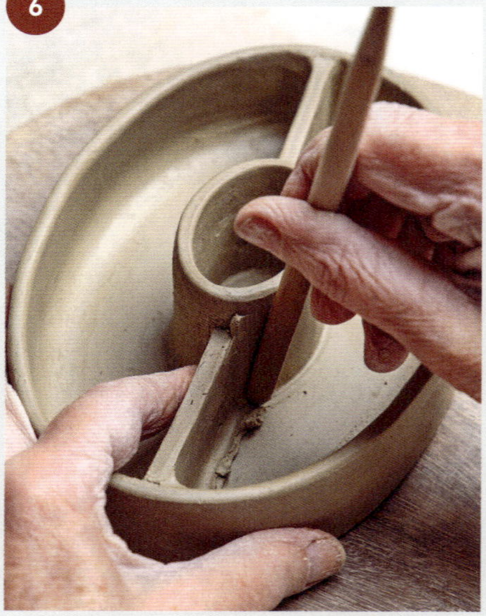

1. Begin by making a paper template for the base of the dish. It can be any shape you like, but oval works well.

   Next roll out a slab of clay (see page 40) large enough to accommodate the template and turn it onto an absorbent board.

   Place the template on the slab and cut the shape out carefully.

2. Roll out another slab, long enough to fit the circumference of the base slab, then cut out a strip 4 cm (1½ in.) wide.

   Score and slip the perimeter edge of the base and the adjoining edge of the wall strip, then fix the wall strip in place, overlapping the ends,

   Cut through the overlap at an angle, then score and slip the ends and join them together securely. Work over the join, inside and out, using a rib until the join is no longer evident.

3. Cut a slightly wider but shorter strip of slab, then curve it around to form a small cylinder. Cut and join the ends, as you did with the wall of the dish, and neaten the join.

4. Carefully squeeze the cylinder into an oval shape to match the dish, then refine the upper rim using a rib to gently round it off.

5. Place the oval in the centre of the dish and mark its position with a pin.

   Score and slip the marked position and the bottom edge of the oval, then fix it in place, making sure it is secure.

   You can reinforce the outer edge of the join with a thin coil of soft clay if you think it needs it. Blend the coil in thoroughly with a suitable tool.

6. Divide the dish in two by securing two more sections of slab strip from the outer wall to the oval at the centre after scoring and slipping all adjoining areas.

   Reinforce the joins on all sides with thin coils of soft clay, blended in with a suitably shaped tool.

   Allow the dish to dry out slowly before bisque firing.

Tea cup and saucer

What pottery project could be more quintessentially British than a tea cup and saucer? It's perhaps not the simplest one in the book: the chances are that you'll want to make a matching set, rather than a single cup and saucer, so it's important to try and keep the sizing and shaping as consistent as you can. Weighing out the clay in advance will help – and if you're new to throwing, it's not a bad idea to have your own version of Keith's 'bucket of doom' to hand for any obvious rejects!

YOU WILL NEED

Clay of choice (preferably stoneware for durability): 300 g (10 oz) for the cup and 300 g (10 oz) for the saucer, plus extra for a handle

Tools for throwing: Water bowl, sponge, rib, cutting wire

Glaze(s) of choice to decorate

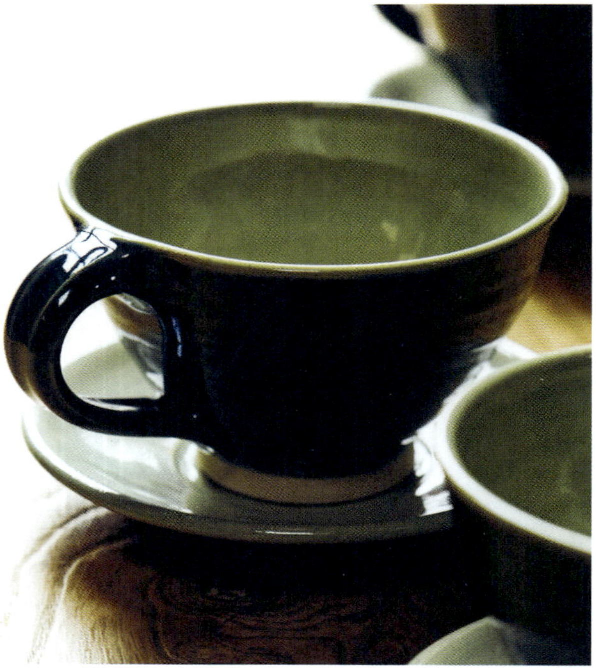

JUDGES' NOTES

The cup can be easily thrown directly on the wheel head, but the saucer is best thrown on a batt – see page 64 for instructions on how to fix one on the wheel.

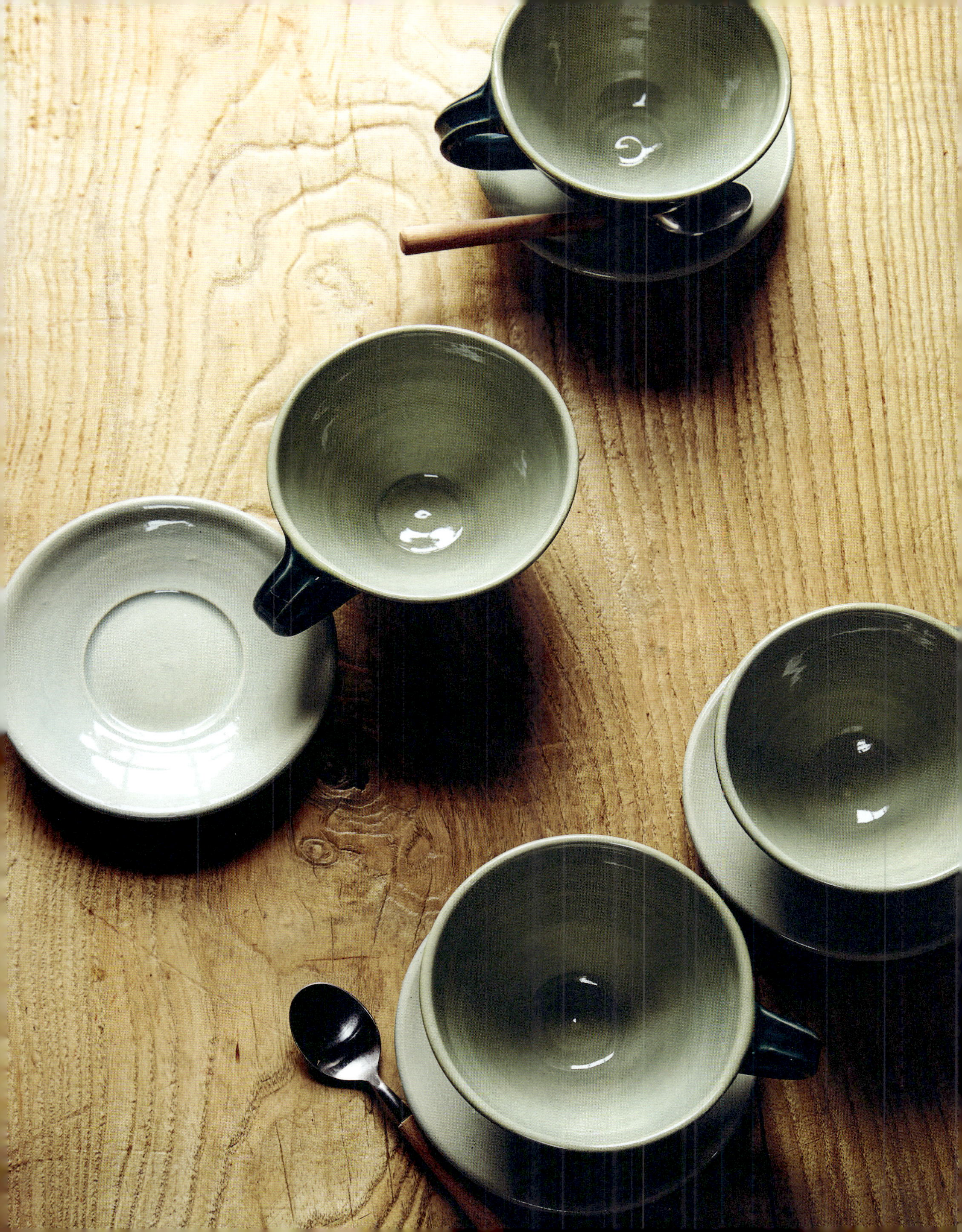

1

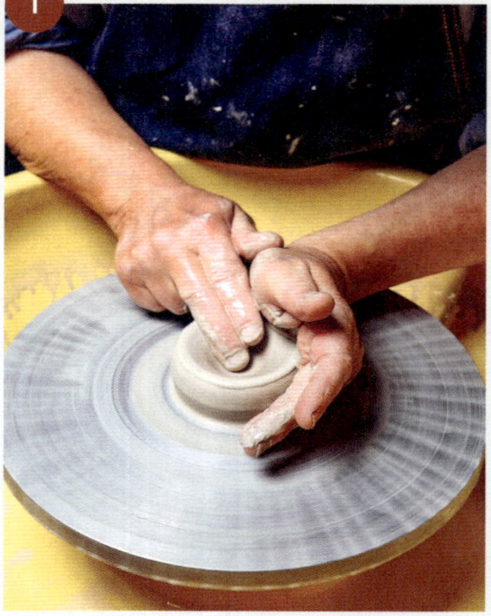

2

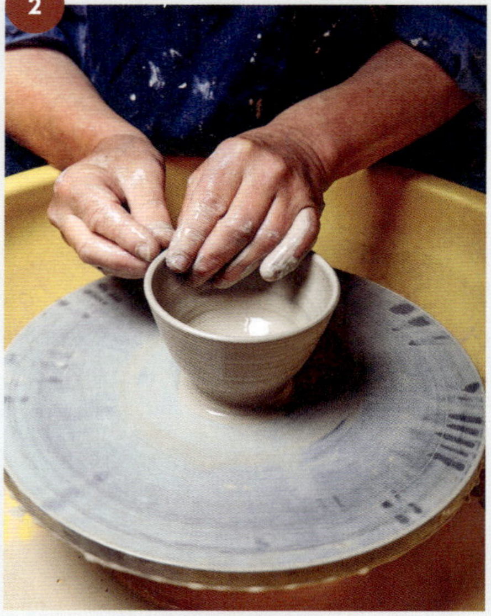

3

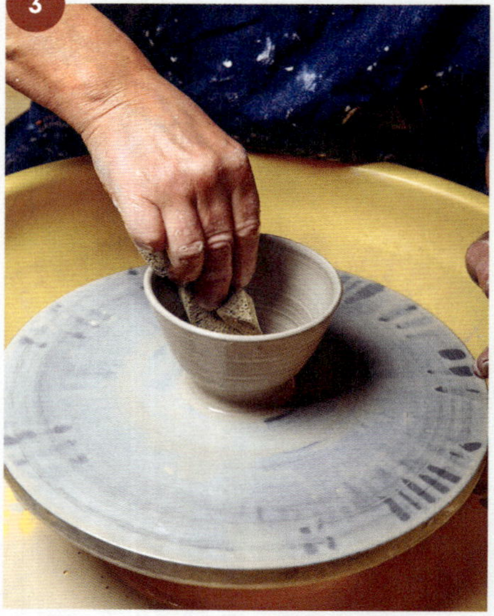

4

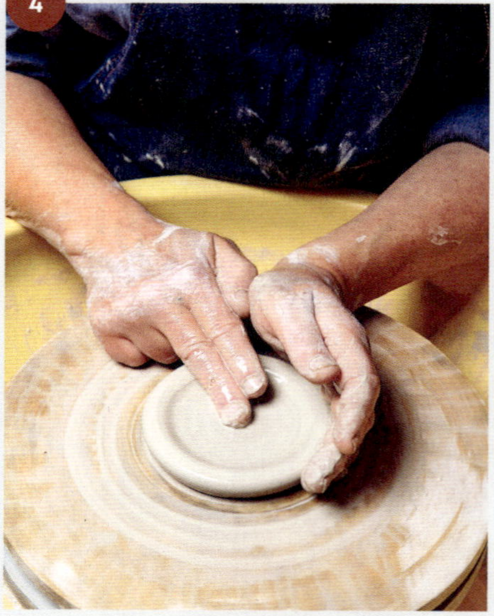

5

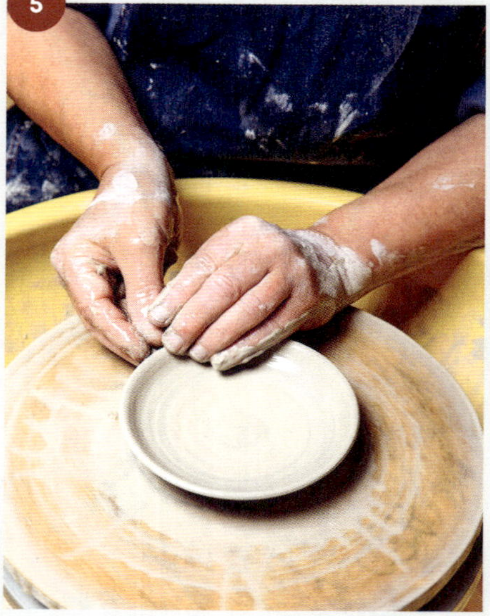

6

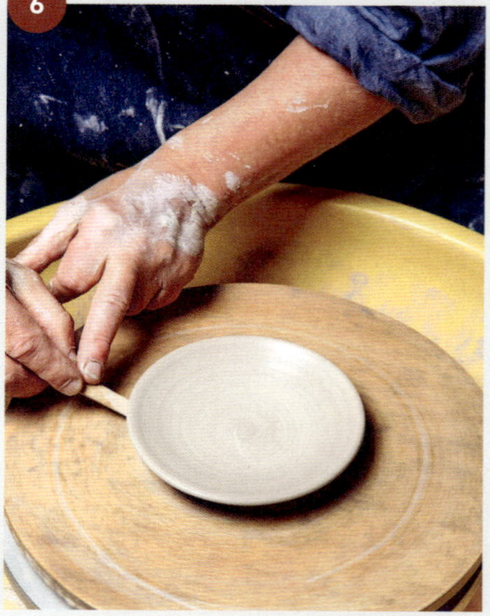

Throwing the cup

1. Centre the given weight of clay (see page 46).

   Open up (see page 50) the centre of the clay, pressing it down to within 10–15 mm (⅜–⅝ in.) of the wheel, then draw the clay back fractionally, maintaining a rounded curve rather than flattening the base.

2. Lift the wall as a cylinder first time (see page 50). Then gently flare the shape out from the rounded base in subsequent lifts, until it has a diameter of 12 cm (about (4¾ in.) and is approximately 7 cm (2¾ in.) high.

3. Mop out the interior of the cup and surface of the wheel around the base.

   Carefully trim away any excess clay around the outside base and cut a shallow bevel with the tip of a rib.

   Clean and dry your hands. Underwire the cup, then holding it as close to the base as possible, transfer it to a board to firm to leather hard.

Throwing the saucer

4. Working on a batt, centre your clay (see page 46). Open it up (see page 50), pressing it down to within 10–15 mm (⅜–⅝ in.) of the batt surface, then draw it out to a diameter of 10 cm (4 in.), leaving a thick rim at the edge.

   Compress the clay in the base by running your fingers over the surface from centre to outside edge three times.

5. With the fingers of your left hand inside the rim and your right-hand fingers opposite on the outside, lift the wall upwards and outwards to a diameter 1–2 cm (½–¾ in.) greater than the rim of the cup, with a gentle curve from the centre.

   When you are happy with the shape, sponge away excess water from the saucer.

6. Clean away excess clay from the underside of the saucer using a wedge-shaped wooden tool, then underwire the base and release the batt from the wheel.

   Allow the saucer to firm to leather hard before attempting to handle it.

TURNING

When both the saucer and cup have firmed to leather hard, turn a foot ring on each piece (see page 66).

Turn the foot ring on the cup first, then measure its diameter.

Leave the saucer *in situ* on the batt to begin with and fix it back onto the wheel, making sure it is central. Carefully turn the central position for the cup to sit in, making it 2–3 mm (about ⅛ in.) wider than the foot of the cup to allow for clay shrinkage. This locating position only needs to be 1 or 2 mm (1⁄16 in.) deep.

Turn the saucer over when finished, centre it, and then turn a suitable width of foot to make the base sturdy for the cup to sit in.

HANDLES

A handle is always applied to a form when it is leather hard to prevent distortion, if applied to a form that has dried too much the handle will crack away from the body. Handles can be attached to thrown forms in several ways, primarily by what is called 'pulling'. This can involve either forming it before attaching it to the vessel or attaching the clay to the vessel first and then pulling the handle from that position.

Another option is to simply hand-build the handle (see page 77).

This method shows how to pull a handle having attached one end to a vessel.

7. Score and slip a position for the handle, just below the rim of the form.
8. Roll a conical-shaped coil of a suitable length and score and slip the fat end. Fix the coil onto the form securely and smooth it onto the wall until it looks seamless.
9. Holding the form in your left hand, wet your right hand and then gently draw it along the length of the coil, applying even pressure to thin and elongate it.

   Repeat this if the handle is not the right thickness first time.

   When you are happy with the handle, draw your thumb along the centre length as a final detail.
10. Turn the handle into a suitable-sized loop to comfortably accommodate fingers or a hand and break off any excess at the end.

    Fix the bottom of the handle onto the wall, again smoothing it until it looks seamless.

7

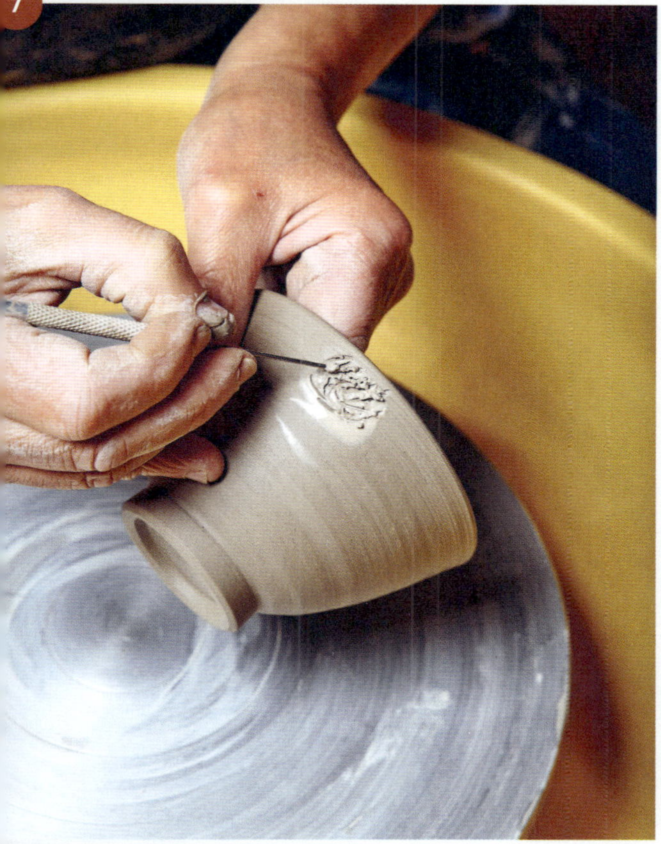

8

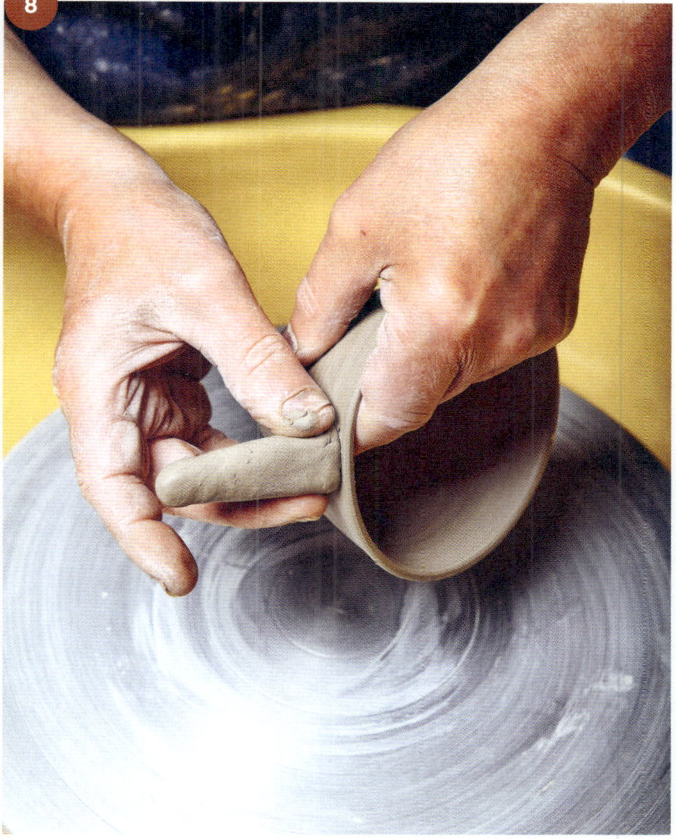

9

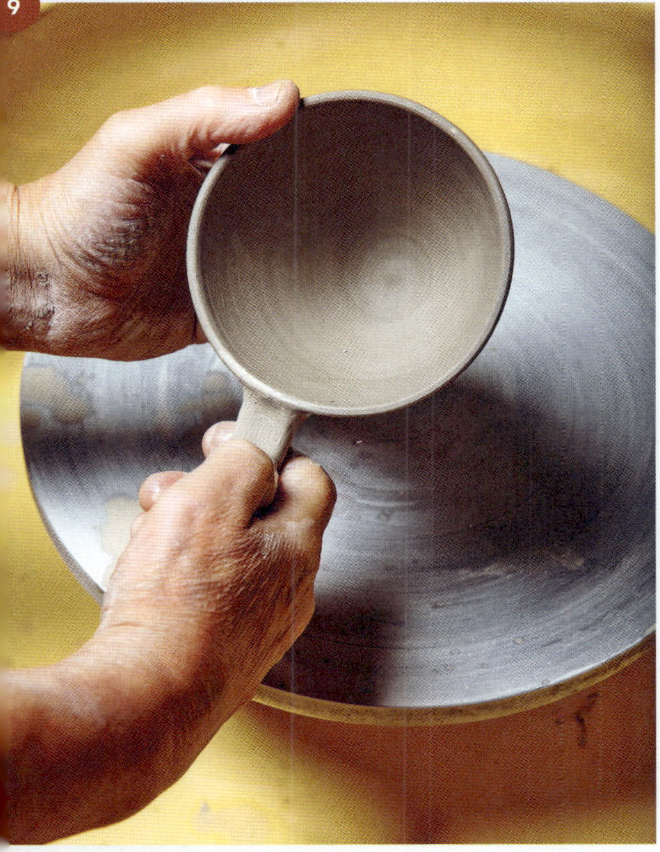

10

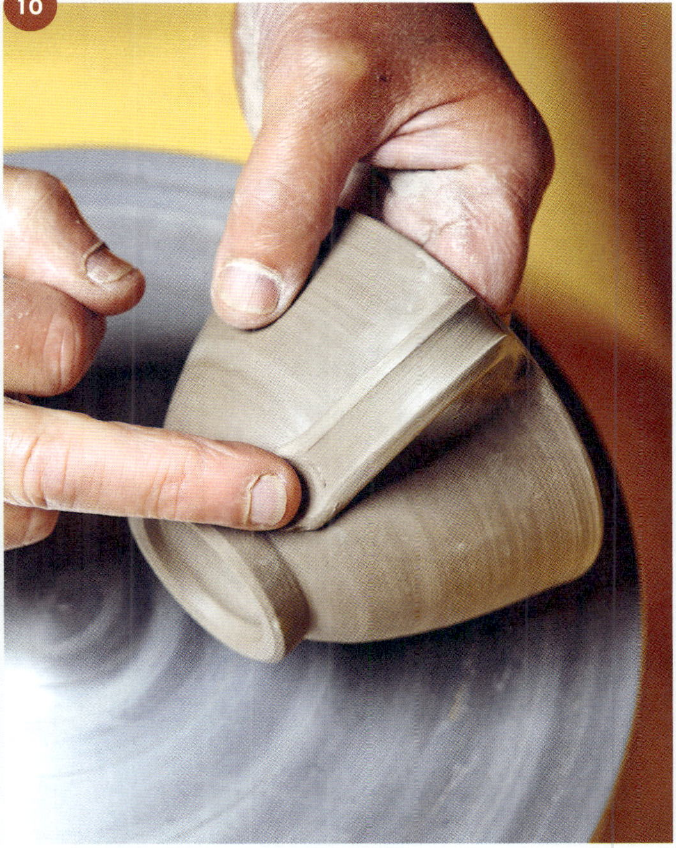

Plant pot

This project shows how to throw a traditionally shaped terracotta flower pot following a time-honoured method. It is essentially a simple adaptation of a cylinder, but differs in that the drainage hole is created in the process of establishing the base. Some surface decoration is added later as an optional extra by scoring lines into the clay.

YOU WILL NEED

Clay of choice (red earthenware or stoneware): 1.5 kg (approx. 3 lb)

Tools for throwing: Water bowl, sponge, metal or wooden rib, cutting wire

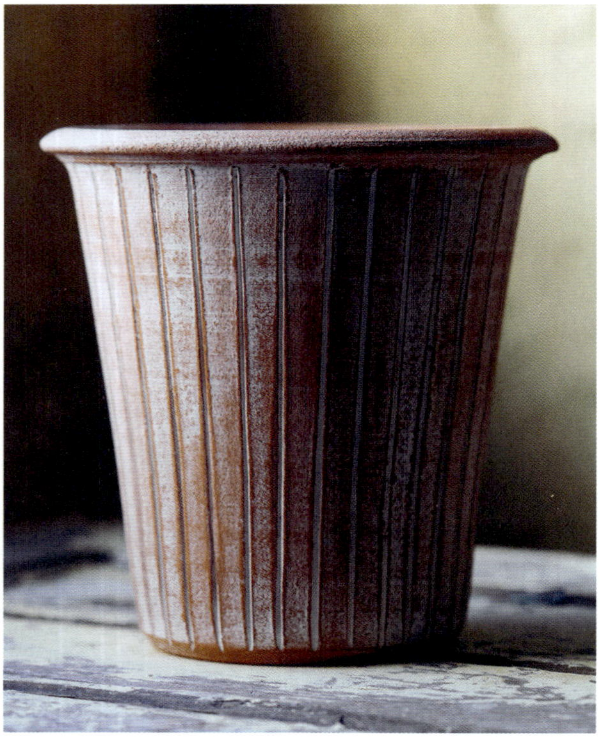

JUDGES' NOTES

Traditionally, red earthenware clay is used for this type of pot, but stoneware clay can be used equally well and has the advantage of being frost proof.

As a general guide, 1.5 kg (approx. 3 lb) of clay will make a pot that is 15–18 cm (6–7 in.) high.

You can centre the clay directly on the wheel head for this project. Traditional makers of this type of ware would throw hundreds in a day and working on a batt would slow the process down, but you can throw on a batt if you prefer.

Be aware that the higher the firing the more the clay will shrink – so take this into account when deciding on the weight of clay (see page 166 for clay shrinkage).

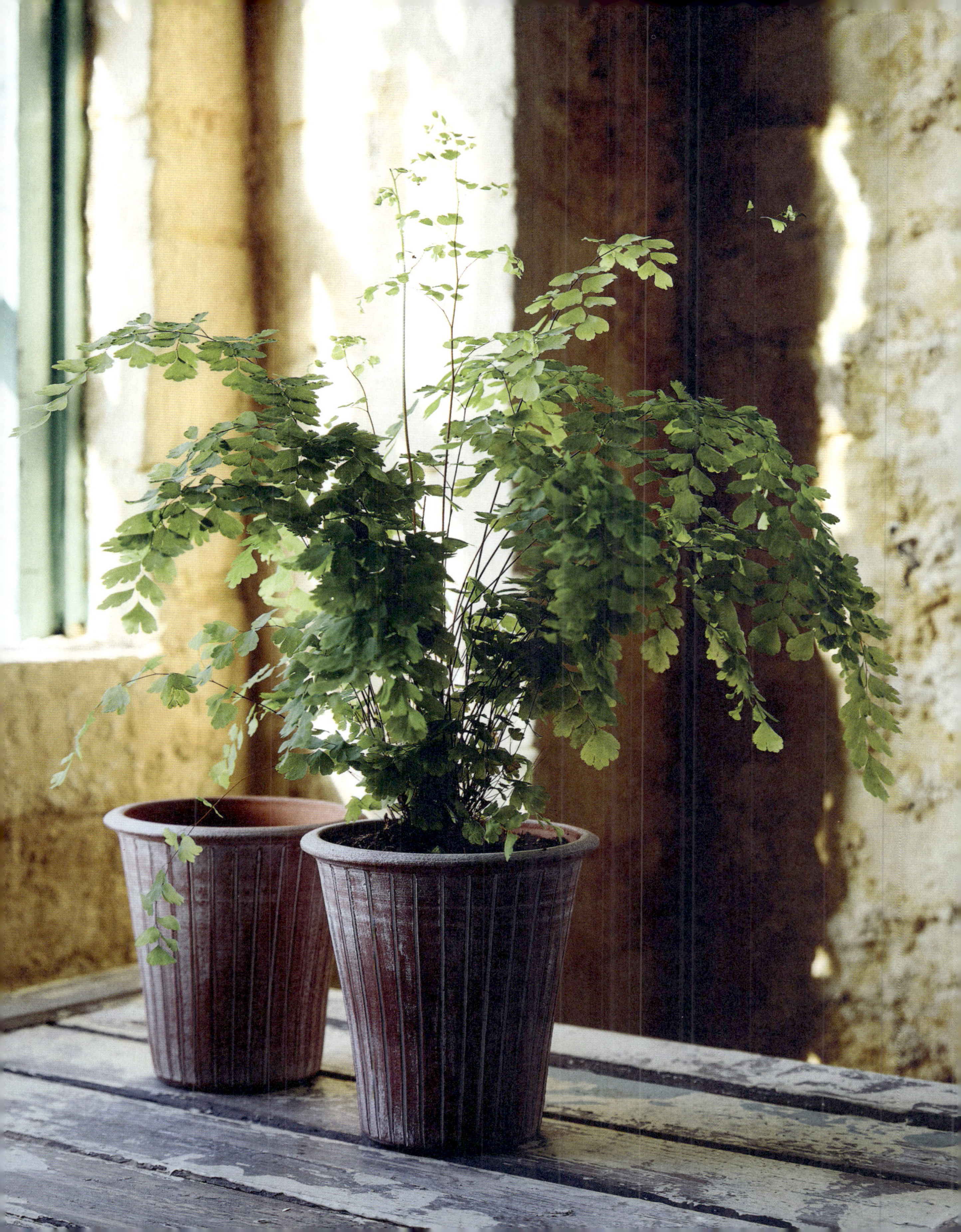

1

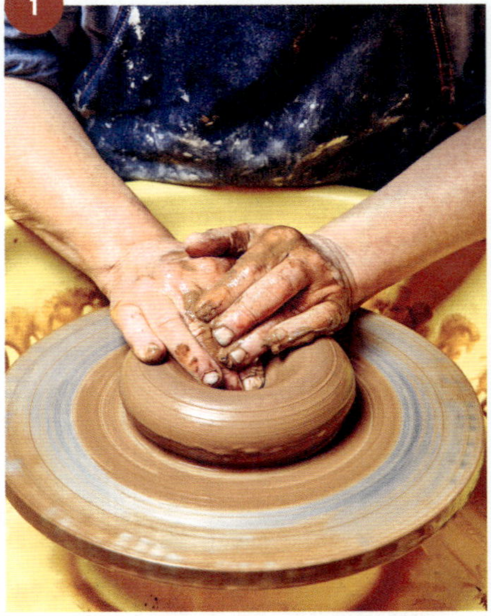

2

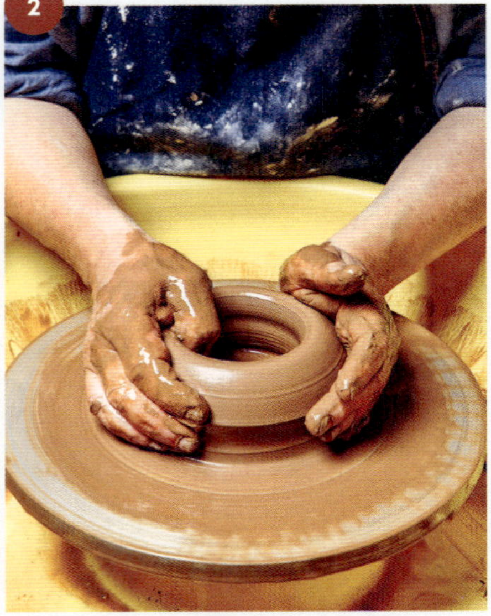

3

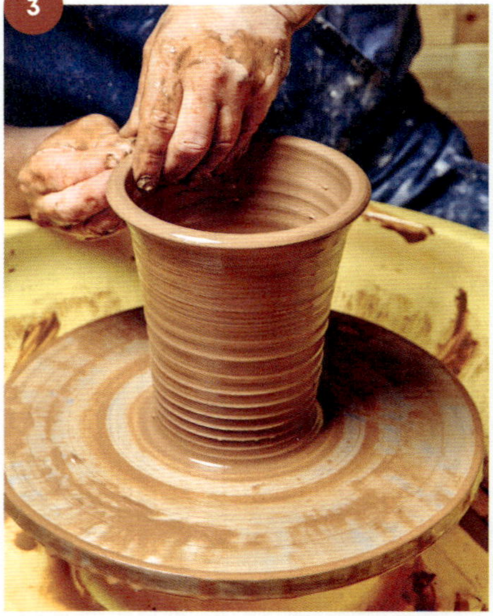

4

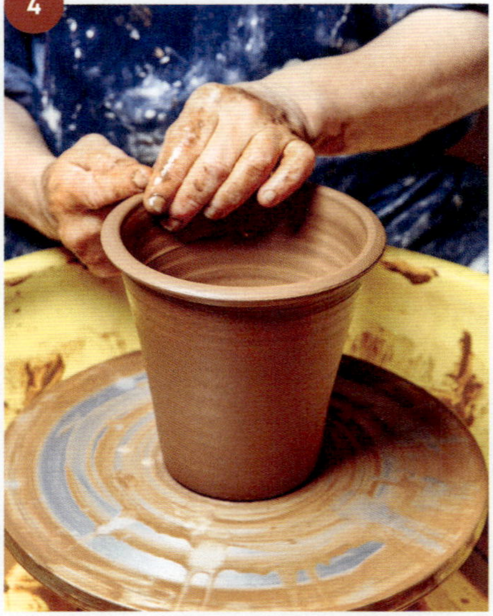

5

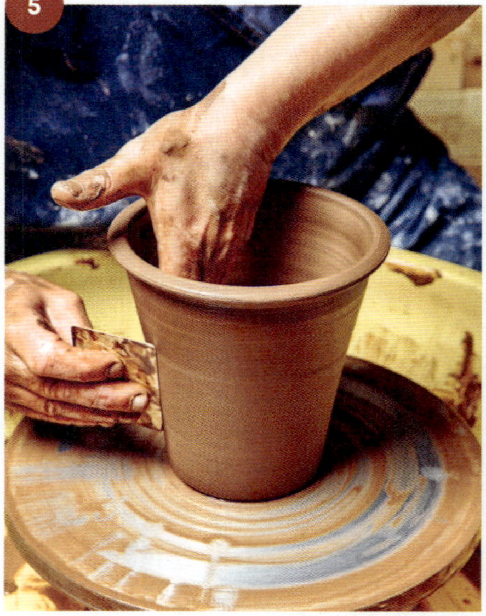

6

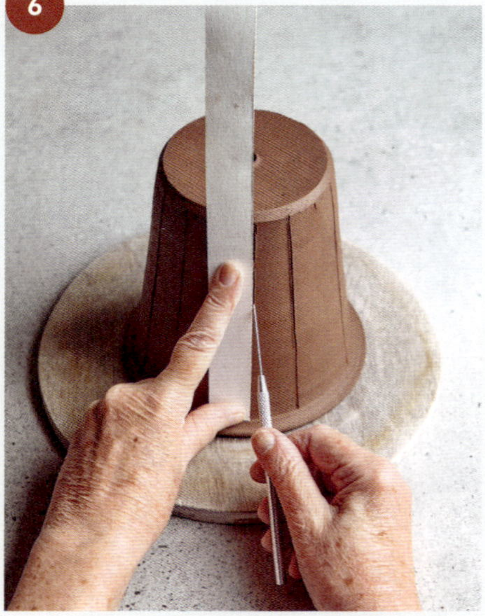

1. Centre the clay (see page 46). Open up (see page 50) the centre of the clay with your right-hand fingers held at the angle shown and supported by your left hand, but, unlike the usual procedure, press down directly onto the wheel head with your second finger at the centre to form the drainage hole. Then lift the finger about 5 mm (¼ in.) from the hole and open out the base of the pot to a diameter of 9–10 cm (3½–4 in.).

   Carefully compress the base with your fingers, maintaining the drainage hole at the centre.

2. Pinch and lift the wall upwards and inwards, holding the fingers and the thumb of your right hand in a pincer position, but leave some thickness at the rim and remember to compress this with your finger after the lift.

   Use your left hand to keep the shape at the side as you lift.

3. Following the instructions for throwing a cylinder on page 50, lift the wall the required number of times to reach a height of 16–18 cm (6–7 in.). Maintain the thick rim and cone-like shape until the last lift, then gently flare the wall outwards to a diameter that equals the height.

   Mop out the interior with a sponge when you've finished.

4. Compress the rim a final time, flattening it off a little more than usual in a slightly downward direction with your finger to form a feature flange as shown.

   Continue the outward flare to sharpen the plant pot shape and redefine the flange when finished.

5. Supporting the wall from the inside with the fingers of your left hand, work over the exterior surface (extending up to the underside of the flange) with a rib to remove the slurry and throwing lines. This is also a good way of refining the shape if required.

   Cut a bevel at the base of the pot and clean away any excess clay and slurry from the wheel head.

   Underwire the base and transfer the pot to a board to firm to leather hard before handling again.

6. Your flower pot is essentially finished at this point, but you can embellish the surface with some feature decoration if you think it looks too generic.

   One option is to score lines around the walls, as shown. Begin by placing a small protractor on the base of the upturned pot, then carefully mark off equally spaced divisions from which to draw the lines.

   Use a flexible card ruler to score the lines down to the underside of the flange from the marked positions at the base.

FIRING INSTRUCTION

Follow the recommended optimal firing temperature for your chosen clay, being aware that it is generally lower for red earthenwares. Pots of this type only need to be fired once if unglazed, as is the tradition.

JUDGES' TIP

Paint a thin wash of white slip on the wall of the flower pot, extending up to but not over the flange, before scoring the lines.

Pet bowl

Although these feeding bowls are a generic shape, you can easily personalize them for a beloved pet through decoration. Bear in mind that feeding bowls should be flat and smooth-walled for ease of cleaning.

YOU WILL NEED

Clay of choice (earthenware or stoneware – the latter will be more hard wearing):
1 kg (2½ lb) for a large bowl – suitable for a dog
700–900 g (1½–2 lb) for a small bowl – suitable for a cat

Tools for throwing: Water bowl, sponge, rib, cutting wire

Glaze(s) of choice to decorate

BEFORE YOU BEGIN

Fix a batt to your wheel following the method on page 64.

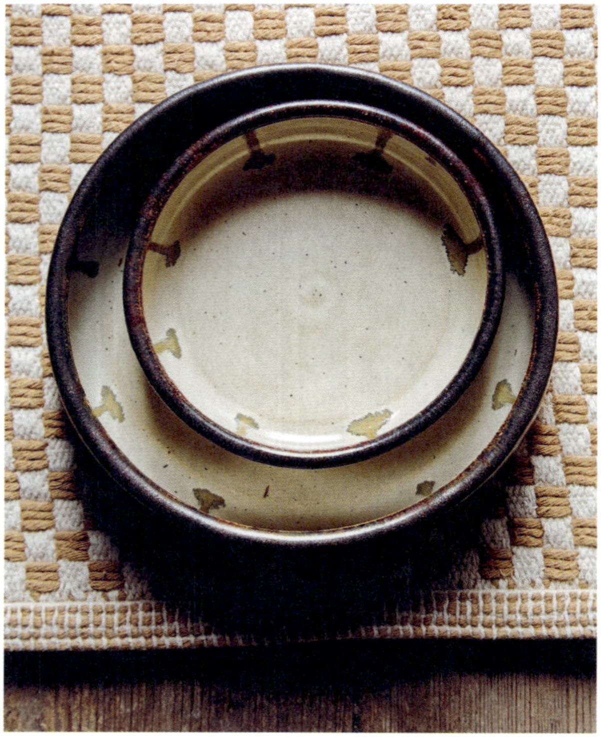

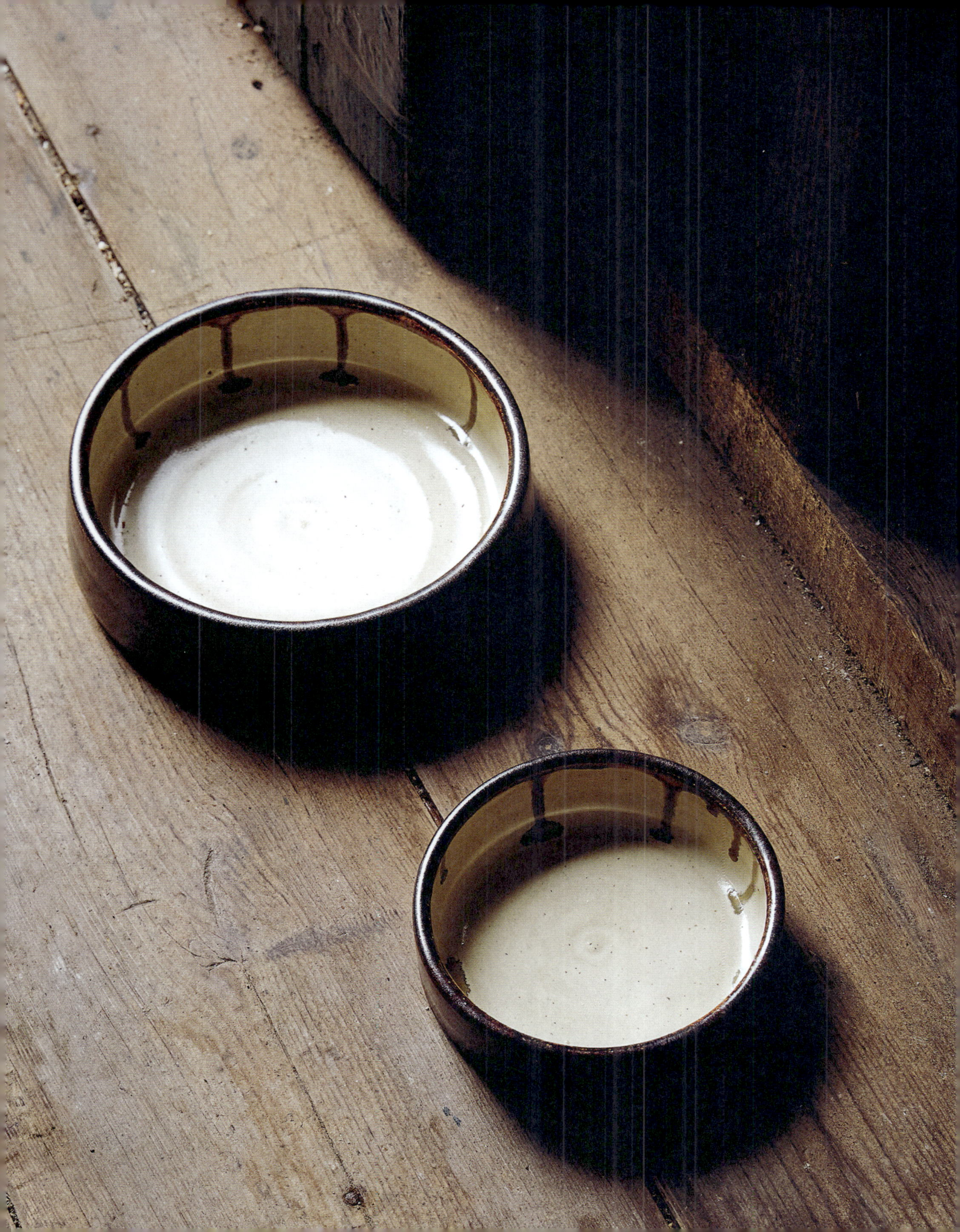

1

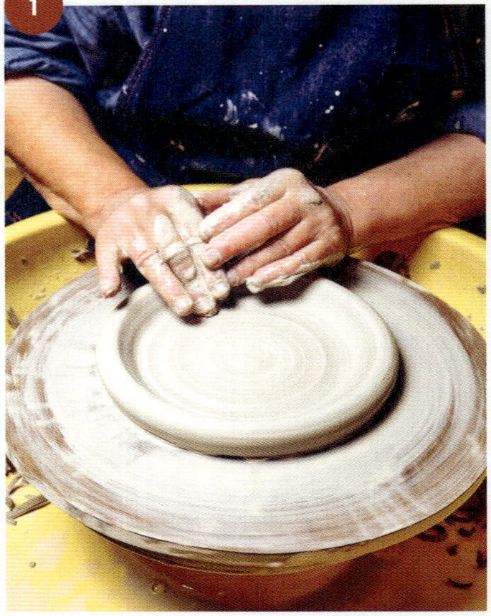

2

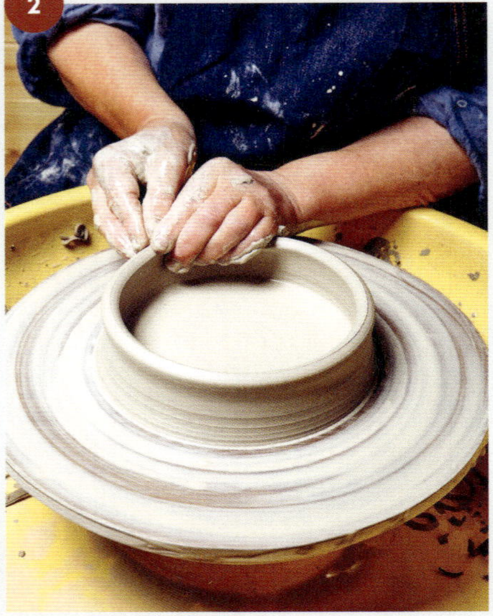

3

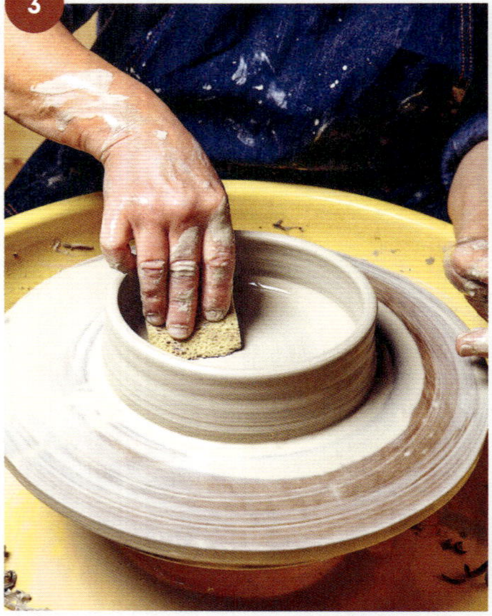

4

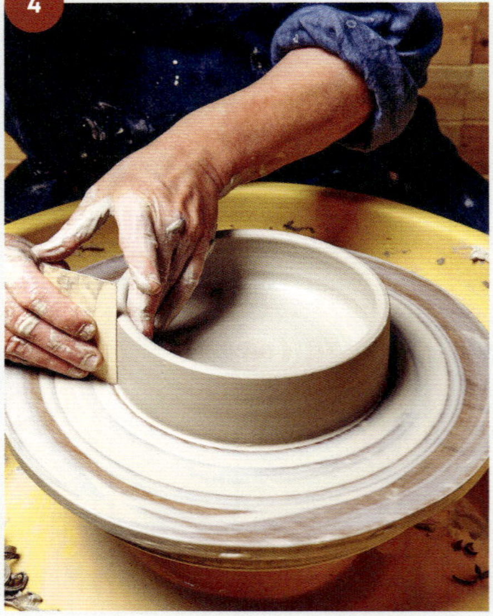

5

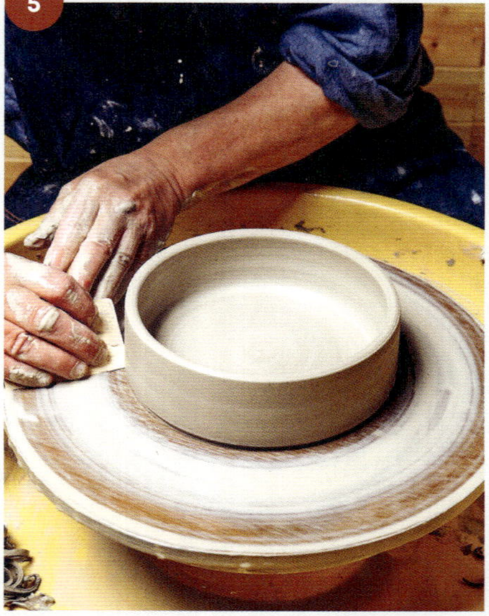

1. Working on a batt, centre your clay (see page 46).

   Open up the centre of the clay (see page 50), pressing down to within 5 mm (¼ in.) of the batt surface and then drawing the base out to a diameter of 18 cm (7 in.) for a dog bowl or 14 cm (5½ in.) for a cat bowl, leaving a thick, doughnut-like ring at the outer edge.

   Compress the clay in the base by running your fingers over the surface from the centre to the outside edge at least three times.

2. With the wheel spinning at medium to fast speed, place the fingers of your left hand inside the fat rim with the fingers of your right hand opposite on the outside, then lift the wall upwards and ever so slightly inwards.

   Repeat until you reach a height of 6 cm (2½ in.) for a dog bowl or 4–5 cm (1½–2 in.) for a cat bowl.

   Remember to compress the clay at the rim after each lift.

3. Mop out the interior of the bowl with a sponge to remove all surplus water, then run the sponge over the batt to remove excess water there.

4. Supporting the wall from the inside with the fingers of your left hand, draw a straight-sided rib around the exterior to remove the throwing lines and completely smooth the surface.

5. Using the tip of the rib, cut a bevel around the outside base edge, then briefly run the rib over the batt to remove any excess clay around the bowl.

   Underwire the bowl once, then lift the batt carefully off the wheel.

   Allow the bowl to firm to leather hard before removing it from the batt.

Dinner plate

Dinner plates are generally around 27 cm (10½ in.) in diameter and, because of the wide expanse of clay involved, are prone to cracking in the drying and firing processes. To avoid this, try to ensure an even thickness in the base and compress it really well. To make plates of different sizes in this contemporary style, simply increase or decrease the weight of clay accordingly.

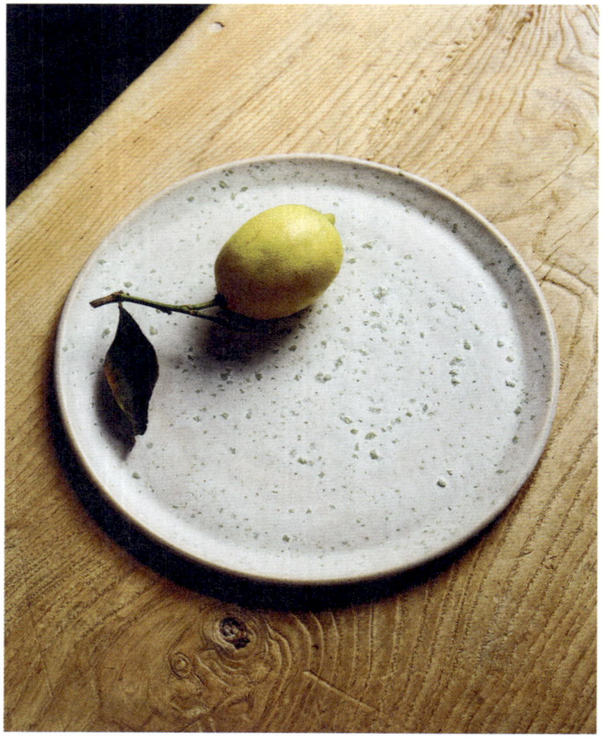

YOU WILL NEED

Clay of choice (earthenware or stoneware): 1.5 kg (approx. 3 lb) for a 27-cm (10½-in.) diameter plate with no foot ring

Large batt

Tools for throwing: Water bowl, sponge, straight-sided rib, cutting wire

Glaze(s) of choice to decorate

BEFORE YOU BEGIN

Fix a batt to the wheel head (see page 64), making sure it is large enough to accommodate the width of the plate if working to the suggested dimensions and weight of clay.

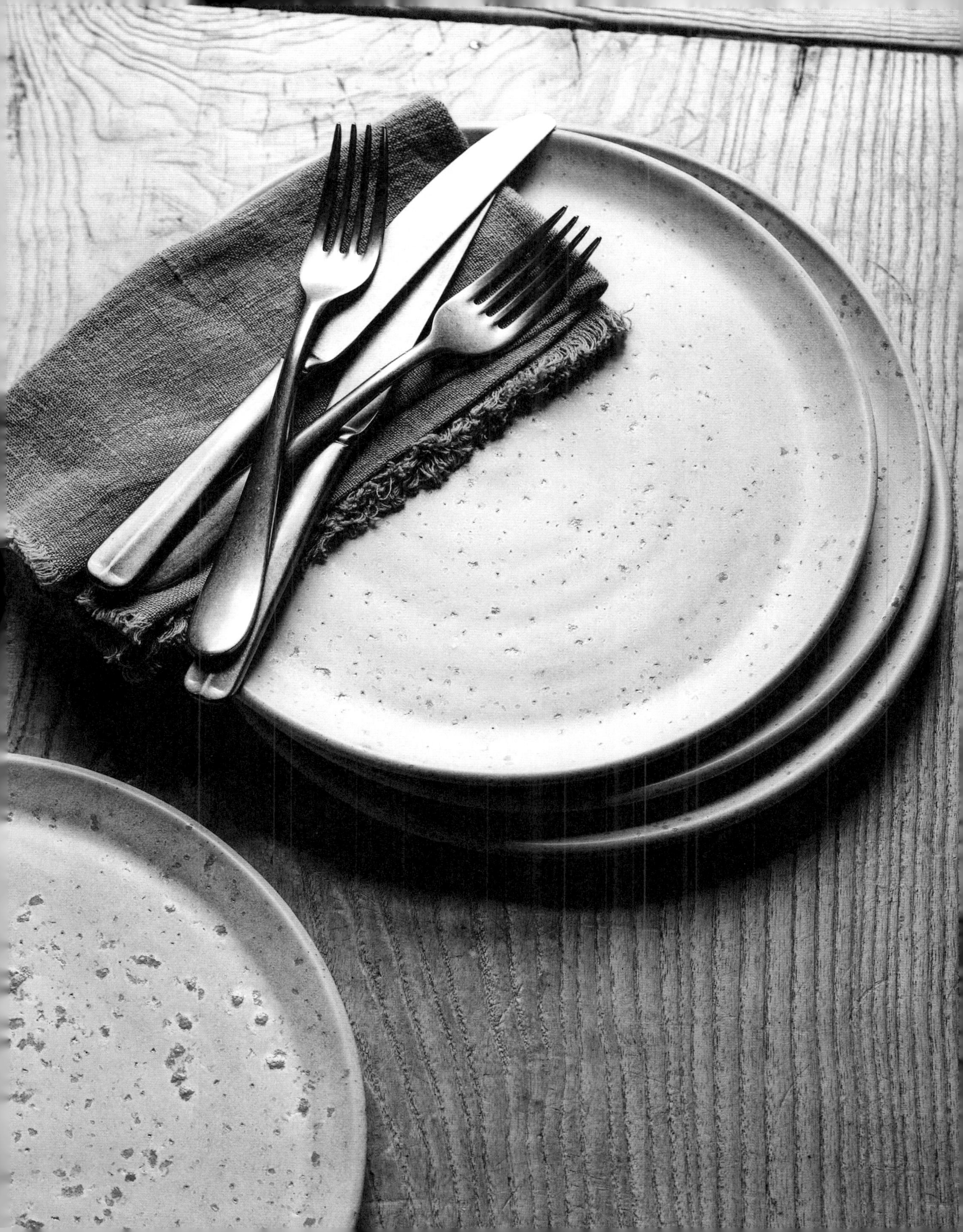

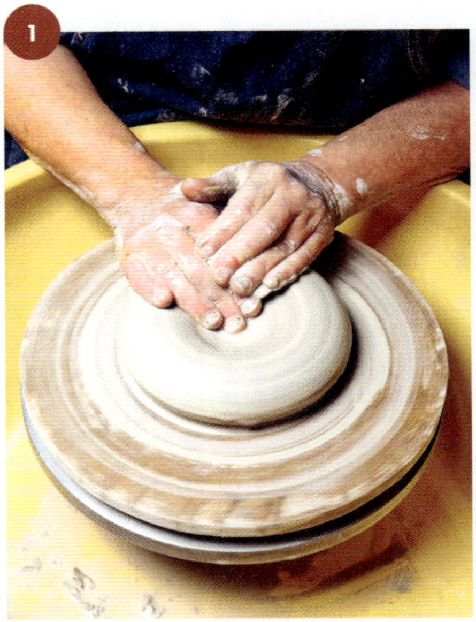
1

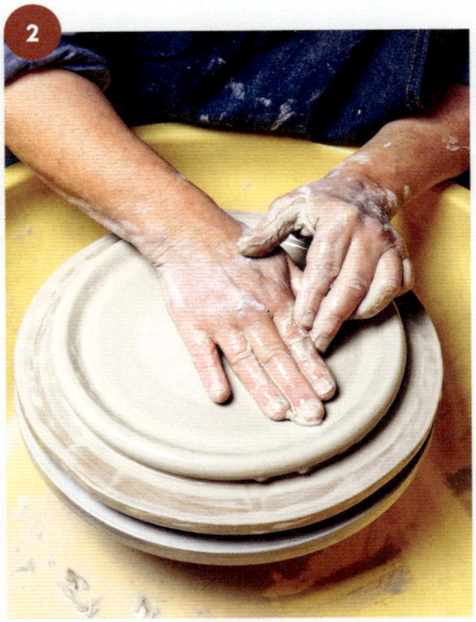
2

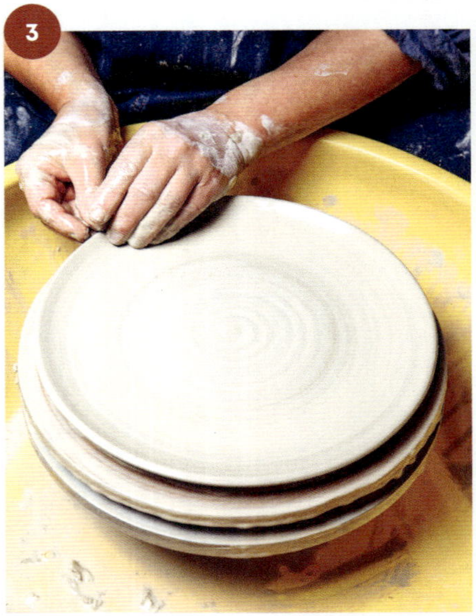
3

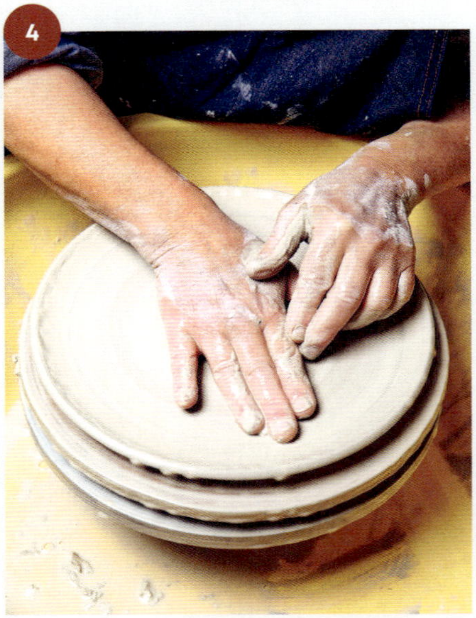
4

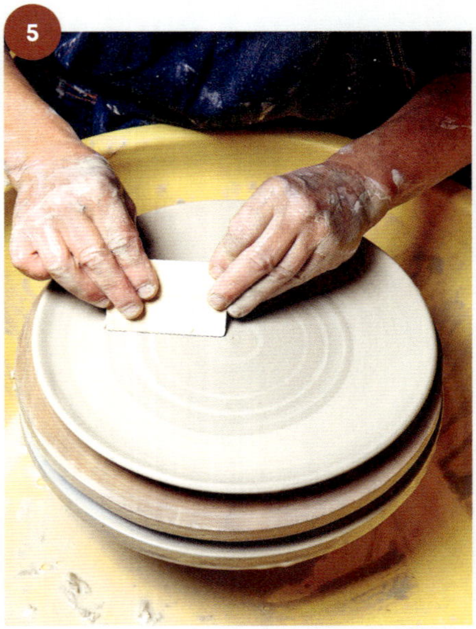
5

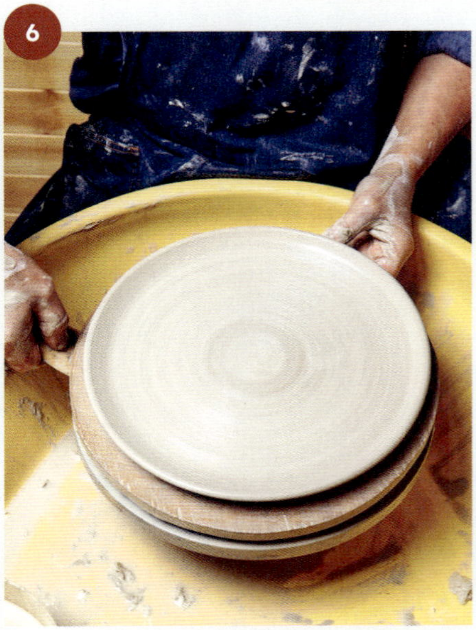
6

1. Centre (see page 46) your well-prepared clay on the batt, then open up (see page 50) the centre to a diameter of approximately 25 cm (10 in.), leaving a thick rim at the edge.
2. Pay particular attention to compressing the clay in the base of the plate by running the fingers of your right hand, supported by the left, over the surface several times, working from the centre to the thick rim.
3. With the fingers of your left hand inside the thick rim and your right-hand fingers opposite on the outside, lift the wall upwards and outwards until it measures 27 cm (10½ in.). Remember to compress the clay at the rim by pinching it gently between the finger and thumb of your left hand, then applying gentle pressure with a right-hand finger.
4. Work over the surface of the plate again with your fingers to ensure there is a gentle curve up from the base to the rim and that the clay is an even thickness throughout. Mop up excess water from the surface of the plate using your sponge.
5. Very carefully work over the surface of the base of the plate with a straight-sided rib to remove any inconsistency of thickness and excess moisture, and to fully compress the clay.
6. Underwire the base of the plate once, holding the wire really taut, then carefully remove the batt from the wheel by prizing it off with a sturdy tool at several points around the edge.

Allow the plate to firm to leather hard before handling it.

JUDGES' TIP

You can delay underwiring large, flat surfaces such as plates if you prefer – it is often better to wait a few hours until the clay has firmed up a little, because wide bases like this often seal up again if cut when freshly thrown. The underside of the plate will seal back onto the batt if wired off when still very wet, hence why it is better to wait.

Nesting bowls

Bowls that can nest inside one another are the perfect solution when storage space is limited. And because they vary in size you can be sure you always have one that is just right for your requirements.

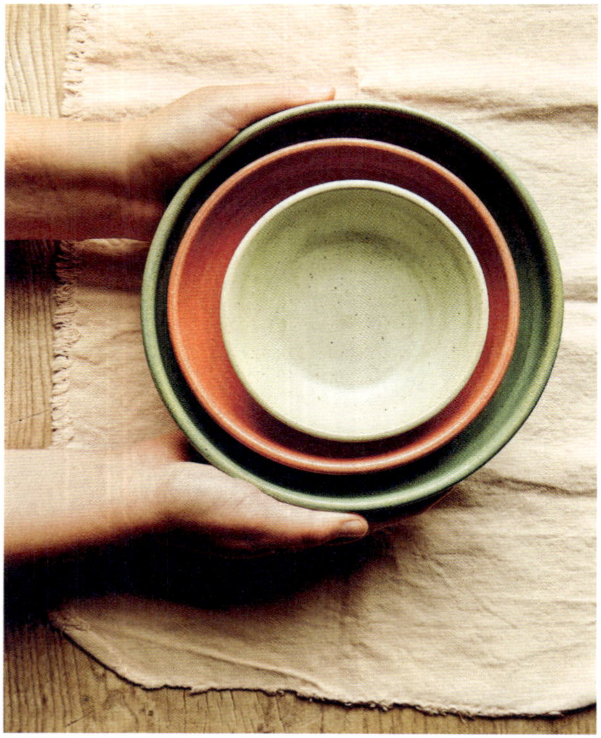

YOU WILL NEED

Clay of choice: (earthenware or stoneware): our three bowls are made from 1.5 kg (3 lb), 900 g (2 lb) and 500 g (1 lb) of clay respectively.

Batt

Tools for throwing: Water bowl, sponge, rib, cutting wire

Glaze(s) of choice to decorate

BEFORE YOU BEGIN

Fix a batt to the wheel head following the method on page 64. For the largest of the nesting bowls, the batt will need to be at least as large as the wheel head – our example has a finished diameter of 24 cm (9½ in.) to give an indication of the size of batt required.

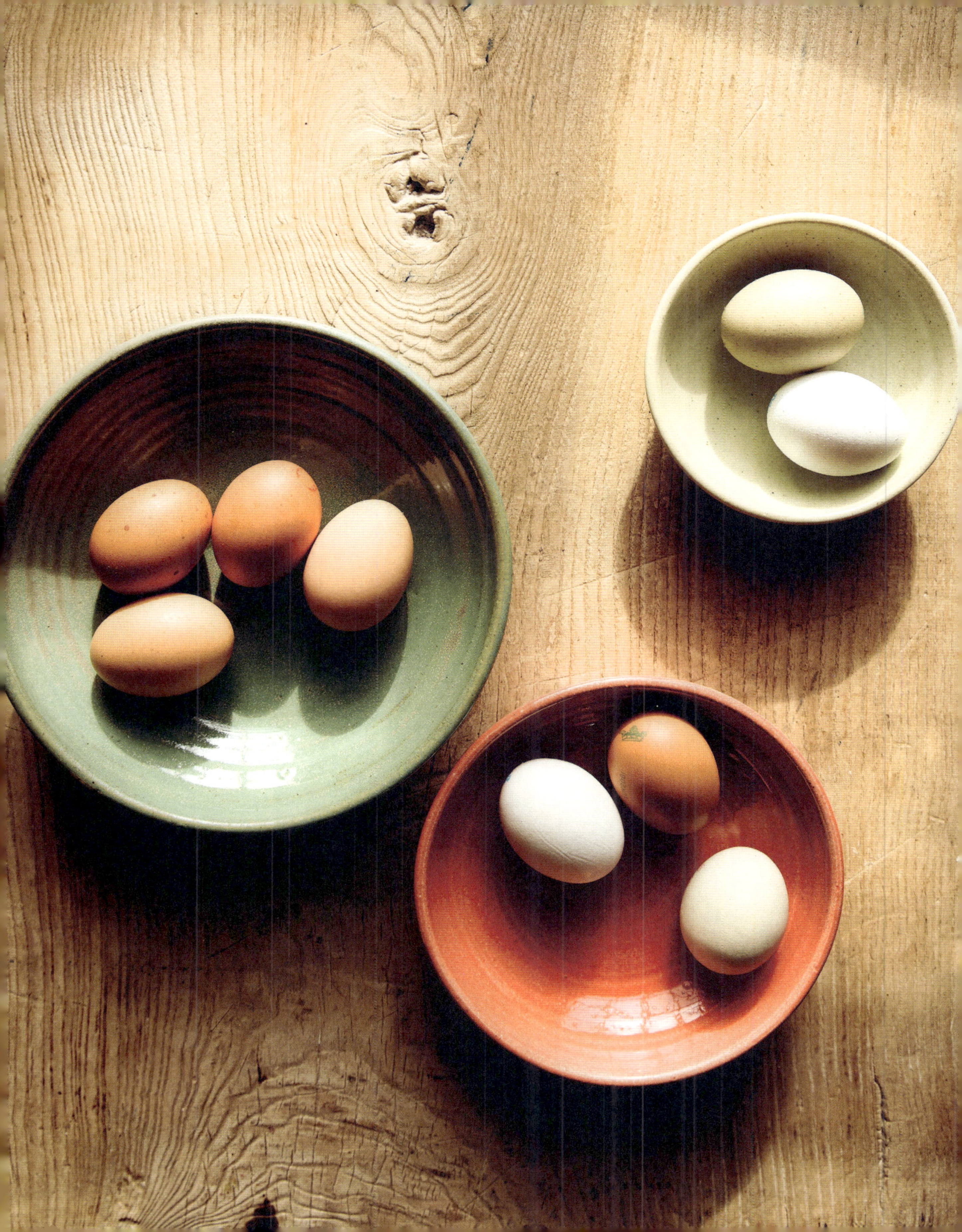

1

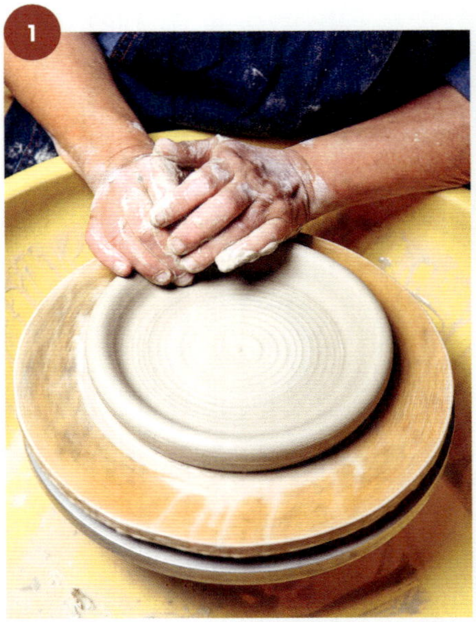

2

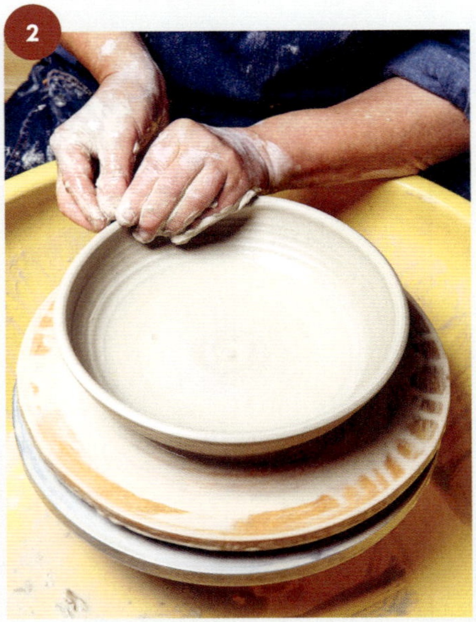

3

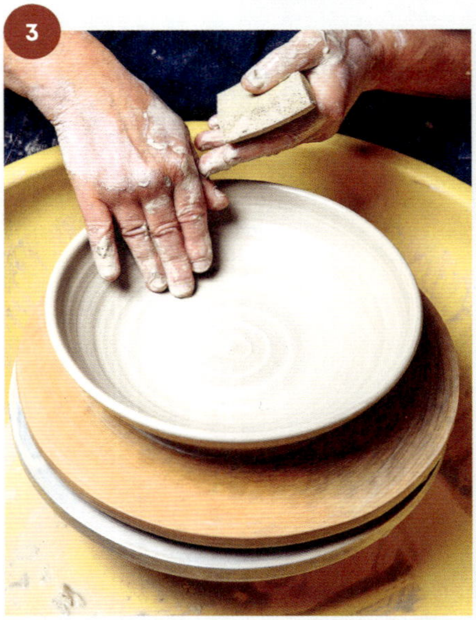

4

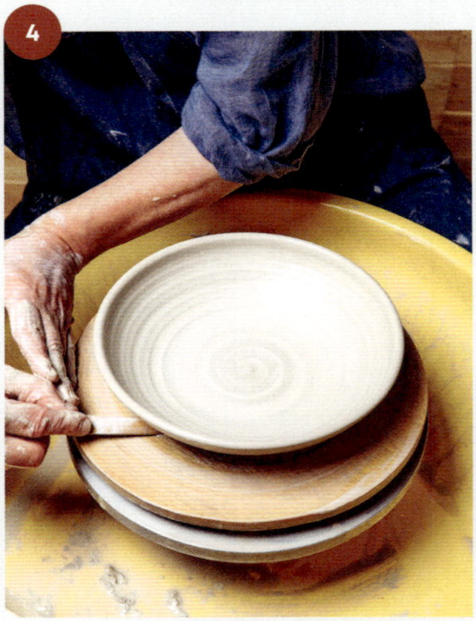

5

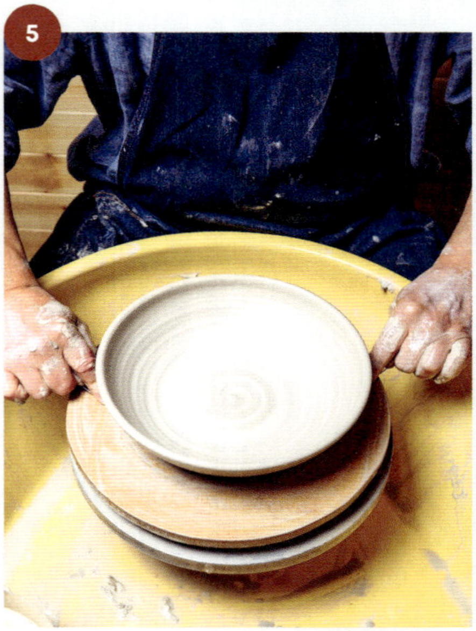

1. Prepare 1.5 kg (3 lb) of clay by kneading it well to remove any possible trapped air then form it into a rough cone shape and centre it (see page 46).

   Now open up (see page 50) the centre by first pressing the fingers of your right hand down through the clay to within approximately 8 mm (just over ¼ in.) of the batt, all the while steadying your hand with the left one for a smooth action. Next draw the clay back towards your body until the diameter of the base is approximately 16 cm (6¼ in.), maintaining equal pressure to ensure a flat, even base and leaving a thick, doughnut-like ring at the edge.

   Compress the clay in the base by running your fingers over the surface several times, working from the centre to the outer wall.

> **JUDGES' TIP**
>
> **Test the thickness of the base following the tip on page 53.**

2. Using the fingers of your right hand, cuff the clay in at the base on the outside as a point to lift the wall from, then with your left hand positioned opposite on the inside, raise the wall upwards, in a gentle curve from the base.

   Repeat the lift as required, flaring the wall outwards to a diameter of 24 cm (9½ in.) with a height of 6 cm (2½ in.) to finish.

   Remember to compress the clay at the rim after each lift.

> **JUDGES' TIP**
>
> **Do not splay the wall too far because it will collapse. There is always a point where the clay cannot support itself, so be careful!**

3. Sponge over the interior surface of the bowl to remove excess water and slurry. As an optional extra, beginning at the centre and using a finger, impress a shallow spiral radiating outwards as a feature.

4. Remove the surplus water and clay from the batt around the outside of the bowl and then, using a suitably shaped tool or rib to fit the shallow angle, carefully bevel the underside base edge.

5. Underwire the bowl carefully once, holding the wire really taut, then gently release the batt from the wheel with a knife or other tool.

   Allow the bowl to firm to a point where it won't distort when handled, then turn it over to allow the base to firm sufficiently for trimming.

Adjusting the sizes

Make the remaining bowls in the same way, decreasing the amount of clay used and the dimensions for each subsequent one.

If you are making three bowls, for example, and beginning with 1.5 kg (3 lb) of clay, the largest will be 24 cm (9½ in.) in diameter and 6 cm (2½ in.) high when finished, with the internal wall flaring out from a 16-cm (6¼-in.) base.

The intermediate size would use 900 g (2 lb) of clay and have a finished diameter of 19 cm (7½ in.) and be 6 cm (2⅜ in.) high, with the internal wall flaring out from a 12-cm (4¾-in.) base.

The smallest size would use 500 g (1 lb) of clay and have a finished diameter of 14 cm (5½ in.) and be 4 cm (1½ in.) high, with an internal wall flaring out from an 8-cm (3-in.) base.

Jug

Jugs are addictive things to throw because, no matter how many you make, you never seem to have one exactly the size you require so you need to make another one. Fortunately, they are quick and relatively easy to throw because they are essentially shaped cylinders.

YOU WILL NEED

Clay of choice (earthenware or stoneware): 900 g (2 lb), plus extra for the handle

Tools for throwing: Water bowl, sponge, rib, cutting wire

Glaze(s) of choice to decorate

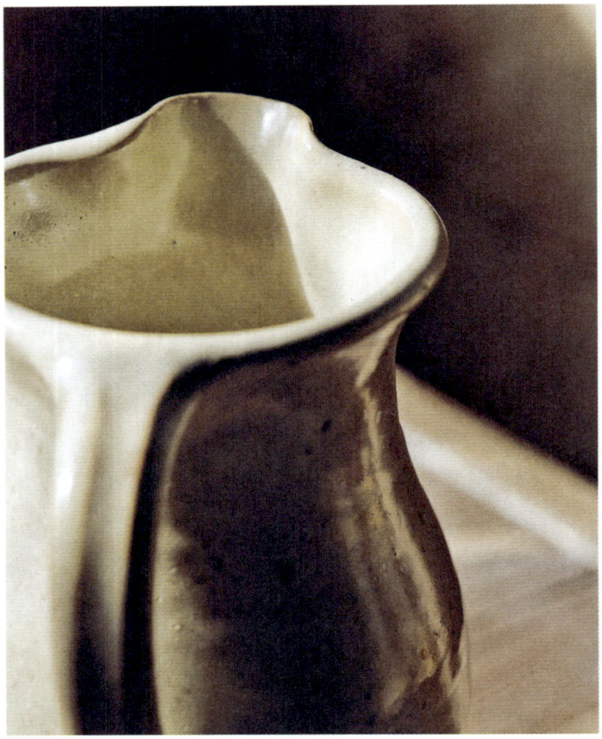

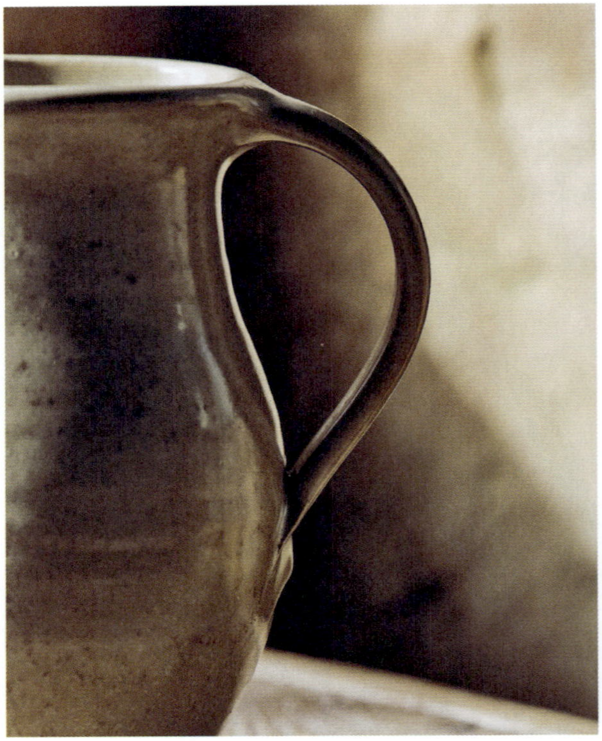

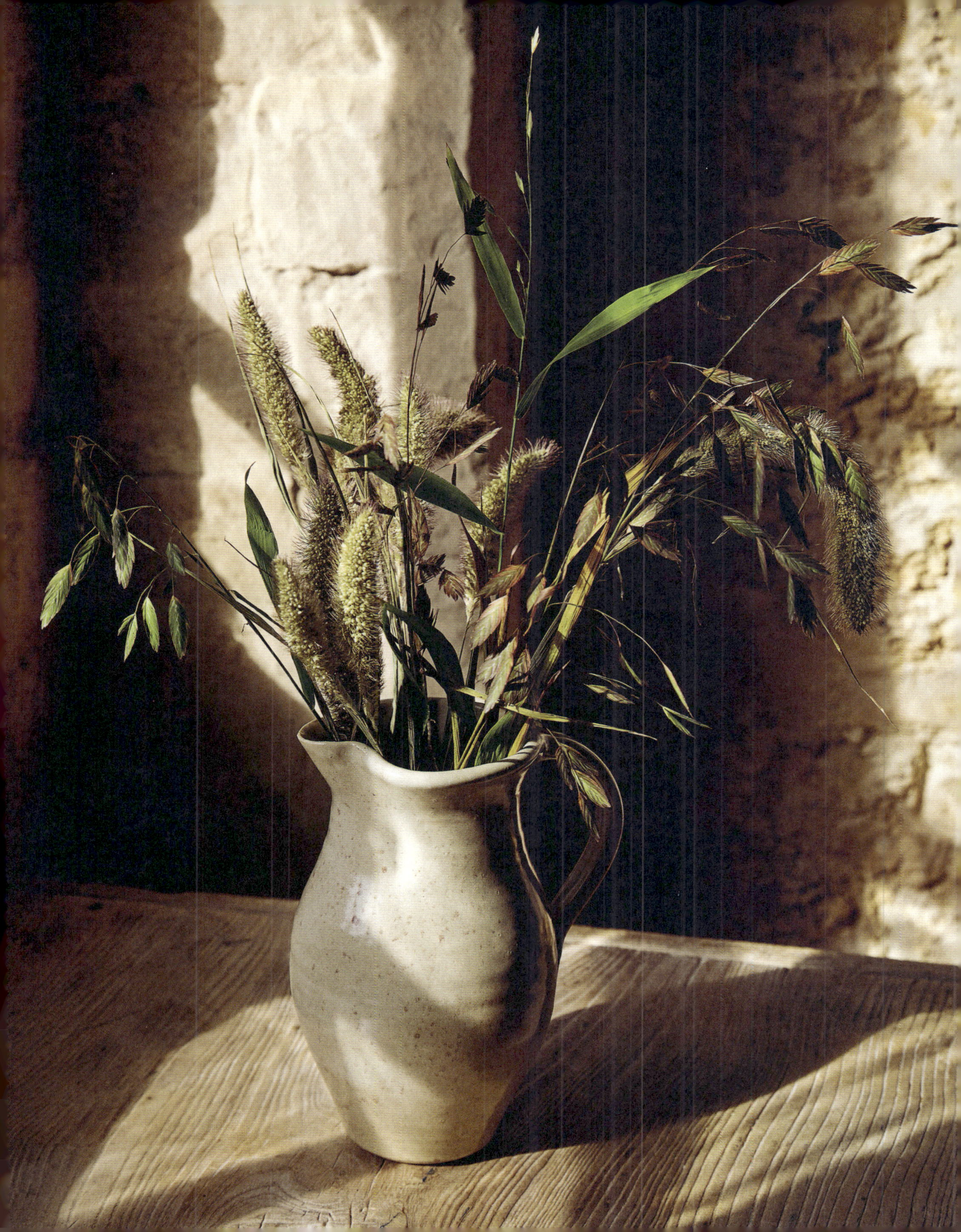

1

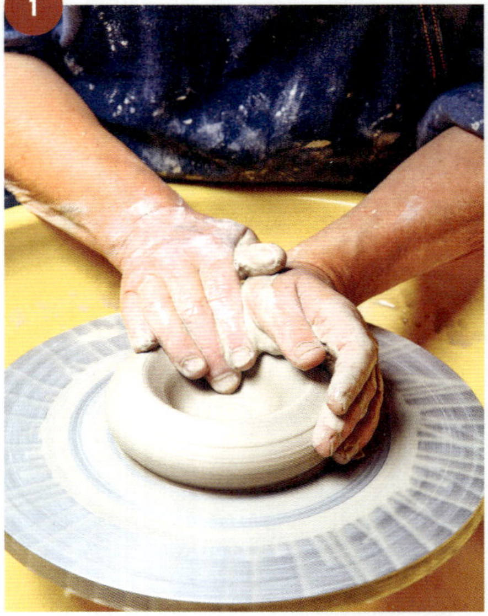

2

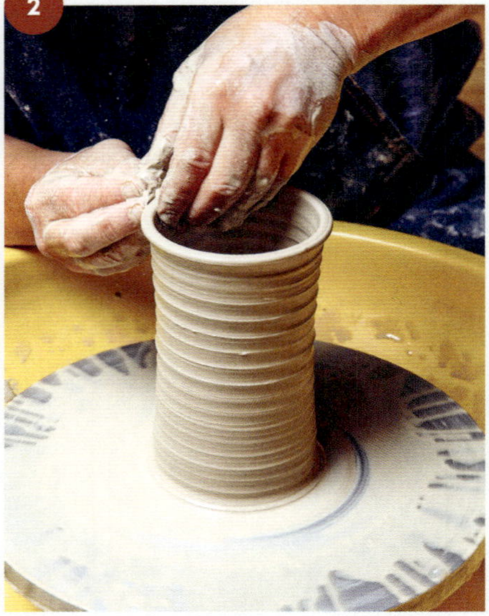

3

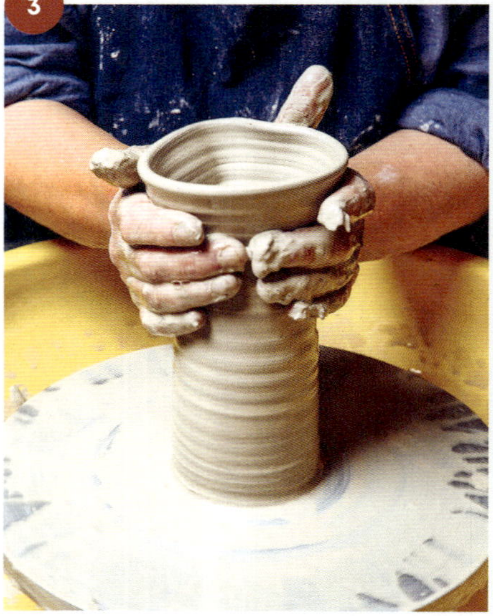

4

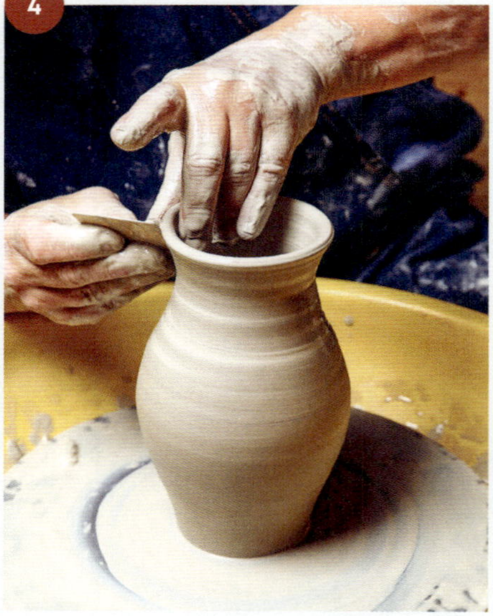

5

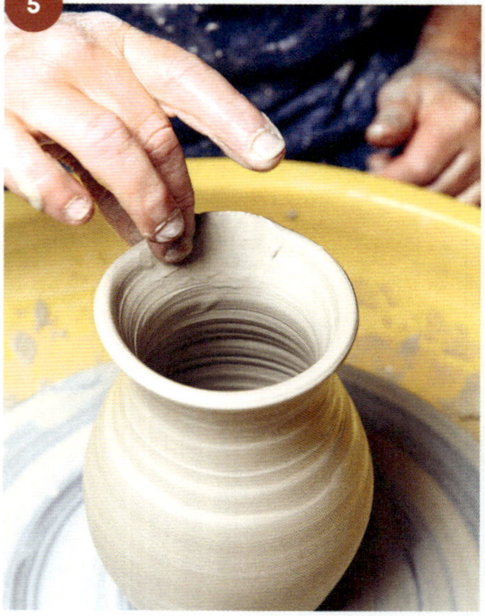

6

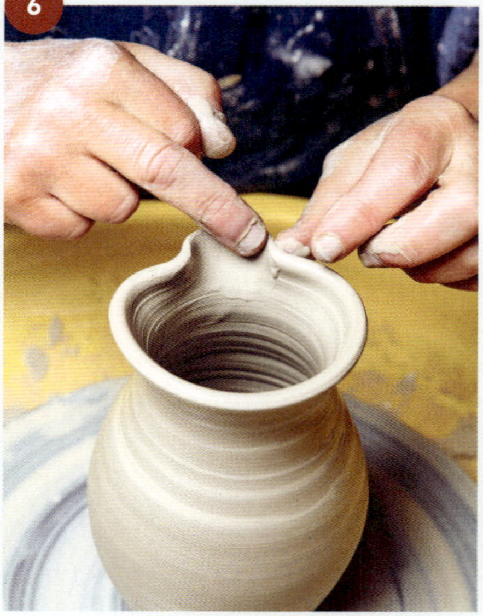

1. Centre (see page 46) your well-prepared clay directly on the wheel head. Open up (see page 50) the centre of the clay, pressing it down to within 5 mm (¼ in.) of the surface, and draw out the base to 7–8 cm (about 3 in.).

   Compress the clay in the base three times.

2. Lift the wall as a cylinder (see page 50), repeating the lifts as many times as required to reach a height of 22 cm (8½ in.) and leaving a slightly thicker rim.

   Remember to compress the clay at the rim when finished.

3. If you feel the shape is flaring out too much, collar the wall in a little between both your hands as shown until the top is narrowed again and you have established the suggestion of a shoulder and neck.

4. Position your left hand inside the cylinder, then gently apply outward pressure to belly the lower two-thirds of the wall onto a rib on the outside. Ease off the pressure as you reach the shoulder to allow the shape to close back in for the upper third.

   Next, collar the neck in carefully between both hands to a dimension that balances with the body, then very carefully work the rib over the outside surface, supporting the wall from inside with your fingers until you can clearly see the shape.

   To improve the definition from shoulder to rim, lift the neck to its final height, giving it a slight outward flare to finish.

5. Clean away all slurry and excess clay from the wheel at the base of the jug, then cut a bevel with the tip of a rib.

   To form the lip of the jug, wet the fingers of one hand, then gently pinch the rim outwards between your finger and thumb to thin it for a width roughly equal to one-fifth of the circumference.

6. When you are happy with the shape and width of the lip, use a finger to push the clay in at either side to further develop the shape. You can hold these positions with the fingers of one hand to further develop the shape of the lip with another finger if required. Simply roll the wet finger from side to side until you have the shape you like.

   Continue to shape the lip in this way until happy with the outcome, then finish by pushing the clay in at the sides with both thumbs to ensure the shape is balanced.

   Holding the cutting wire taut, underwire the jug just once and then lift it off with clean hands and place it on a board to firm to leather hard.

   When the jug is firm enough to handle without distorting, attach a handle (see page 110).

Olive oil bottle

This stylish oil bottle is elegant enough to grace any table, but requires a slightly more advanced throwing technique to make successfully.

YOU WILL NEED

Clay of choice (earthenware or stoneware): 500 g (1 lb)

Batt (optional)

Tools for throwing: Water bowl, sponge on a stick, cutting wire, rib or old bank/store card

Glaze(s) of choice to decorate

BEFORE YOU BEGIN

If you are confident about lifting forms off the wheel after throwing, you can work directly on the wheel head for this project. If not, fix a batt in place (see page 64).

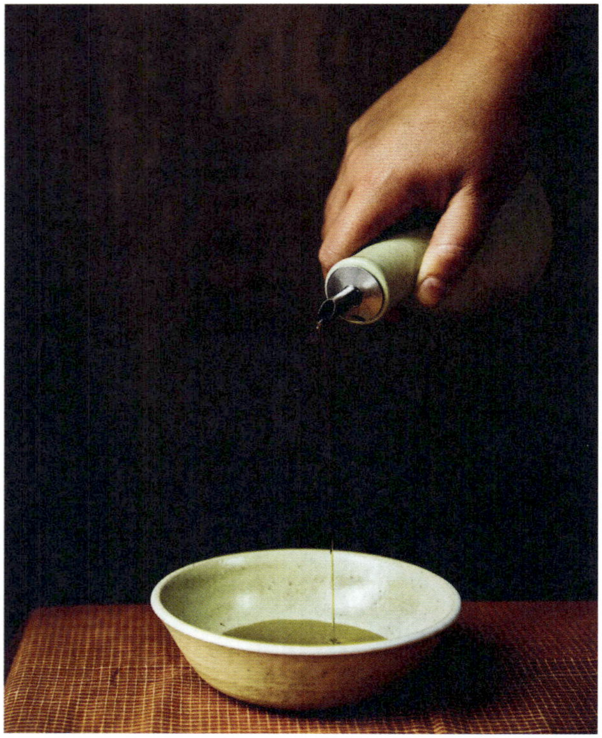

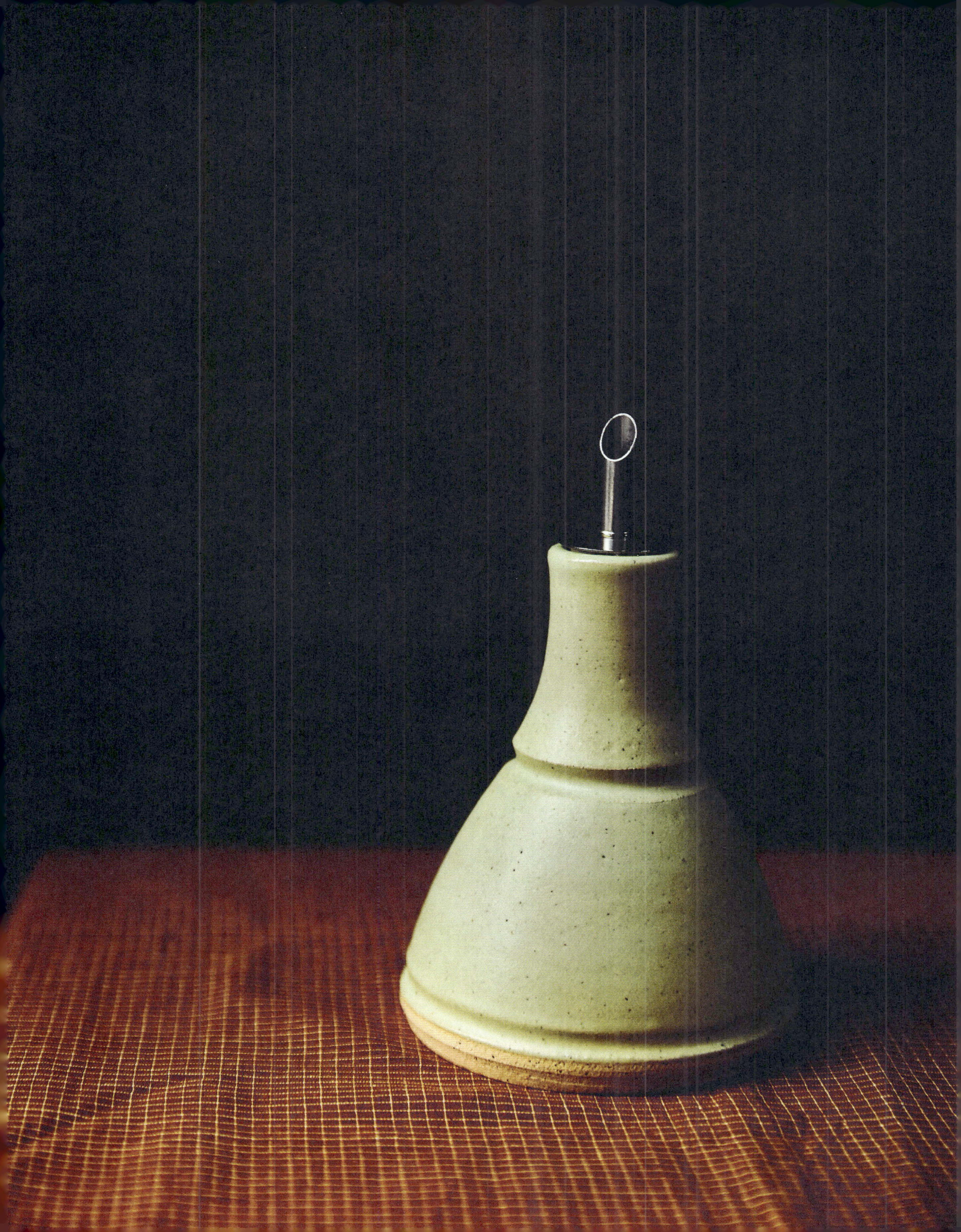

1
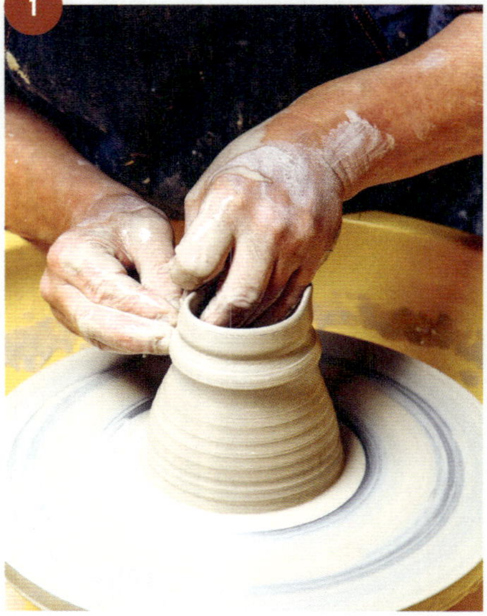

2
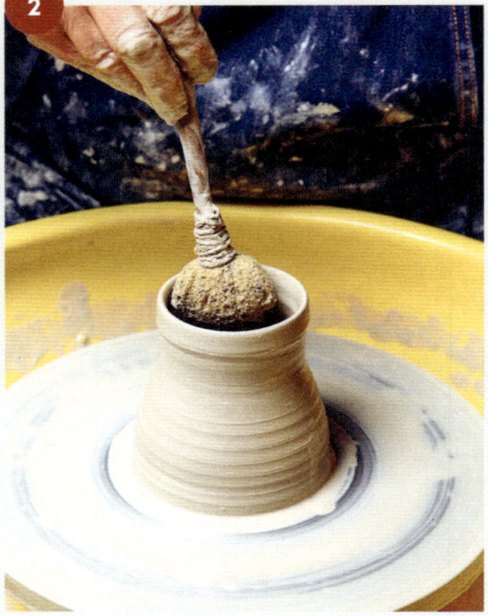

3
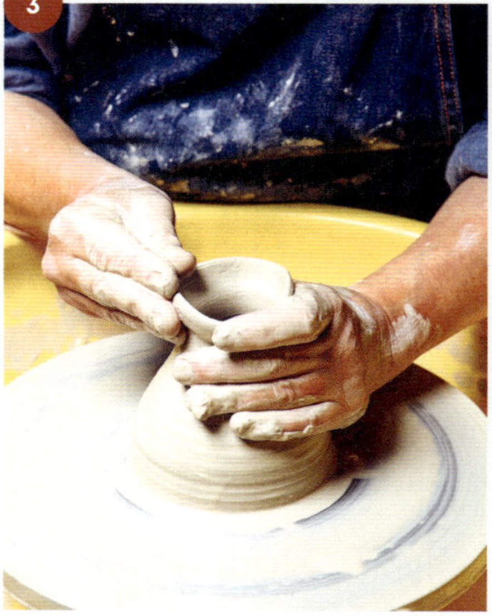

4
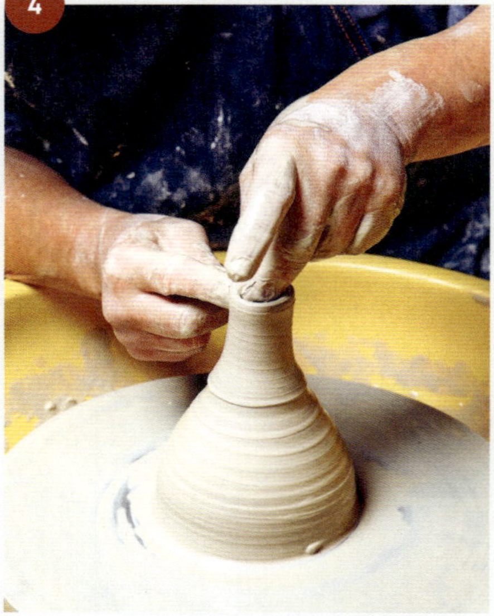

5
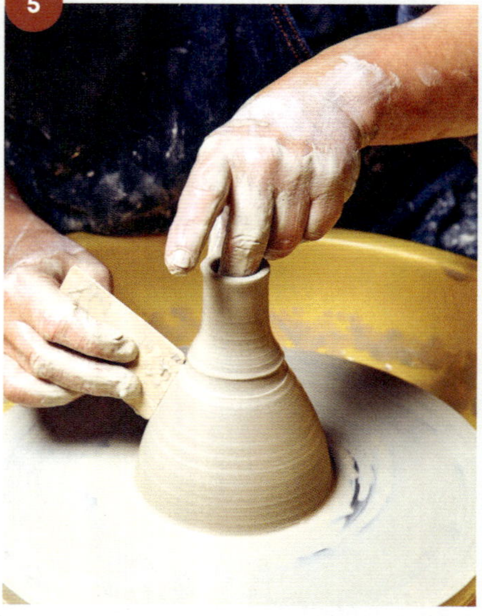

6
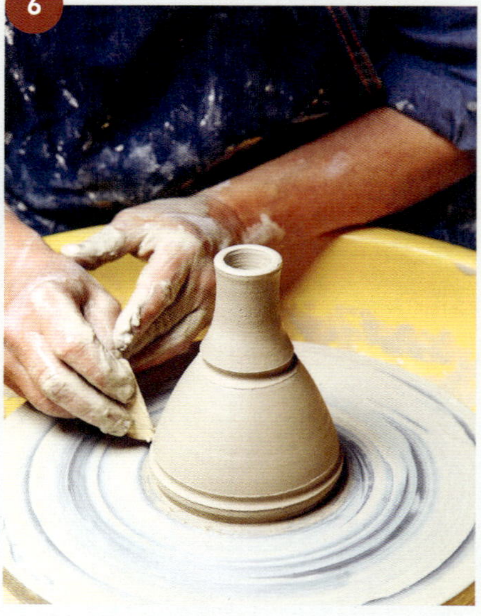

1. Centre the clay (see page 46).

   Open out (see page 50) the base with the fingers of your right hand, pressing it down at the centre of the clay to within 5 mm (¼ in.) of the wheel head and steadying your right hand with the left as you work to widen the base to 10 cm (4 in.) in diameter.

   Compress the clay in the base, then lift the wall to a cylinder (see page 50), narrowing it considerably towards the rim and leaving a slight thickness at this point to extend the neck later.

   Remember to compress the clay at the rim after each lift.

2. Mop the interior of the form out with a sponge on a stick to remove all excess water and slurry, because once the neck has been narrowed you will no longer have access to the inside.

3. With the wheel spinning at slow to medium speed, collar the neck of the form in by wrapping your left hand around it while at the same time easing the clay inwards with the fingers of your right hand; place the tips of your fingers over the rim to keep it level.

   It is important to keep the interior of the neck straight so that you can correctly fit the pouring device after firing, so pay close attention to this detail.

4. Place a finger of your left hand inside the neck, with a finger of your right hand opposite on the outside, and carefully lift the wall vertically until the remaining clay is an even thickness.

5. Continue to work on the spout until you are completely happy with it, ensuring that it is neat, of an even thickness and perfectly straight. Then, holding a finger of your left hand inside the spout as support, work over the surface of the bottle with a rib or an old store card to remove excess slurry and water.

   Work from the base upwards, taking care not to distort the shape.

6. Bevel the bottom edge of the bottle with the tip of the rib, then carefully cut a groove at shoulder height and another above the bevel at the base as decorative features.

   Clean up the area around the bottle, then wire off the underside, holding the wire taut.

   Quickly transfer the bottle to a board, lifting it carefully with two hands positioned as close to the base as possible, then allow it to firm to leather hard before handling it again.

CLOSING THE NECK

The neck must be closed to a size that will accommodate your pouring device after firing – allowing for clay shrinkage. This will vary according to the type of clay you use and the size of your fitting, so you must work it out accordingly (see page 166). The pouring stoppers usually have a rubber or plastic fitting that allows for some leeway, but you still need to be as close to the correct size as possible.

Moon jar

Although *The Great Pottery Throw Down* is filmed in the heart of the British Potteries, the programme frequently refers to other cultures and ceramic traditions, both in terms of the challenges set and in the way the contestants take inspiration from their own travels. This project is inspired by Korean pots known as 'moon jars' – wide-bellied pots traditionally made of porcelain – although we suggest you use stoneware or earthenware until you've gained more experience. The name comes from both the rounded shape and the traditional white glaze, which is reminiscent of the colour of the moon in the night sky.

Moon jars can be made in one or two parts, depending on their size. However, learning to 'belly' a shape successfully in a single form is best done on a small scale to begin with.

YOU WILL NEED

Clay of choice (earthenware or stoneware, preferably a smooth body): approx. 900 g (2 lb)

Batt (optional)

Tools for throwing: Water bowl, sponge, rib, cutting wire

Glaze(s) of choice – white is not a hard-and-fast rule!

BEFORE YOU BEGIN

You can throw this size of moon jar directly on the wheel head. However, if you aren't confident about doing this, you can throw it on a batt (see page 64).

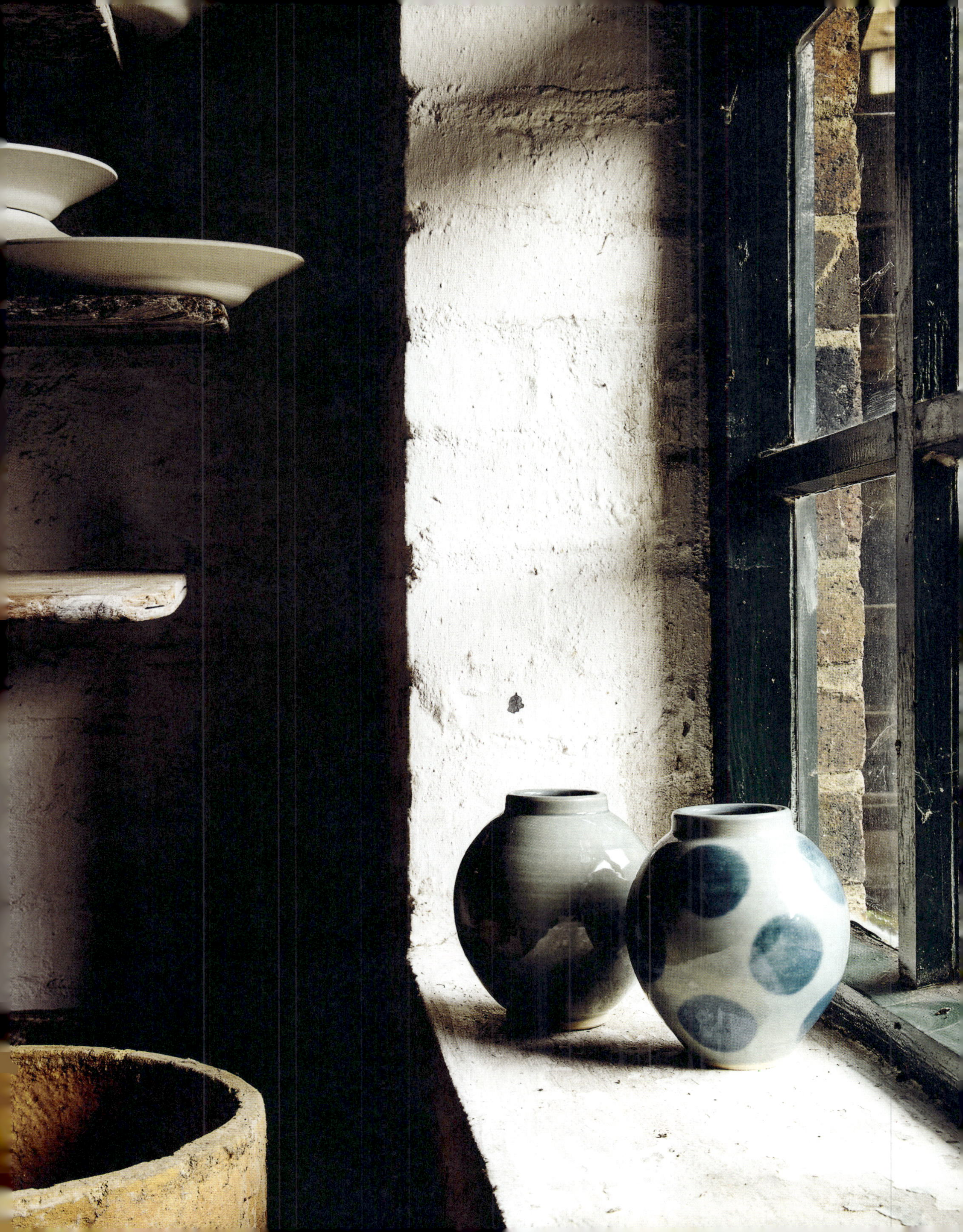

1

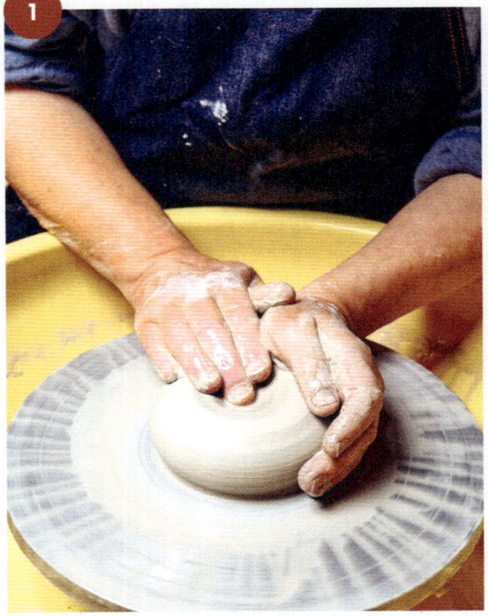

2

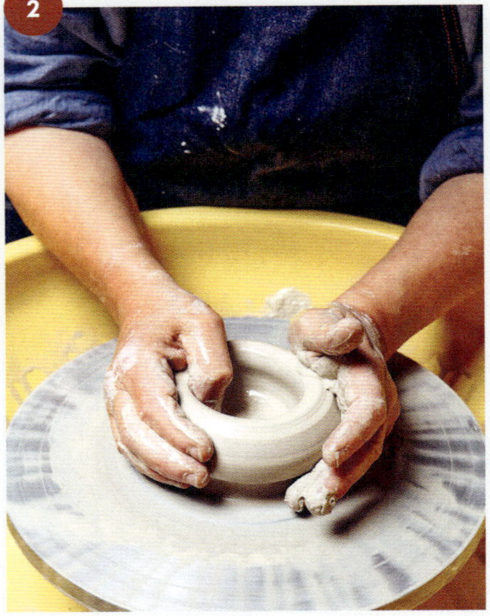

3

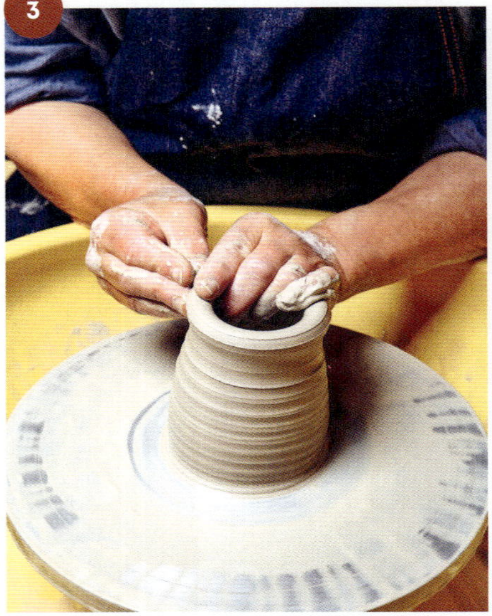

4A

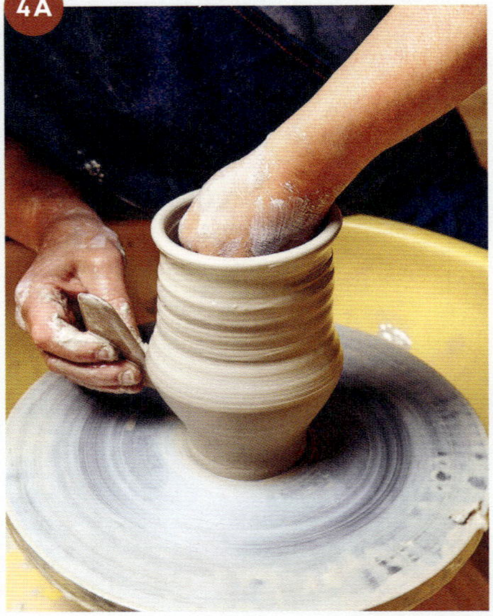

4B

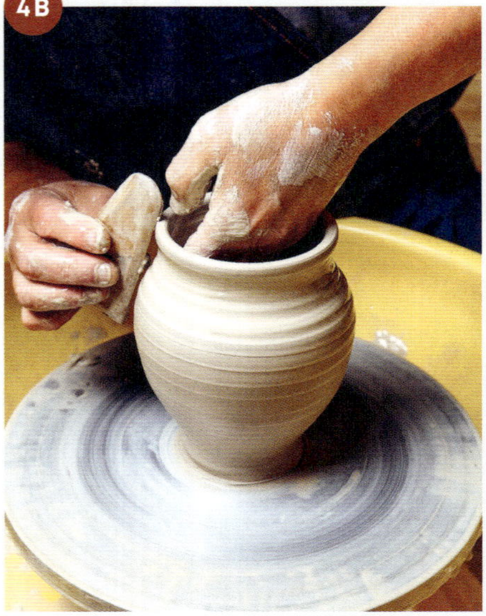

1. Centre your well-prepared clay (see page 46). Then open up (see page 50) the centre, pressing it down to within 5 mm (¼ in.) of the wheel head and drawing the base out to a 7-cm (2¾-in.) diameter.

   Compress the clay in the base of the pot three times with your fingers or thumb, working from the centre to the outside edge.

   Remember to lubricate the clay from time to time.

2. To position the clay correctly before raising the wall, pinch and lift the doughnut-like ring at the side a few centimetres (an inch or so) using the pincer-like position of your right hand, while maintaining your left hand on the opposite side to keep the clay centred.

3. Next, lift the wall to a narrow cylinder (see page 50) 20 cm (8 in.) high with a slightly chunky rim; this will allow for the reduction in height caused by the bellying process. Ease off the pressure slightly as you reach the mid-point of the lift so that the clay remains a little thicker here to allow it to be bellied out in the next step.

MEASURING BASE THICKNESS

This moon jar does not have a turned foot at the base, so the thickness at the base should be roughly equal to the thickness of the wall when the form is fully thrown. Use a pin to check if you are unsure (see page 53).

4. Place your left hand inside the form again, then gently apply outward pressure onto a wooden throwing rib – with a straight or curved edge as preferred – held against the outside of the wall.

   Apply light pressure from within to begin from the base, increasing as you reach the centre point (photo 4A), then ease off again as the form closes in towards the top (photo 4B).

   Compress the rim again when you have finished.

5. Repeat the process again to improve the shape of the jar (this time using a metal kidney-shaped rib for greater surface refinement), bellying out further where required to create a more moon-like shape but remembering to ease off towards the rim so that the shape remains relatively closed.
6. Now carefully mop out the water from the interior of the form using a sponge.

   Place the fingers of your left hand inside the jar. Carefully applying gentle pressure, work over the shoulder with a rib on the outside to round the shape in balance with the rest of the body, closing to a small flange or neck.
7. Use a flexible rib or an old store card to clean around the outside base of the jar and cut a shallow bevel. The resulting shape should be beautifully rounded, smooth and clean with an opening of approximately 7 cm (2¾ in.) and a finished height of 17 cm (6½ in.).
8. Holding your wire taut, pass it under the base once, then quickly lift the jar off the wheel, holding it in two clean hands as close to the base as possible, and place it on a board.

   Allow the jar to firm to leather hard before handling it again.

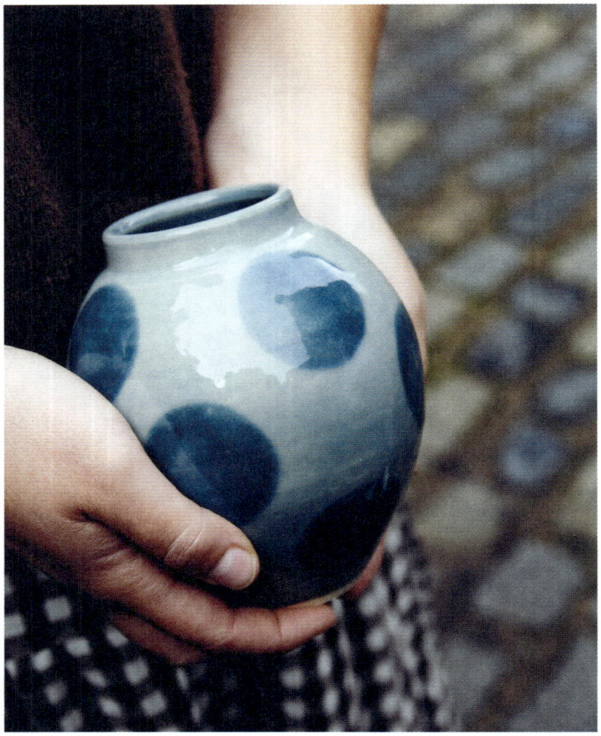

MOPPING OUT

Mopping up water from the inside of a form with a sponge at regular intervals will prevent the base from saturating. If your hand will not reach all the way inside to the base, use a sponge on a stick.

5

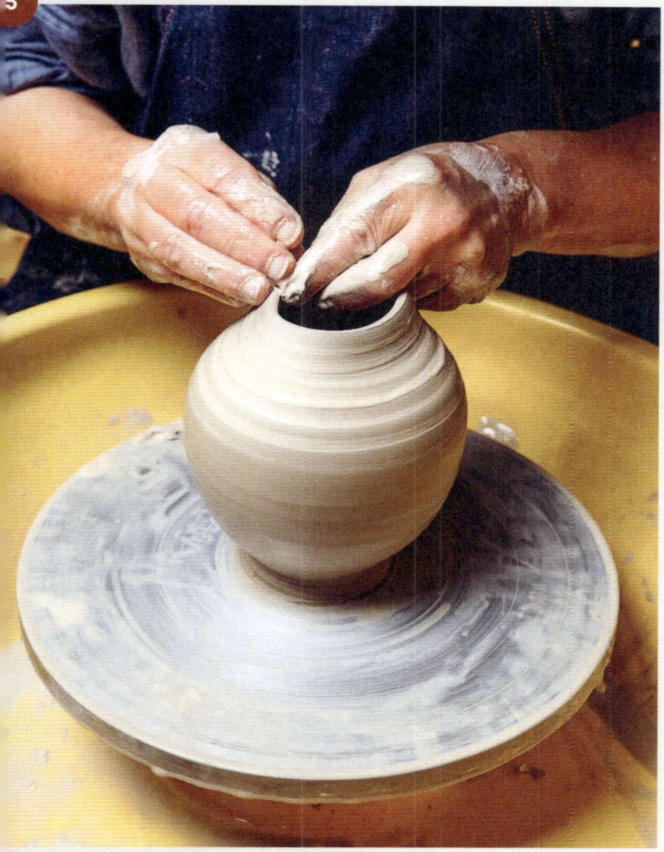

6

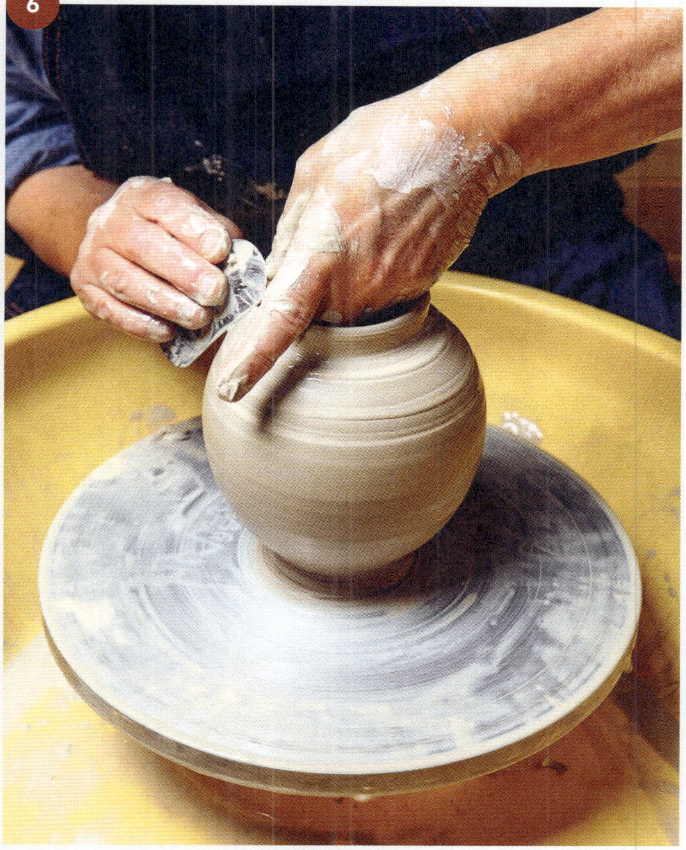

7

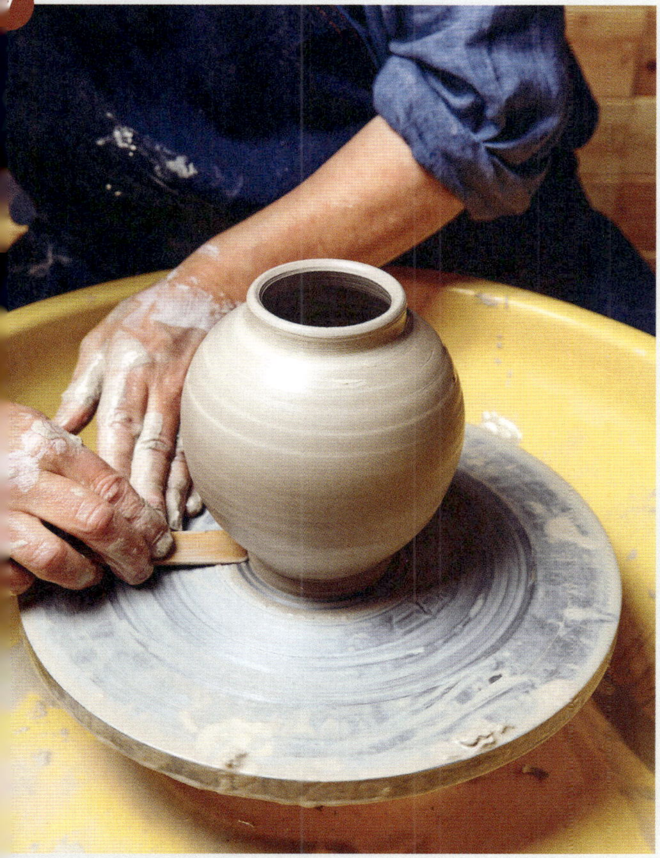

8

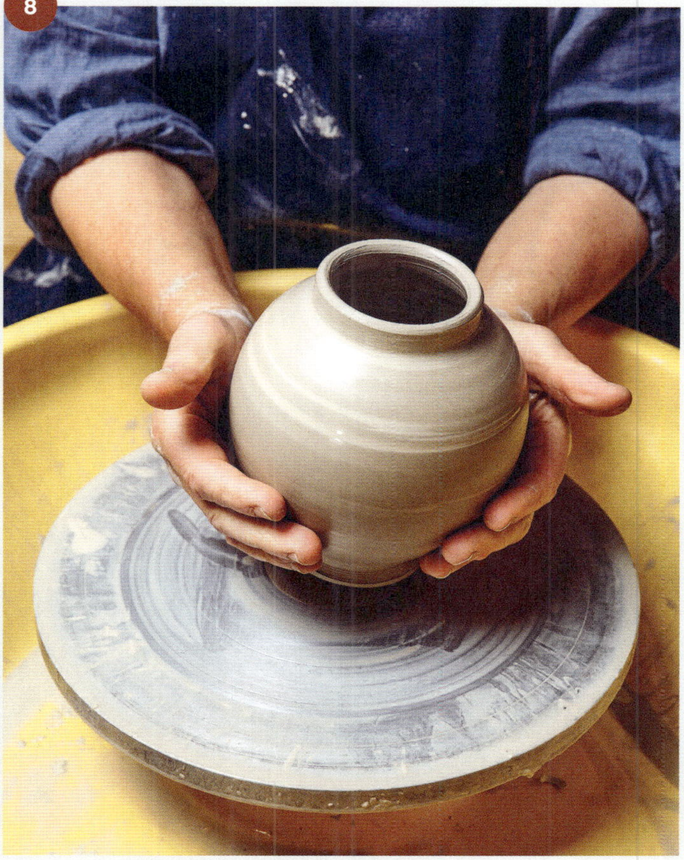

Salad bowl

This is a perfectly practical deep bowl for serving salads or vegetables, but it could be used equally well for mixing cakes or batters.

YOU WILL NEED

Clay of choice (earthenware or stoneware): approx. 1.8 kg (4 lb)

Batt

Tools for throwing: Water bowl, sponge, rib, cutting wire

Glaze(s) of choice to decorate

BEFORE YOU BEGIN

Fix a batt to the wheel head (see page 64).

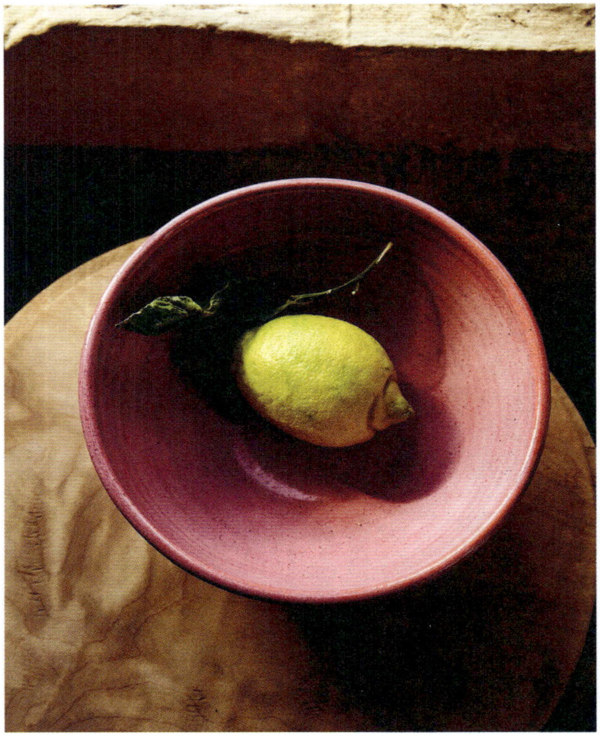

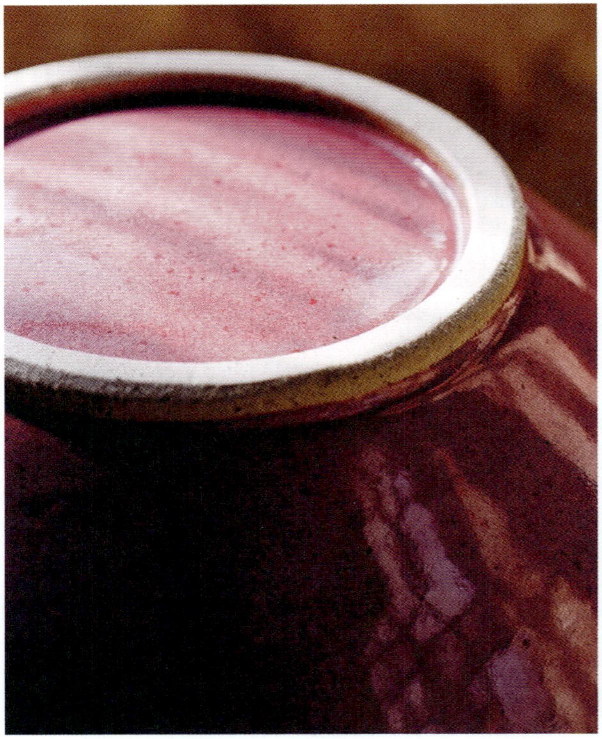

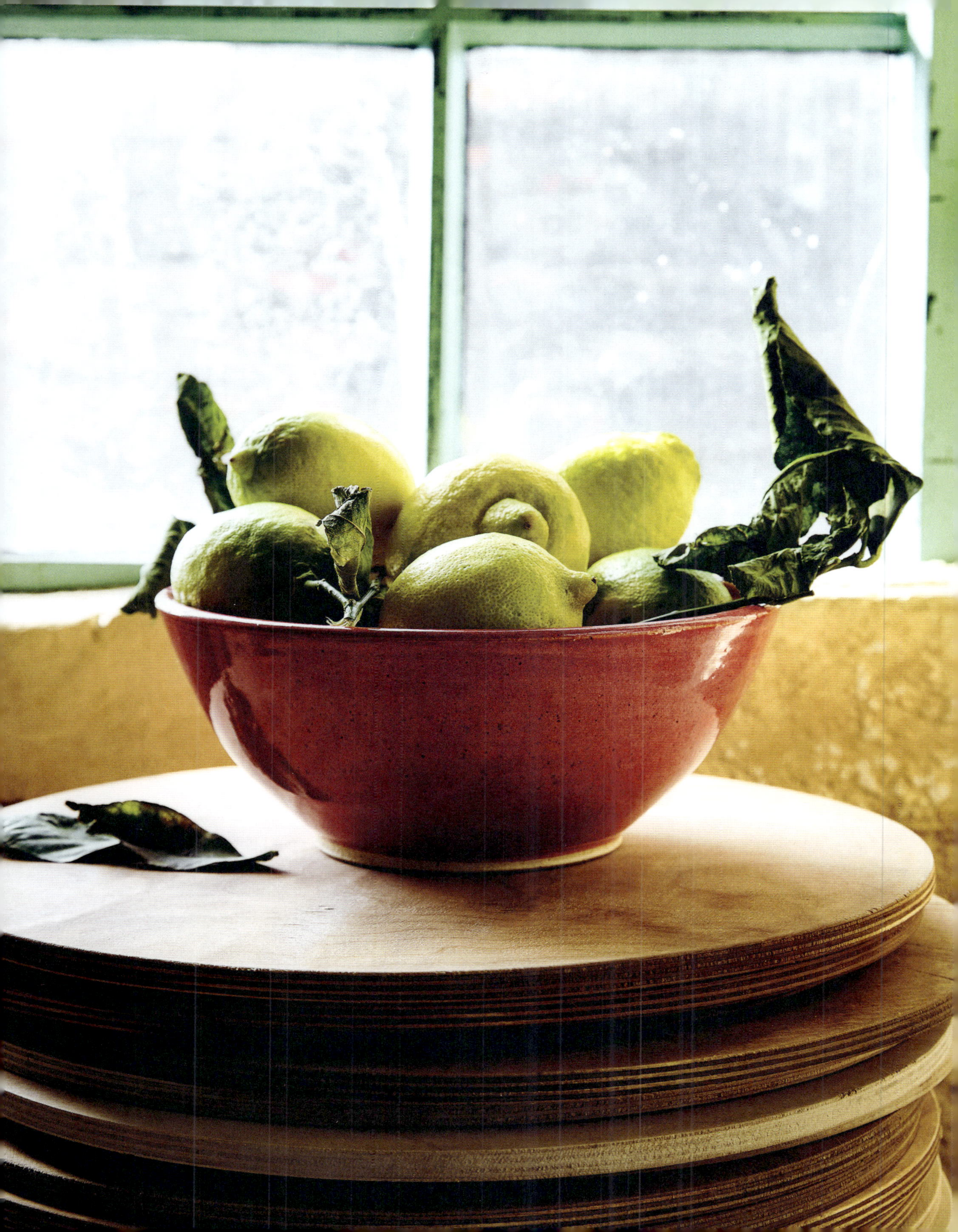

1

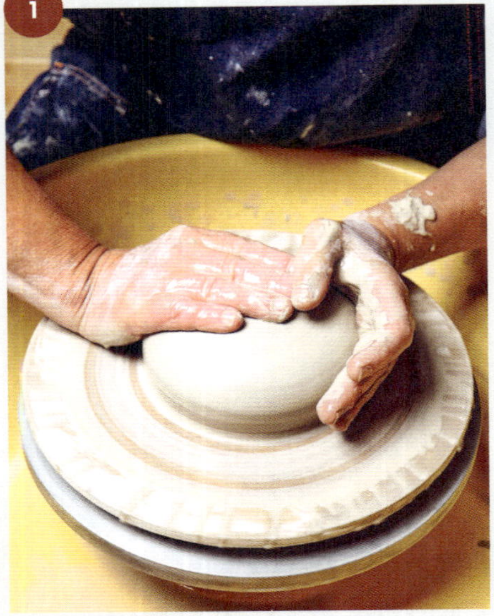

2A

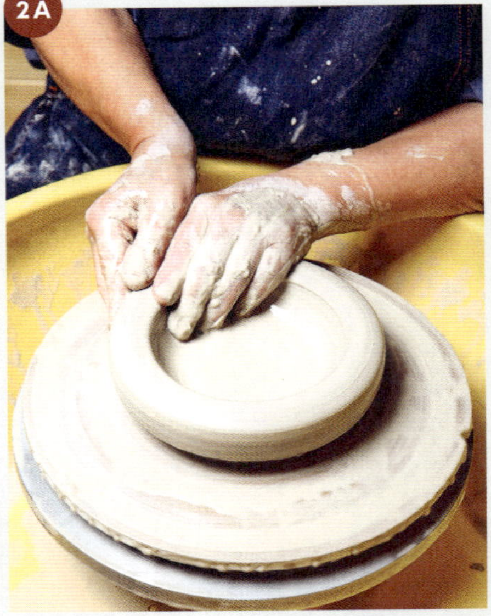

2B

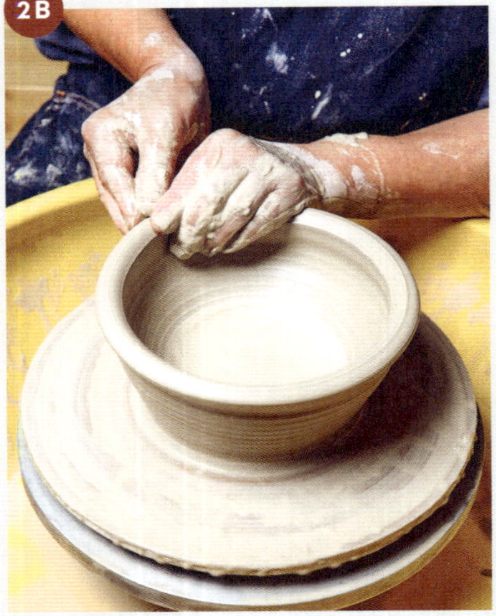

3

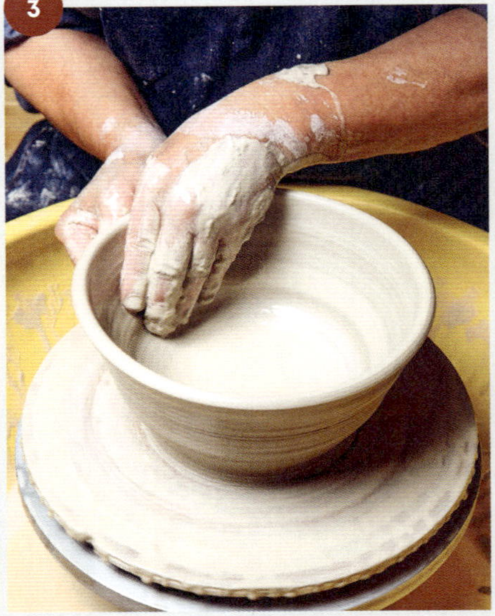

4

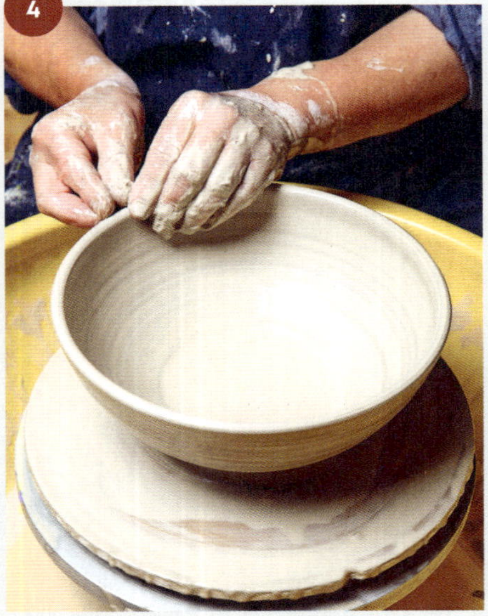

5

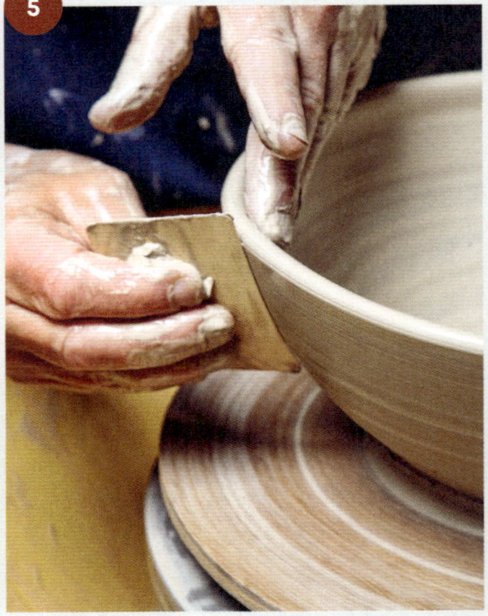

THROWING BOWLS – COMMON FAULTS

› Making the base too narrow is the most common cause of issues when throwing bowls. You need a wide foundation to prevent the walls from drooping outwards – usually an irretrievable problem once it happens, because it results in the walls collapsing.

› Thin points in the wall caused by the clay being off centre will also cause collapse in the thin area.

› Failure to create a good curving base creates a weakness in the clay because the section is uneven. This often results in cracks later if you don't turn right through the base when creating the foot ring.

1. Prepare the clay and centre it on the batt (see page 46).

   Open up (see page 50) the centre of the bowl, gently pressing it down to within 10–15 mm (⅜–⅝ in.) of the wheel head.

   Now widen the base to 10 cm (4 in.) in diameter, with a slightly curved surface.

   Compress the clay at the base, maintaining and refining the curve in the process.

   Use your left hand to keep the form centred as you form the base.

2. Dribble a little water over the wall of the clay, then lift the wall with your left-hand fingers inside and your right-hand fingers opposite on the outside (photo 2A).

   Keep this first lift relatively vertical, as though you are forming a cylinder, and leave a thick rim at the top rather than thinning the clay right through from base to tip (photo 2B).

3. Lift the wall again in the same way, but this time gently flare the shape by curving it upwards and out from the gently rounded base. Do not flare it too far at this stage and remember to compress the clay at the rim with tip of a finger after the lift.

4. Lift the wall a final time until the bowl is approximately the shape you see in the image. It should be about 25 cm (10 in.) in diameter at the rim and 10 cm (4 in.) high.

   Remember to compress the clay at the rim before carefully mopping out the interior with a sponge, then clean up the batt around the base.

   Cut a shallow bevel around the base, using the tip of a rib or similar tool.

5. Supporting the wall from the inside with your left-hand fingers, carefully work over the exterior with a rib to remove the throwing lines and smooth the surface.

   Carefully wire off the underside of the bowl and release the batt from the wheel.

   Leave the bowl to firm up on the batt until you can handle it without distorting the shape, then carefully turn it over for the base to firm up a little before trimming.

TURNING THE BASE OF THE BOWL

The method for turning a foot ring on the bowl is exactly the same as that shown on page 66, but you need to ensure the diameter of the foot relates to the rest of the form so that the bowl is in proportion and sturdy enough for practical use.

JUDGES' NOTE

A greater weight of clay than used in previous projects is required to throw this bowl, so make sure it is a good, smooth throwing body and of the correct consistency to hold the shape well as it is formed. Be aware that it may take a little longer and a little more effort to centre than usual, but don't move on to the next stage until you are sure that the clay is running freely through your fingers.

JUDGES' TIP

If you feel confident, you can use a kidney-type rib to work over the interior surface of the bowl. This will refine the shape of the curve on the inside, remove excess slurry and compact the clay for a good surface (important for domestic ware). However, you must do this without touching the exterior wall if that has already been refined.

Bud vase

Bud vases are perfect for single stems or small bunches of flowers such as sweet peas and they look especially good grouped together when made in multiples of different sizes. Although the shape and construction method are simple, it's amazing how varied they can be – and that's all down to how you choose to embellish them. Many *Throw Down* contestants have their own unique tools for creating texture and decoration, often improvised from household items like cutlery, lollipop sticks, or even pen tops for embossing tiny circles into the clay. Make a note of any unusual textural tools that you see on the programme and gradually collect your own.

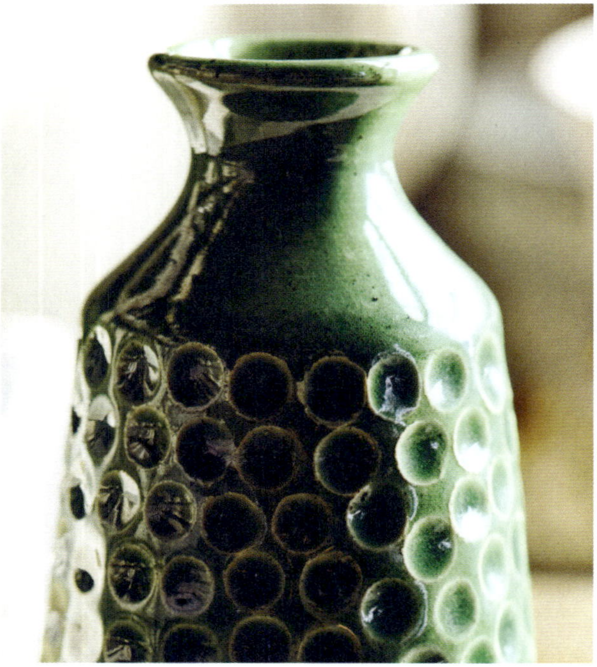

YOU WILL NEED

Clay of choice (earthenware or stoneware): 500 g (1 lb)

Tools for throwing: Water bowl, sponge on a stick, rib, cutting wire

Tool to texture the surface (optional)

Glaze(s) of choice to decorate

BEFORE YOU BEGIN

This little vase is essentially a narrow cylinder and can be thrown directly on the wheel head.

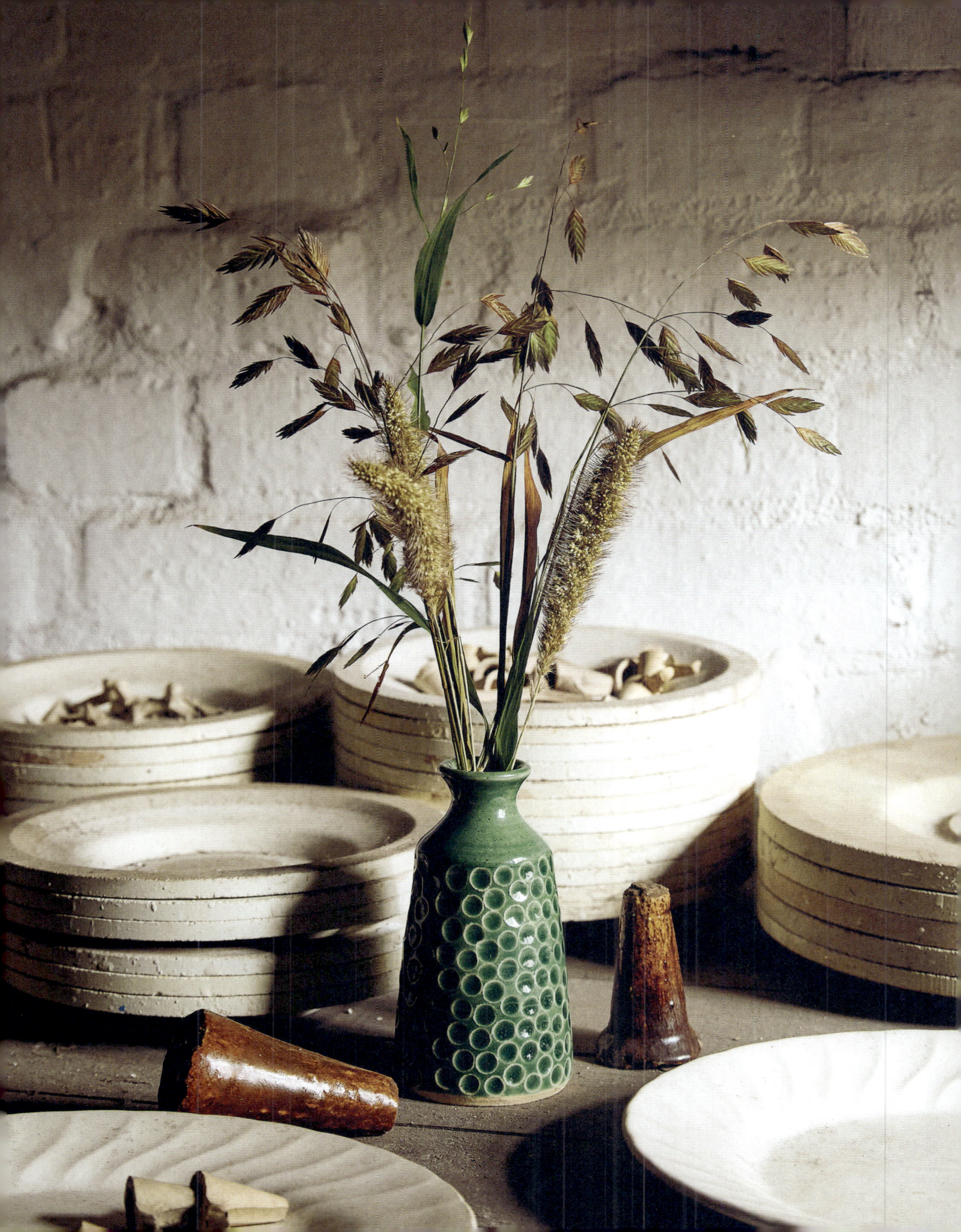

1

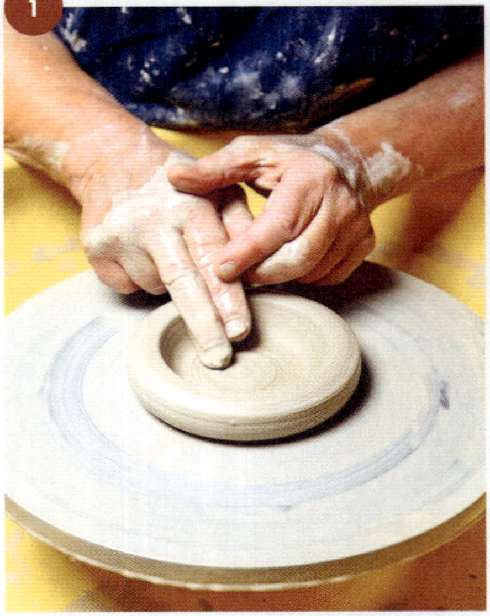

2

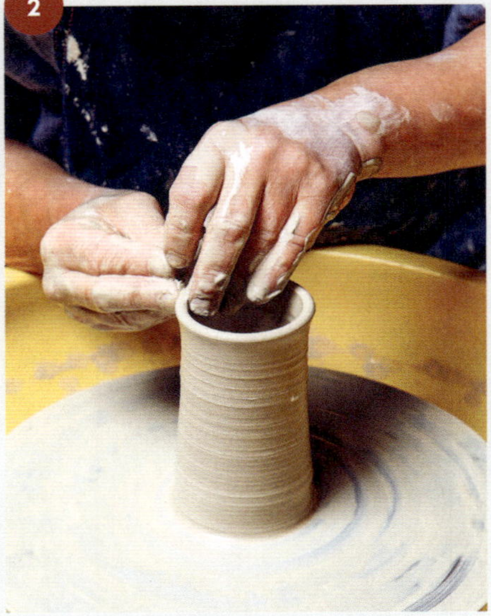

3

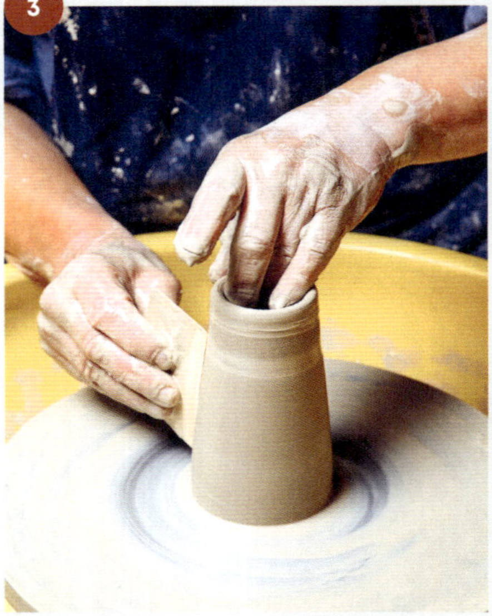

4

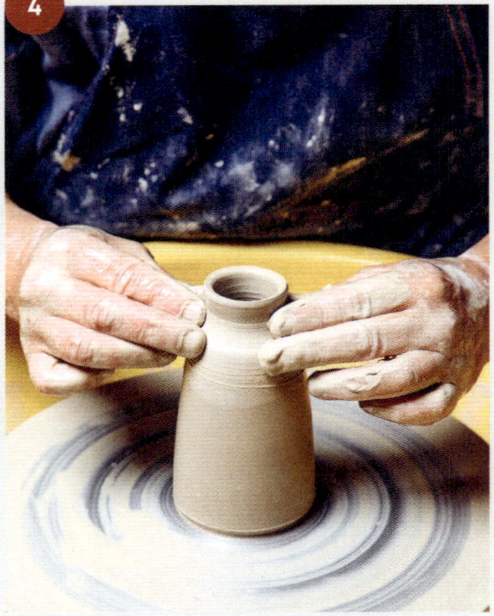

5

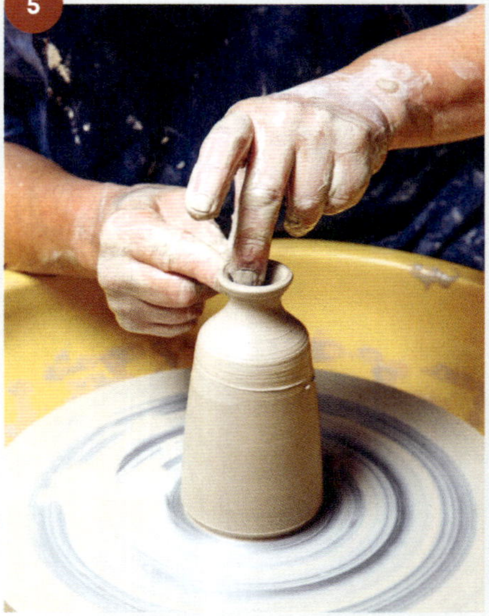

6

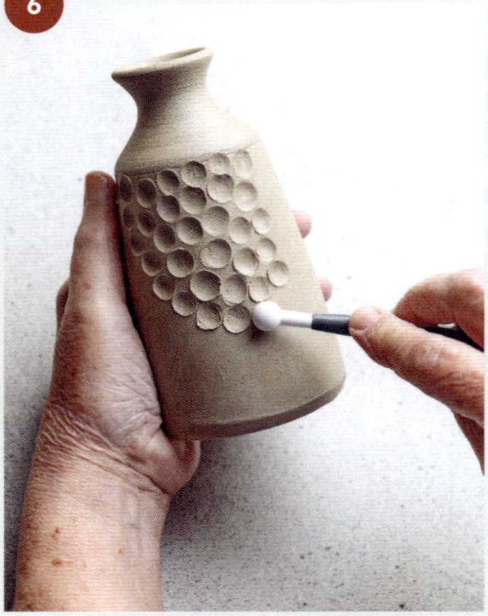

1. Centre the clay (see page 46). Open out the base (see page 50), pressing your fingers down to within 5 mm (¼ in.) of the wheel head.

   Draw the base out to a diameter of 8 cm (just over 3 in.), leaving a thick rim for the wall.

   Compress the base with your fingers.

2. Raise the wall the required number of times to form a slim cylinder (see page 50) 15 cm (6 in.) tall and narrower at the rim than at the base.

   Mop out the interior with a sponge on a stick when you have reached the required height.

3. With the fingers of your left hand inside the cylinder for support, work over the exterior wall with a rib to remove the surface water and throwing lines and fully straighten the wall, still maintaining the narrow rim.

4. Hold the first finger and thumb of each hand in a pincer position and place them 1–2 cm (½–¾ in.) below the rim of the vase, then collar the neck in, applying equal pressure from both sides as the wheel turns slowly.

   Continue until you are happy with the size of the aperture.

5. Very carefully, flare the rim outwards slightly, supporting the wall from inside with the tip of a finger and shaping it onto a finger on the outside.

   Cut a shallow bevel around the base of the vase and clean off the surrounding surface of the wheel.

   Clean and dry your hands, underwire the vase once, then quickly lift it off the wheel and place it on a board to firm to leather hard.

6. Once the vase has firmed up, you can decorate the surface with impressed texture if you choose.

   One simple technique to try is to create a bubbled surface by pressing a ball-ended tool into the clay. This type of tool is sold for cake decorating, but works equally well for clay.

Teapot

A teapot is probably the most challenging of all thrown items to make because of the many techniques involved in making the component parts (body, spout, lid, handle etc.). One of the keys to success is to make all the parts in one session, so that they all firm up at the same rate to reduce the chance of joints cracking.

A project like this has to be fit for purpose, so whenever one features on *The Great Pottery Throw Down*, Keith and Rich make a point of testing how it pours. It's always a nerve-wracking moment, but pay attention to the height and angle of the spout and you'll be fine.

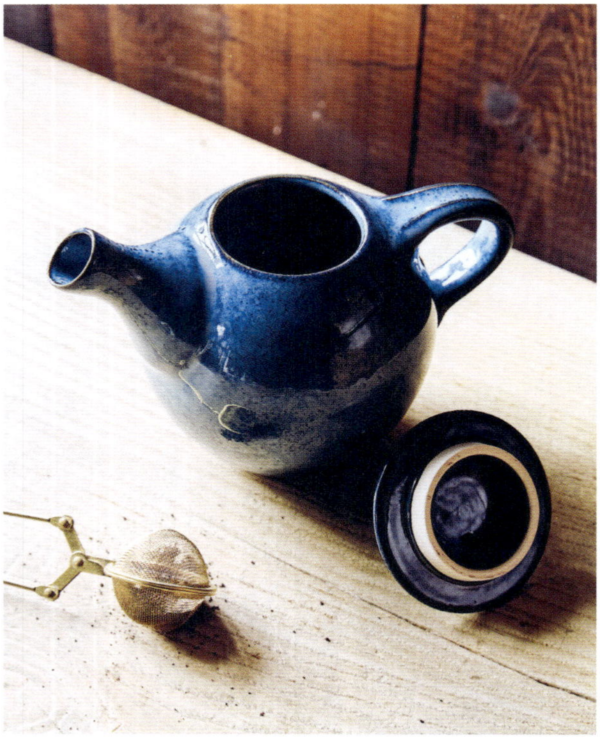

YOU WILL NEED

Clay of choice (earthenware or stoneware): 700 g (1¾ lb), plus extra for the handle

Tools for throwing: Water bowl, sponge, rib, cutting wire

Turning tool

Hole-making tool

Glaze(s) of choice to decorate

CLAY WEIGHT

Much will depend on the clay you are using. Earthenware will shrink less than stoneware, so the suggested weight will alter the size of the finished product – 700 g (1¾ lb) of clay for the main body will make a four-cup teapot 13 cm (just over 5 in.) high.

THROWING NOTES

This teapot is made using a technique called 'throwing off the hump', which involves making all the component parts of the pot except the handle from a single, centred cone of clay. It is tricky and will take practice, but it will open up many options for other forms once you have mastered it.

You can throw the teapot directly on the wheel head.

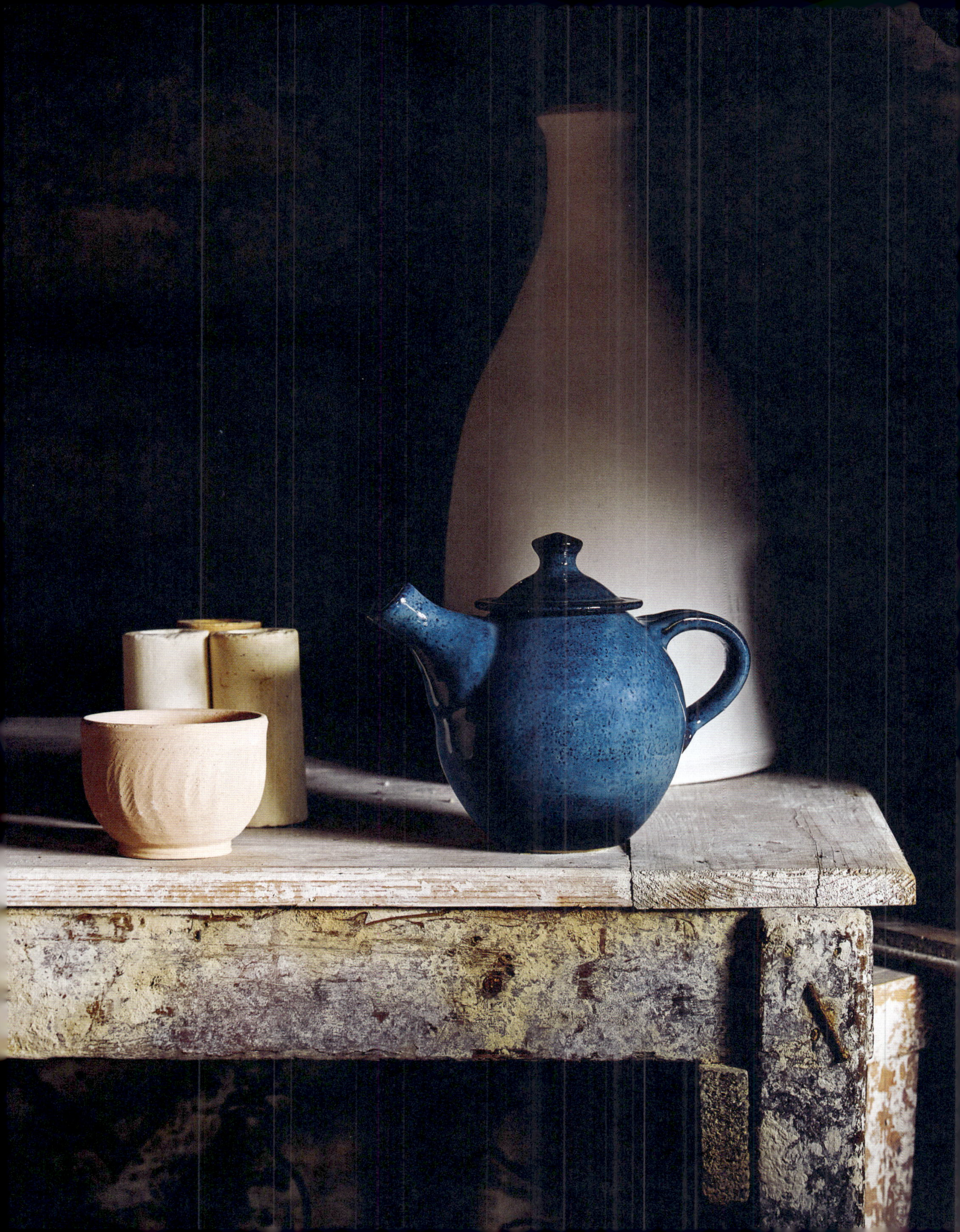

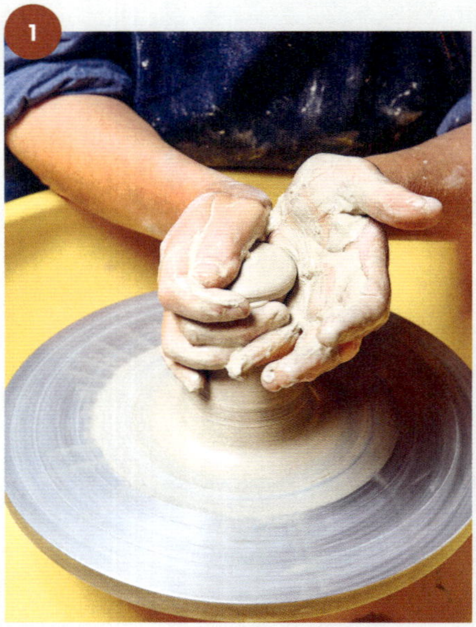
1

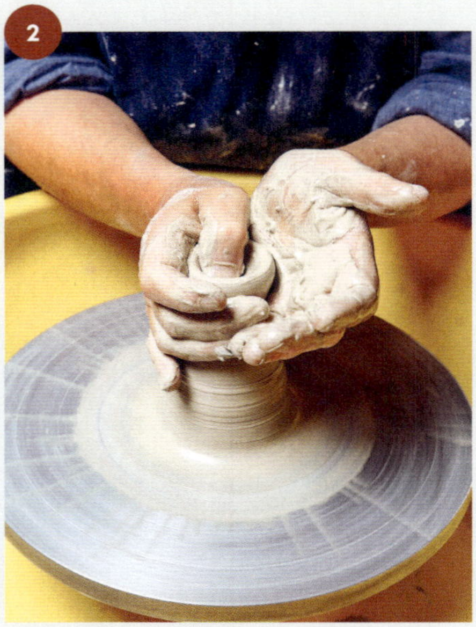
2

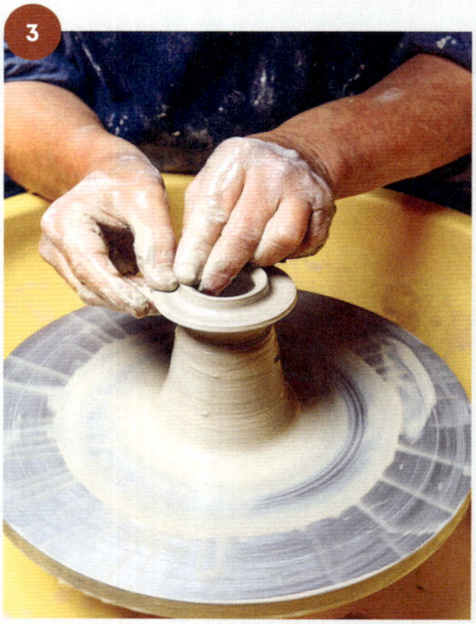
3

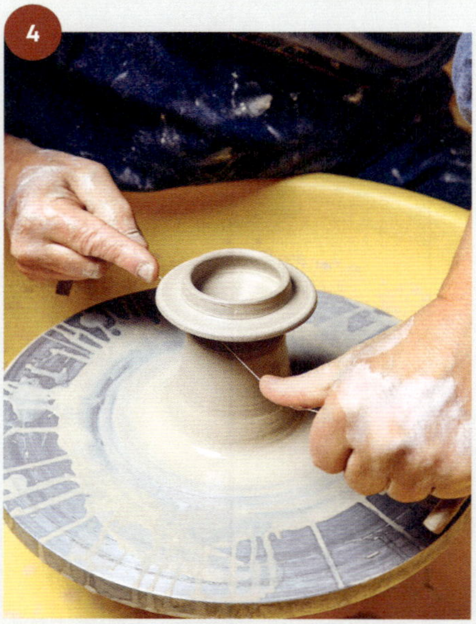
4

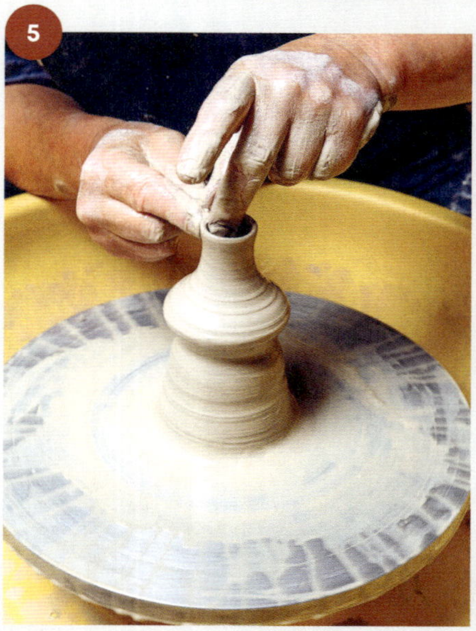
5

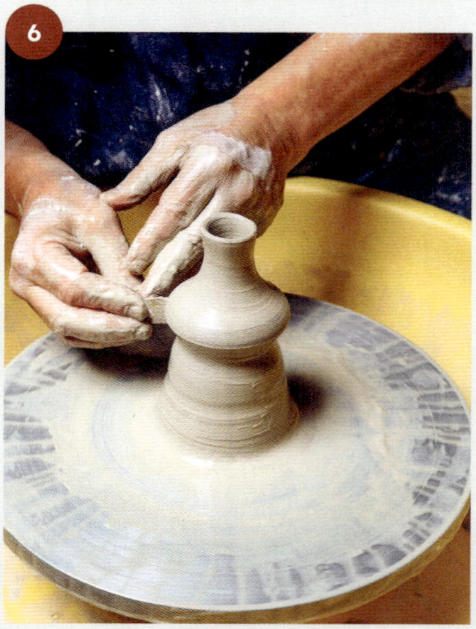
6

Throwing the lid

1. Centre the suggested weight of clay on the wheel head (see page 46), but don't flatten off the cone after raising it a second time. Instead, carefully isolate a knob at the top with the sides of your hands, using your right-hand fingers to flatten off the surface in the process.

2. Maintaining your hand positions at the side of the knob, carefully open up (see page 50) the centre, using the thumb of your right hand and pressing it into the clay to a depth of approximately 3 cm (just over 1 in.).

3. Position your left-hand finger inside the opening, with your thumb opposite on the outside, and carefully pinch the locating flange upwards to a sufficient height to sit stably on the body of the pot once thrown. At the same time, draw the clay beneath the flange outwards with the fingers of your right hand.

   Remember to compress the clay on the rim of the flange when finished, then run a sponge briefly over the entire surface to remove excess water.

   Measure and record the diameter of the flange, as you will need this measurement when throwing the body.

4. Carefully underwire the lid, then lift it off the hump and place it on a board to firm to leather hard for turning.

Throwing the spout

5. Re-centre the remaining clay and then, with it still in a coned-up position, isolate another knob at the top and open out the centre, as you did for the lid.

   Next, position your left-hand fingers inside the clay and your right-hand fingers opposite on the outside and first lift the wall to a narrow cylinder.

   With the second lift, belly the wall outwards from the base by applying greater pressure from inside for half its height, then greater pressure from the outside to close the clay to a narrow spout.

   Compress the clay at the rim.

6. Sponge over the surface to remove excess water, then use the tip of a rib to score a line to cut the spout off at.

   Wire through the scored line and carefully transfer the spout to a board to firm up.

Throwing the body

7. Re-centre the clay one more time and, following the method for the moon jar (page 136), throw a bellied shape that closes at the top to a diameter fractionally greater than the diameter of the flange on the lid.

   You can close the opening at the top with or without a raised neck.

   Work over the exterior of the pot with a rib, supporting the wall from inside with your left-hand fingers.

   Cut a shallow bevel at the base, then underwire it and, with clean hands, transfer the pot to a board.

Continued overleaf

Trimming the lid and attaching a knob

8. Using the concentric lines as a guide, centre the flange of the lid on the wheel head after moistening the surface. Check that it is running true with your finger (see page 66); if it is not, reposition it and try again. Apply gentle pressure to secure it to the wheel once centred.

Next, using your chosen turning tool, trim away the clay over the centre of the lid to form a gentle dome.

9. Score and slip a position at the top centre of the lid and on the underside of a small knob of clay, then fix it in place.

10. With the wheel turning slowly and using minimum water, throw the knob to a shape of your liking, making sure it works well as a device to lift the lid.

Sponge over the finished lid to tidy it up when finished.

Preparing and fitting the spout

11. Hold the spout against the side of the pot to determine the angle at which it needs to be cut to fit well. Cut the wide end of the spout at the required angle and take the opportunity to remove any thick excess not already removed in the process.

Sit the spout against the body and score around its outline with a pin.

12. Using a hole-cutting tool, make a series of holes inside the marked position for the spout, allowing enough room around them for it to be fitted.

13. Score and slip around the holes and the rim of the spout, then fix it in place, carefully blending the clay onto the body seamlessly. Wipe around the join with a damp sponge to neaten up.

14. Make another hole in the lid to allow for the release of steam.

15. Following the method for pulling handles (see page 110), attach a coil of suitable length for your pot and then pull it through your wet hand until it is the correct thickness and shape.

Curve the handle around and attach it to the wall of the pot, making sure there is enough space for a hand to lift it without touching the body, which will be hot once boiling water is inside.

Allow the finished pot to dry out slowly with the lid in place, then bisque fire it.

JUDGES' TIP

Remember that the end of the spout should always rise above the pot so that it is higher than the water level when the pot is filled – this is very important.

7

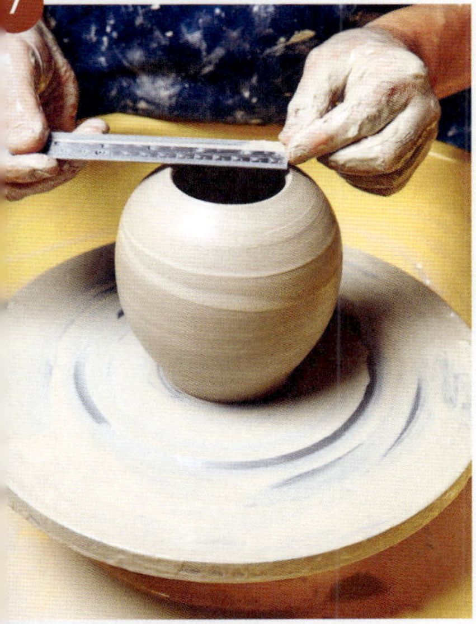

8

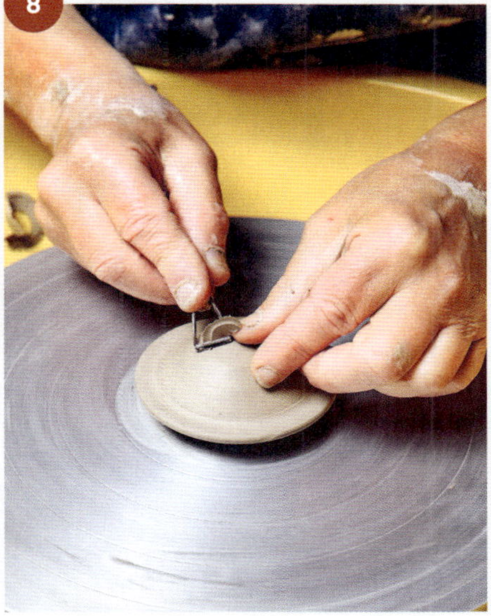

9

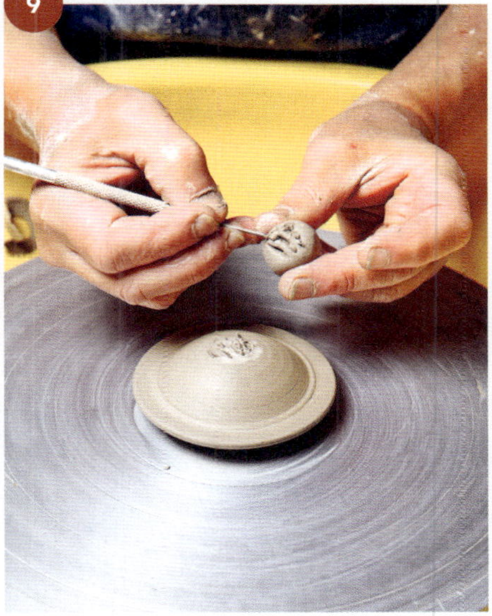

0

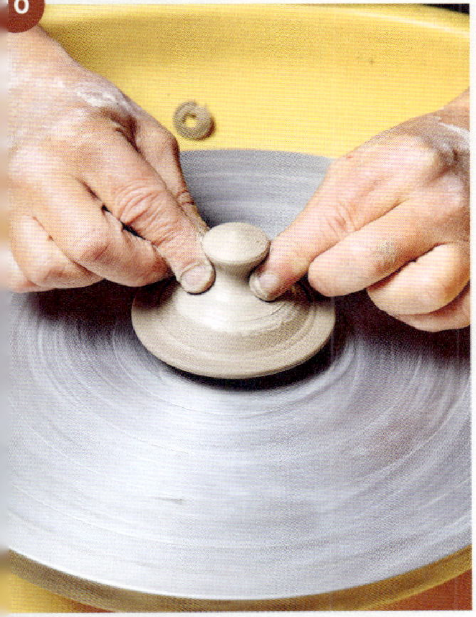

11

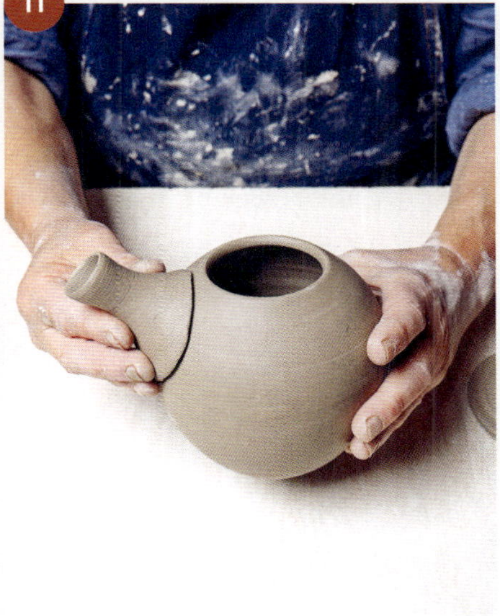

12

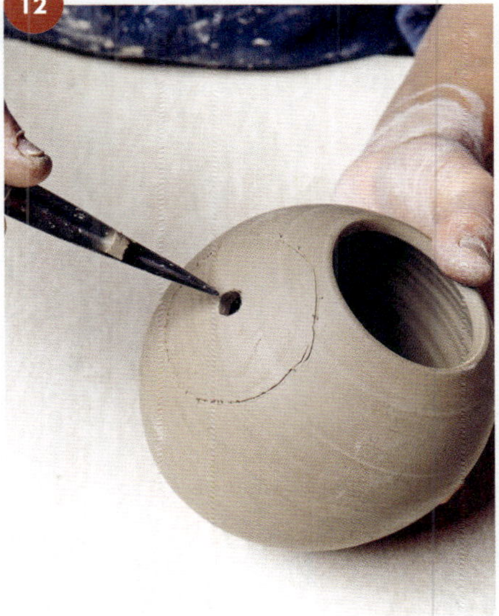

3

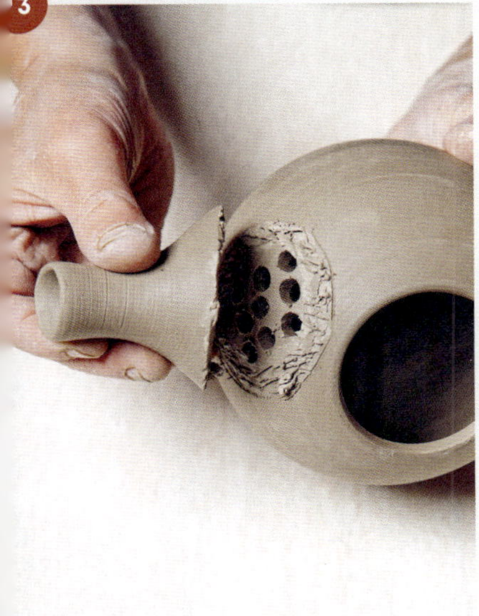

14

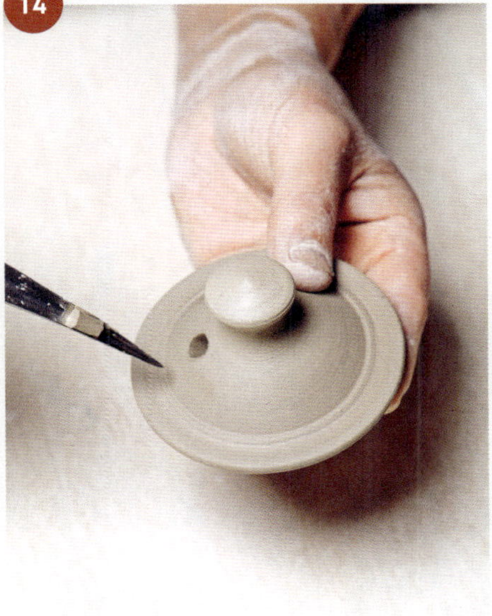

15

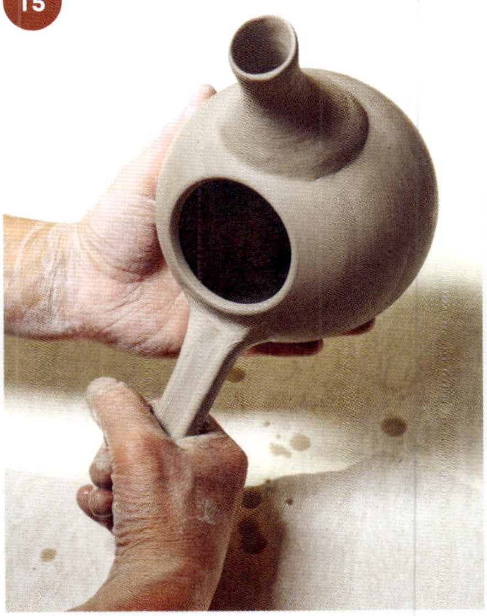

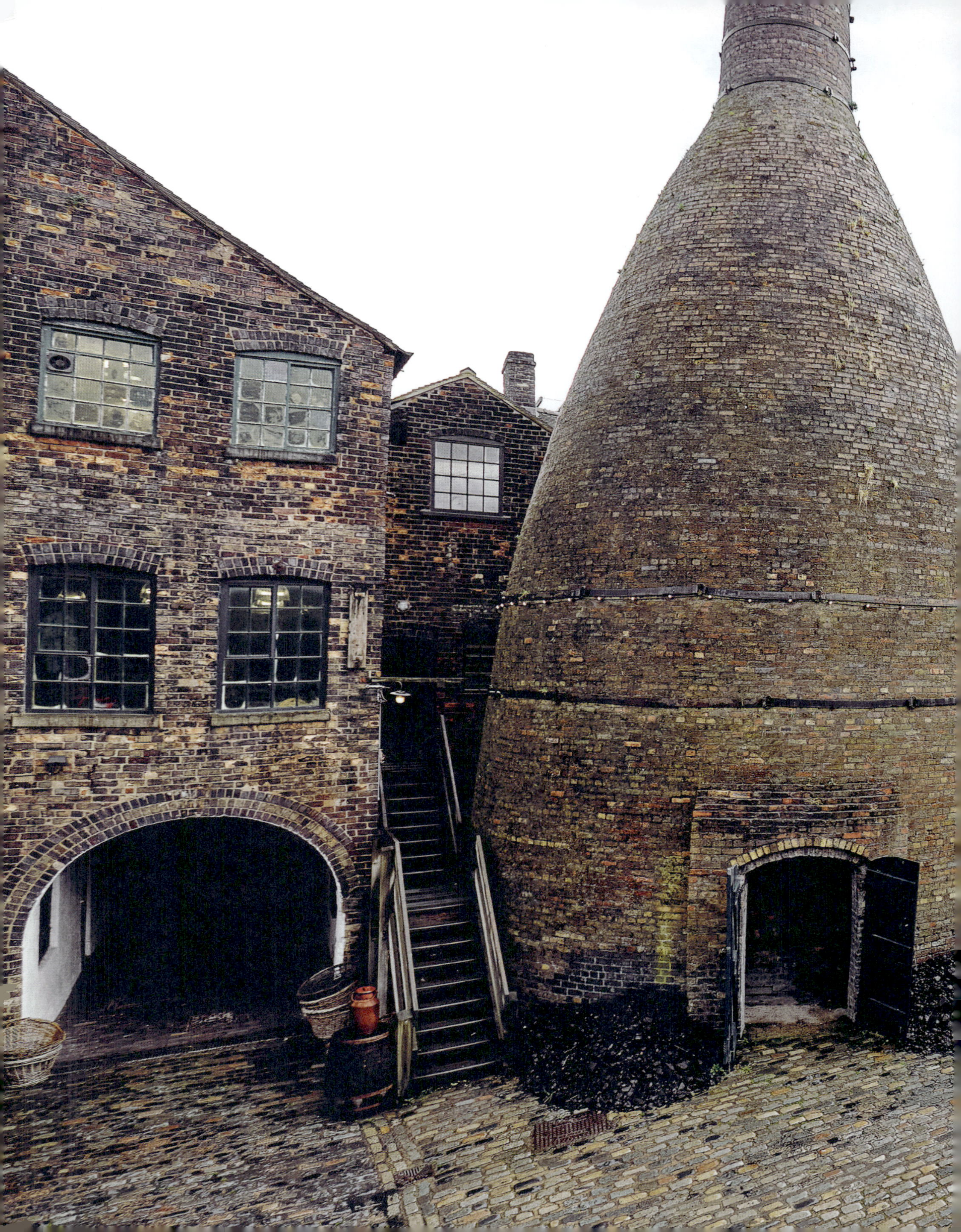

Finishing techniques

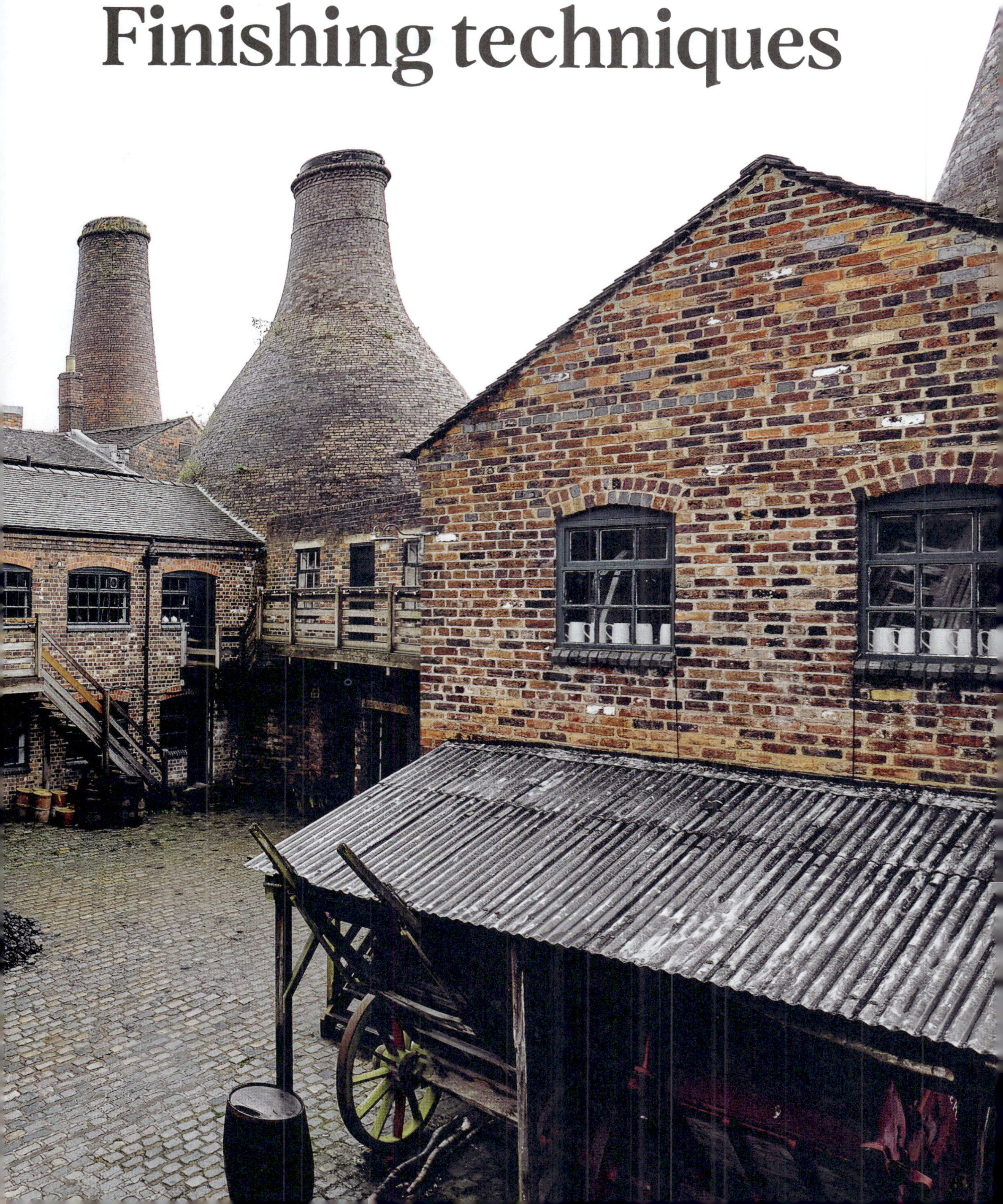

Adding decoration

The options for surface decoration are many and varied. Here, we will take a brief look at several different surface decoration methods.

Slip techniques

PAPER RESIST

A method using paper shapes to form a resist for sponged and painted layering of colour.

SGRAFFITO

A method involving drawing into the clay with specific tools. It can be used on dark clay bodies onto which slip has been applied for contrast.

MISHIMA OR INLAY

A technique that fills in sgraffito drawings and textured impressions with coloured slips, then scrapes back the excess to reveal the design.

SLIP TRAILING AND TUBE LINING

This method uses a trailing bulb to trail a pattern of liquid slip directly onto the raw clay, or over a layer of slip laid down earlier in another colour.

MARBLING AND FEATHERING

In marbling, two or more coloured slips are incorporated to achieve the marbled effect. Feathering is drawing a quill to create a pattern.

Raw clay – pre-construction techniques

These methods are applied to the clay pre-construction and are often used with slab work.

TEXTURE

Wooden stamps and design blocks
These are used to impress patterned detail.

Bisque rollers and stamps
Great for the Mishima inlay technique.

Textured wallpapers and fabrics
These can be used really creatively with templates to build complex surface designs.

Organic materials
You can create botanical-style surfaces with leaves, flowers and seed heads.

Rubber/silicone texture mats
These are used to impress a design but also for underglaze printing and glaze-on-glaze printing.

Techniques for bisque ware

These can form the decoration in their own right or be applied as a base for transparent or opaque glaze.

OXIDE

Used as a base for designs in wax and glaze, plus oxide washes in texture.

UNDERGLAZE

Underglazes are used extensively on *The Great Pottery Throw Down* for their vibrant colours. Application can be by brush, sponge or trailing and while regularly applied to a bisque fired surface, they can also be used on green ware.

The colours are made even more vibrant when covered with a transparent glaze, which can be either brushed on or dipped.

Spattering

You will need to release your inner Jackson Pollock to master this decoration method, but it is a simple technique that can be used with slips, underglazes or glazes. Here we outline two approaches to the technique using glaze.

YOU WILL NEED

Glazes in colours of your choice

Piece of foam to support the pot as you work

A length of batten or a long paintbrush

A soft brush with long head and/or a stiff brush (an old toothbrush will also work)

1. You can spatter directly onto a bisque-fired surface as a base for transparent glaze or spatter over a base glaze. Whichever you choose, secure the vessel on a bed of foam, then load a soft brush with glaze (in an alternative colour if the vessel has been glazed in advance).

   Hold your length of batten close to the surface of the vessel and tap the loaded brush vigorously on it.

   Allow the spattering to dry before turning the vessel and repeating the process until the entire surface has been covered to your satisfaction.

2. Alternatively, load a stiff brush with glaze, then again with your vessel sitting on a foam bed, draw the bristles back and release them to spatter the surface in a more speckled way.

1

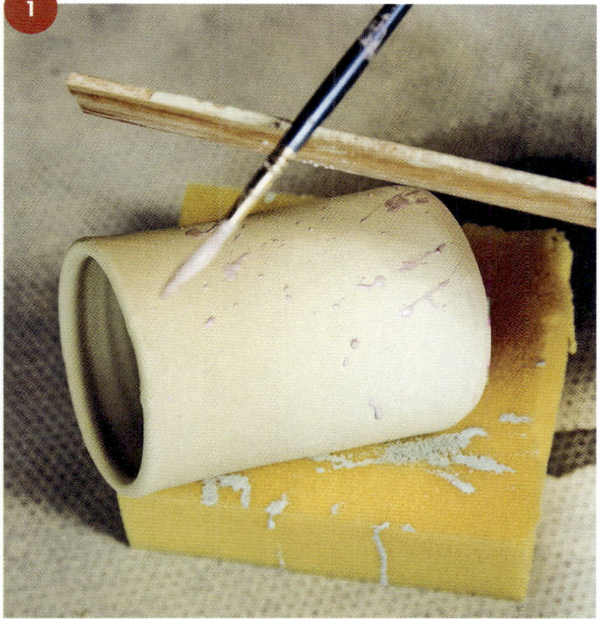

2

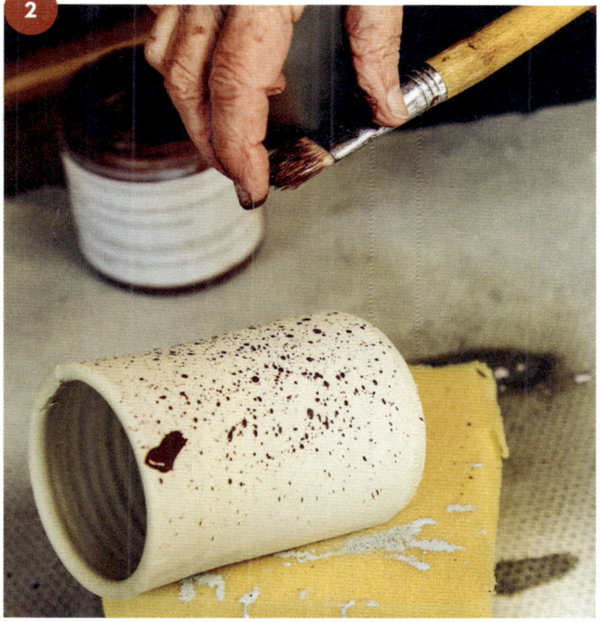

Paper resist

Continuing on from page 86 where we showed you a simple approach to tile making, the following technique demonstrates just one possible method for decorating the surface of your tiles. Apply it at the green stage, prior to bisque firing.

YOU WILL NEED

A selection of slip or underglaze colours that will contrast well

A fan-shaped brush

Newspaper or blank newsprint paper (available from craft outlets and other paper suppliers)

Craft knife for cutting the paper templates

A selection of natural sponges with different surface qualities – fine, open etc.

1. Paint the surface of the tile in your base colour of slip or underglaze, using a fan-shaped brush for even application.

   Allow the surface to dry to the touch, then re-apply the colour if it looks thin or patchy.

   Again, allow the surface to dry to the touch – base coat the rest of the tiles while you are waiting.

2. Using newspaper or blank newsprint paper, carefully cut out a series of shapes to fit your tiles, then place one of the paper templates on the tile and seal it to the surface using a brush dampened with water.

3. Load a sponge (or a brush if you prefer) with a contrasting colour of slip or underglaze and carefully sponge over the paper design (photo 3A), working deftly to prevent the paper from lifting.

   Allow the surface to dry to the touch, then sponge or brush further colours in selected areas to build up a pleasing arrangement of colour (photo 3B). Note – if you are using a sponge, there will also be a textural quality to the surface.

4. Carefully lift one end of the paper template with a pin and remove it. You will find there is something very satisfying about doing this!

5. If you want to develop the design further, you can paint more detail into the surface using a fine brush, as shown here.

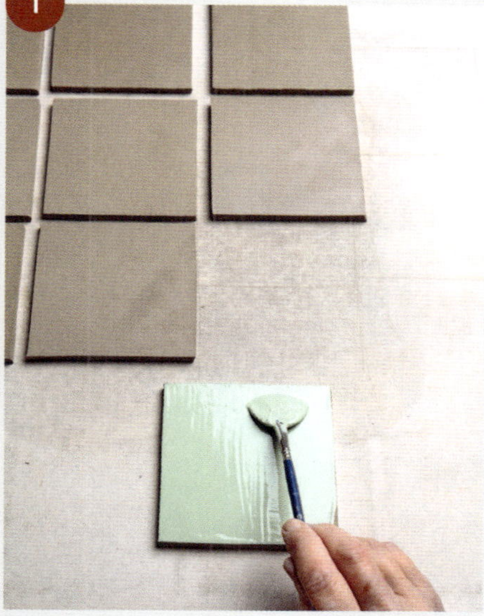
1

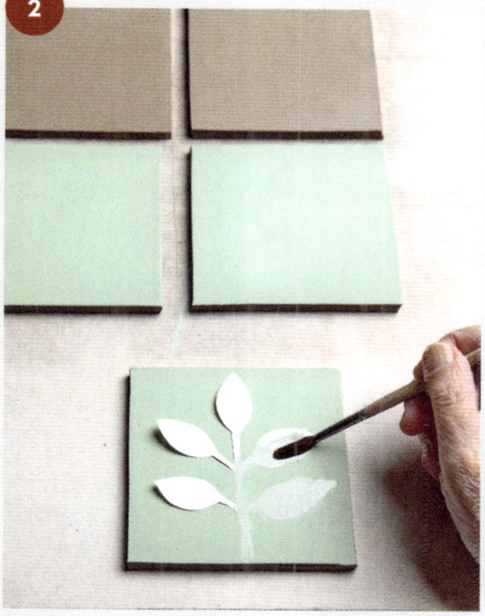
2

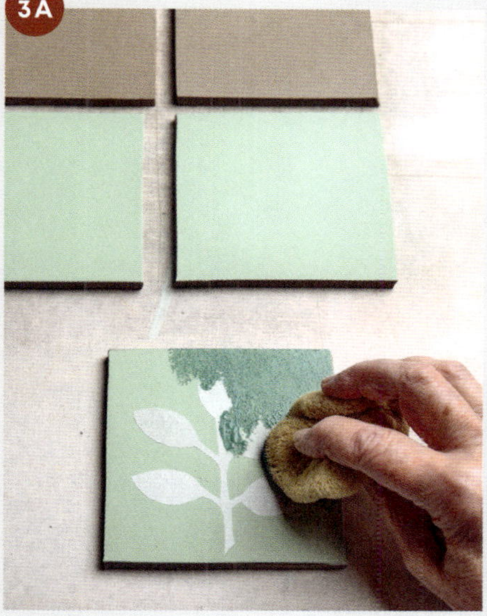
3A

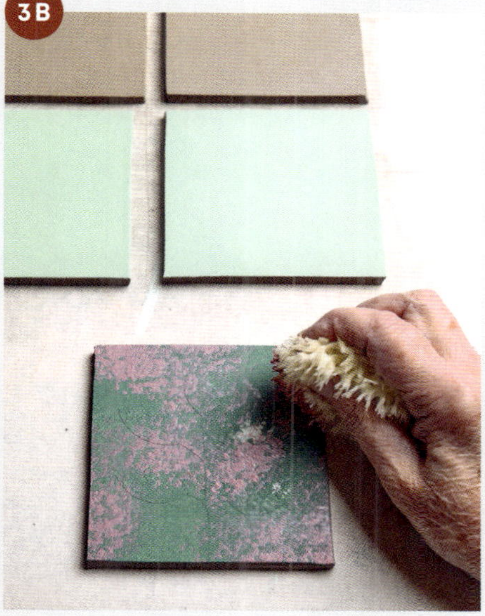
3B

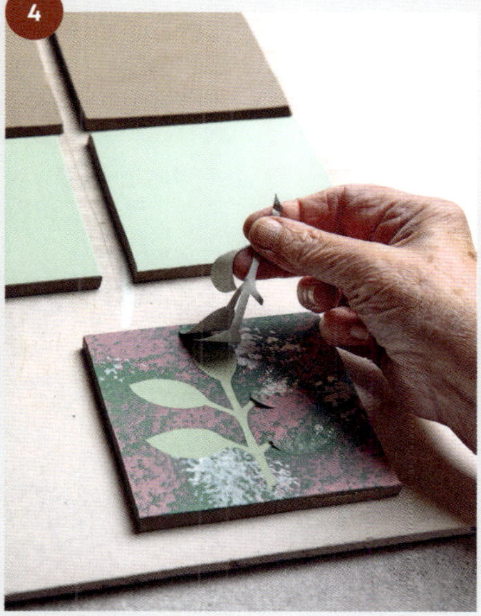
4

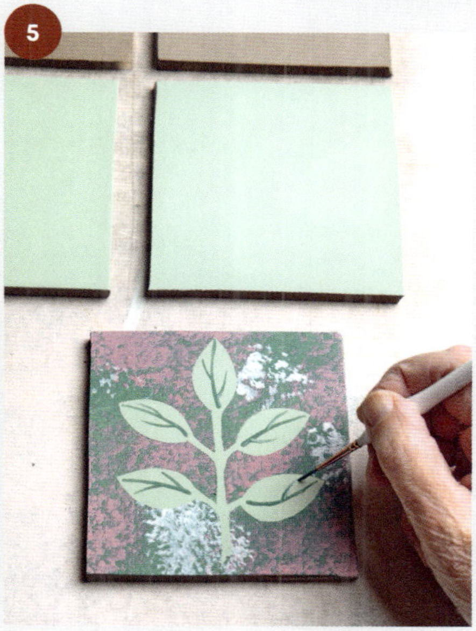
5

Glazing

The main purpose of glaze is to make ceramics functional by forming a seal over the clay to make it non-porous and hygienic to use. However, glaze is also a surface decoration method and can be formulated in many ways to create a variety of finishes for both functional and decorative wares.

When you first begin working with clay, most of your efforts will be focused on learning how to make and build pottery. At this stage it would be too daunting to also have to learn about the chemical composition of glazes and how they work. Fortunately, many commercially prepared glazes are available from pottery suppliers in liquid or powder form, including brush-on glazes that have been tried and tested to produce guaranteed, foolproof results. However, varieties that are likely to be used in large quantities – such as transparent glazes – are best mixed from dry ingredients to save on cost.

TO PREPARE A COMMERCIAL POWDER GLAZE YOU WILL NEED

A large, sealable bucket

A mixing spoon

An 80-, 100- or occasionally a 120-mesh sieve

A glaze brush or large rubber kidney

A dust mask – very important!

Preparing the glaze is simply a matter of mixing the dry ingredient with water and putting it through the sieve with a glaze brush or a large rubber kidney, making sure you are wearing a face mask to avoid inhaling potentially toxic ingredients.

The glaze should be the consistency of single cream when mixed. A good way to test the density of the glaze, other than using a hydrometer, is to dip your finger in it. The mixture should cover your finger thinly, so you can see the wrinkles through it. If it covers your finger thickly, water it down a little and test it again.

Making a glaze from individual ingredients

If you want to experiment with making a glaze from individual ingredients, the principle for mixing is the same. However, you will need to weigh out the ingredients exactly prior to mixing, otherwise the glaze could be compromised and not fire as you had hoped.

There are many books of glaze recipes out there to inspire you. It is always a good idea to make up the minimum amount to begin with so that you can test fire it first. Many things can affect the way a glaze behaves, including the source of the raw materials (they often come from different parts of the world and therefore have slightly different chemical structures), miscalculations in weighing, and even the conditions within your kiln.

Brush-on glazes

Brush-on glazes are a popular and simple way to decorate your projects. They are quick and easy to use because you don't need to make and test the glazes before you use them.

Many established potters are quite purist about glazes, preferring to make their own to create a unique surface finish or to cut down on costs because commercially available brush-on glazes can be expensive. But here's the thing: brush-on glazes come in a vast range of colours, with different ones to accommodate all firing temperatures, in shiny or matt finishes, with specific qualities such as speckles or crystals, or textured for volcanic or crawled effects, and they can be combined to create wonderful special effects. They have also been thoroughly tested to very high standards so are totally reliable and invariably come out of the kiln looking as they are meant to. And, unless otherwise stated, they are almost always food safe if fired to the manufacturer's specifications. Obviously they are not cost effective for mass production, but for those working on a small scale who don't have the time or inclination to mix their own glazes, they are a marvel.

APPLYING BRUSH-ON GLAZE

1. Prepare your glazes by mixing them thoroughly before use. If the glaze seems too thick, simply add sufficient water to make it brushable.

   Be sure to use a separate brush for each glaze you apply to avoid cross contamination.

2. Full instructions for applying the brush-on glaze will be on the jar, but a fan-type brush tends to give the best coverage and two or more coatings will be required for best effect.

JUDGES' NOTE

Brush-on glazes can thicken over time if they are not used regularly, but they can always be restored by adding water.

1

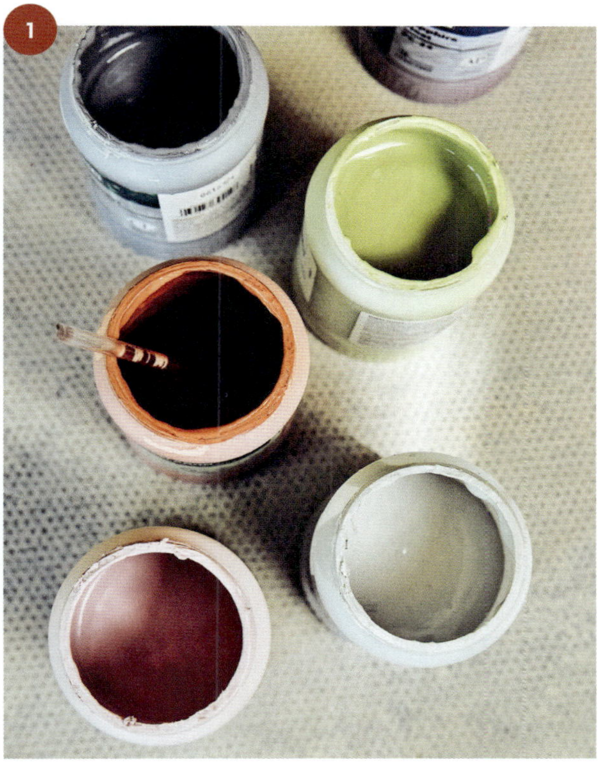

2

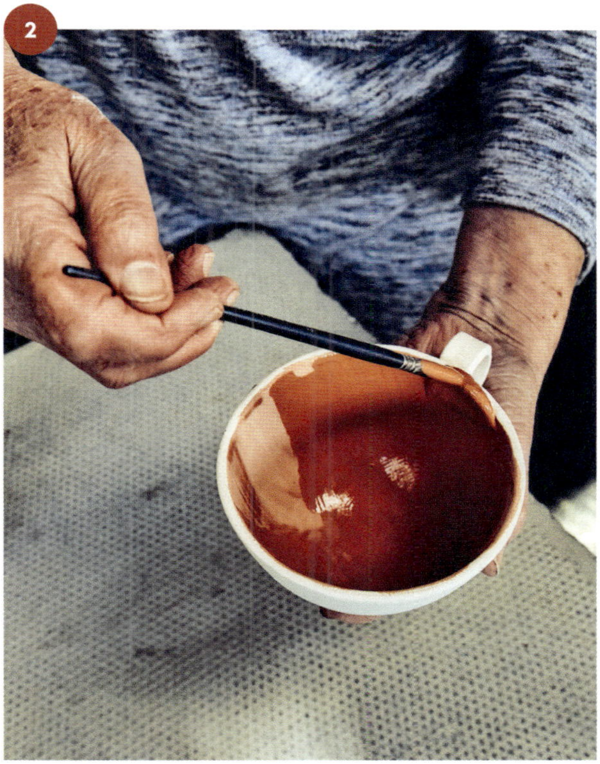

Dipping glazes

This application method requires a large bucket of glaze, generally one big enough to fully immerse your wares. It is a quick glazing technique ideal for production potters who simply want to repeat the same finish and worth practising if you intend to make items in quantity.

Because glaze can be harmful to the skin you can wear gloves to practise this technique. Alternatively you can use glaze tongs, which are available from most ceramic suppliers.

1. Holding your pot firmly at the rim and base with the least possible contact of your fingers, quickly dip your pot in the glaze and then pour out any excess.

   Don't leave the pot in the glaze for more than a couple of seconds, otherwise the coating will be too thick.

2. Allow the surface to dry to the touch on the pot, then dip a finger back into the glaze and dab it onto the finger mark at the rim to cover it. The base doesn't matter because the glaze will be removed from here next.

3. Next 'clean your bottoms!' – using a kidney, scrape away all glaze from the base of the pot, including the bevel around the edge, so that there is at least 5 mm (¼ in.) of unglazed surface around the base wall. The glaze can be scraped directly back into the bucket.

4. Having scraped as much glaze off the base as possible, wipe over the surface with a damp sponge to remove all remaining traces. Failure to do this could result in the pot sticking to the kiln shelf as the glaze melts in firing, so pay close attention.

5. Allow the glaze to dry out completely until powdery when handled. Wearing a dust mask and using a metal kidney, gently work over the raised glaze where you held the pot as it was dipped to reduce it to the level of the rest of the surface and even out the thickness.

JUDGES' NOTE

Some potters choose to wax the undersides of their wares prior to glazing, which minimizes the amount of cleaning up you need to do afterwards, but the wax is unpleasant when it burns off in firing, especially if there is a lot of it in the kiln.

JUDGES' NOTE

Other glazing methods to consider when a piece of work is too large to hold in the hands to dip include:

Pouring: The vessel is suspended on battens over a container large enough to contain the run-off, then the glaze is poured over the surface.

Spraying: This is only realistic if you have access to a spray booth.

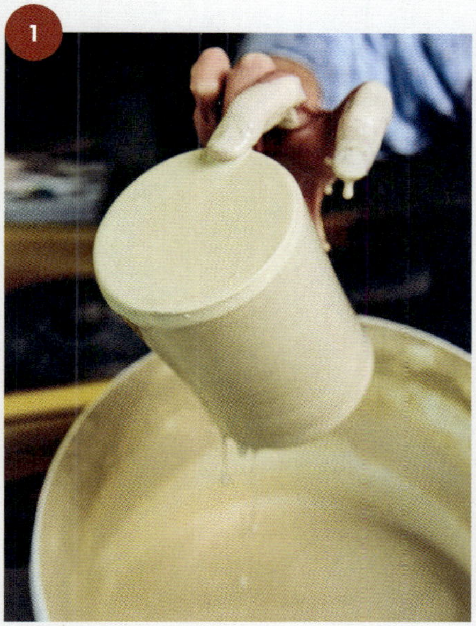
1

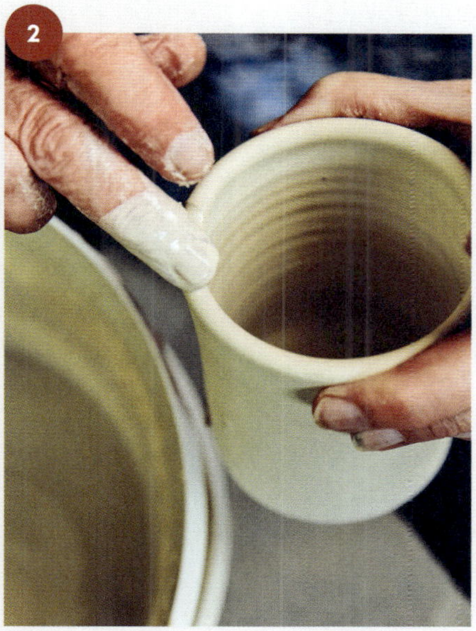
2

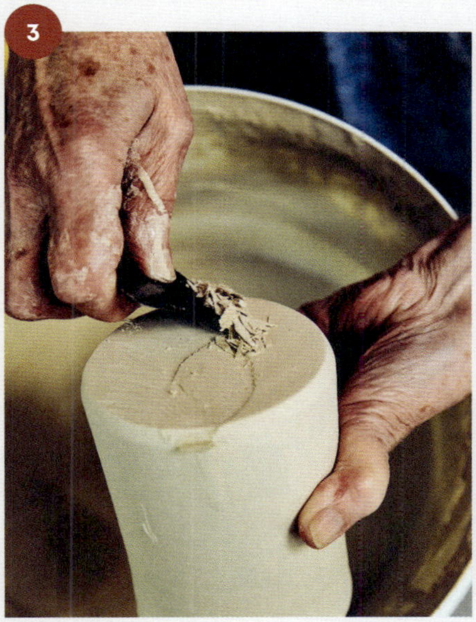
3

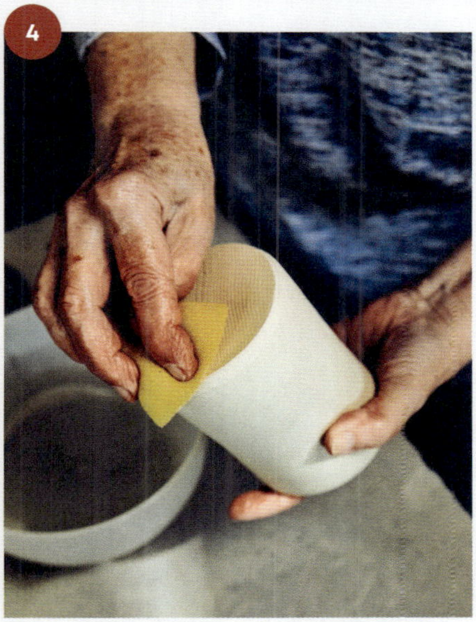
4

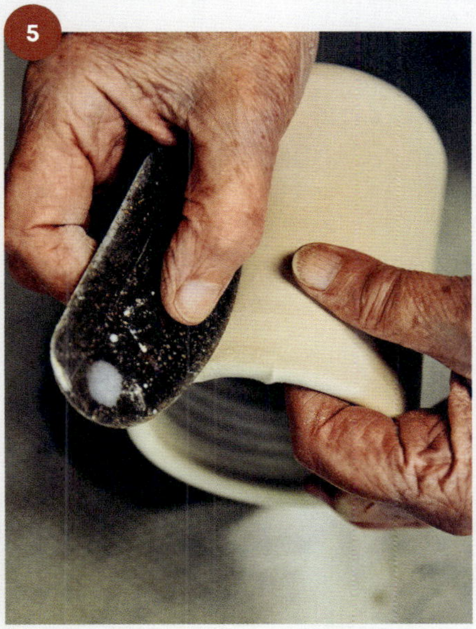
5

Firing

Firing your work for the first time in your own kiln can be nerve-wracking and there is much to learn. As with domestic ovens, no two kilns ever fire quite the same and it takes time to get used to an individual kiln's quirks. However, the most important thing is that you understand what is happening in the firing process so you can make informed decisions about what needs to change if you are not satisfied with the outcomes you are getting.

Clay shrinkage

Clay shrinks in three stages: first, as it dries; second, in bisque firing (where shrinkage is greatest); and finally in firing to its top temperature. On average, clays shrink between 10% and 15% from its raw state to its mature fired state, depending on the type. As a general rule, the higher the temperature at which a clay is fired, the more it will shrink.

JUDGES' NOTE

We are only referring to electric kiln firings in this book, as that is how all of the projects featured were fired and it is the method beginners are most likely to use because of its relative simplicity.

Firing stages

There are usually two stages in the firing process (although there can be more, depending on the nature of the surface decoration). The first stage is known as the **bisque** or **biscuit firing** and it is at this stage that the shape of the clay is made permanent by an irreversible chemical process, although it remains porous. The main purpose of bisque firing is to make pots easier to handle for glaze application.

A bisque firing should be started slowly, so that the temperature rises at 100–150°C (210–300°F) per hour until it reaches 500°C (930°F). At this temperature the chemically held water in the clay molecules is mostly driven off, so the temperature can be raised to the final temperature more quickly. Within this general rule there can be variations according to the type of clay you are working with, but the clay manufacturer should be able to advise on the best schedule.

The second stage – known as the **glost** or **glaze firing** – melts a glaze onto the surface of the clay. This can be achieved using a range of atmospheres and techniques such as oxidation, reduction or raku. This said, the most likely firing method for the beginner is in an electric kiln, which is an oxidation atmosphere. The adequate supply of oxygen during firing ensures that any oxides present in the glazes remain intact, resulting in oxidation colour responses – for example, copper oxide will produce greens. The firing schedules for glaze will vary according to clay type but you can find a rough guide over the page.

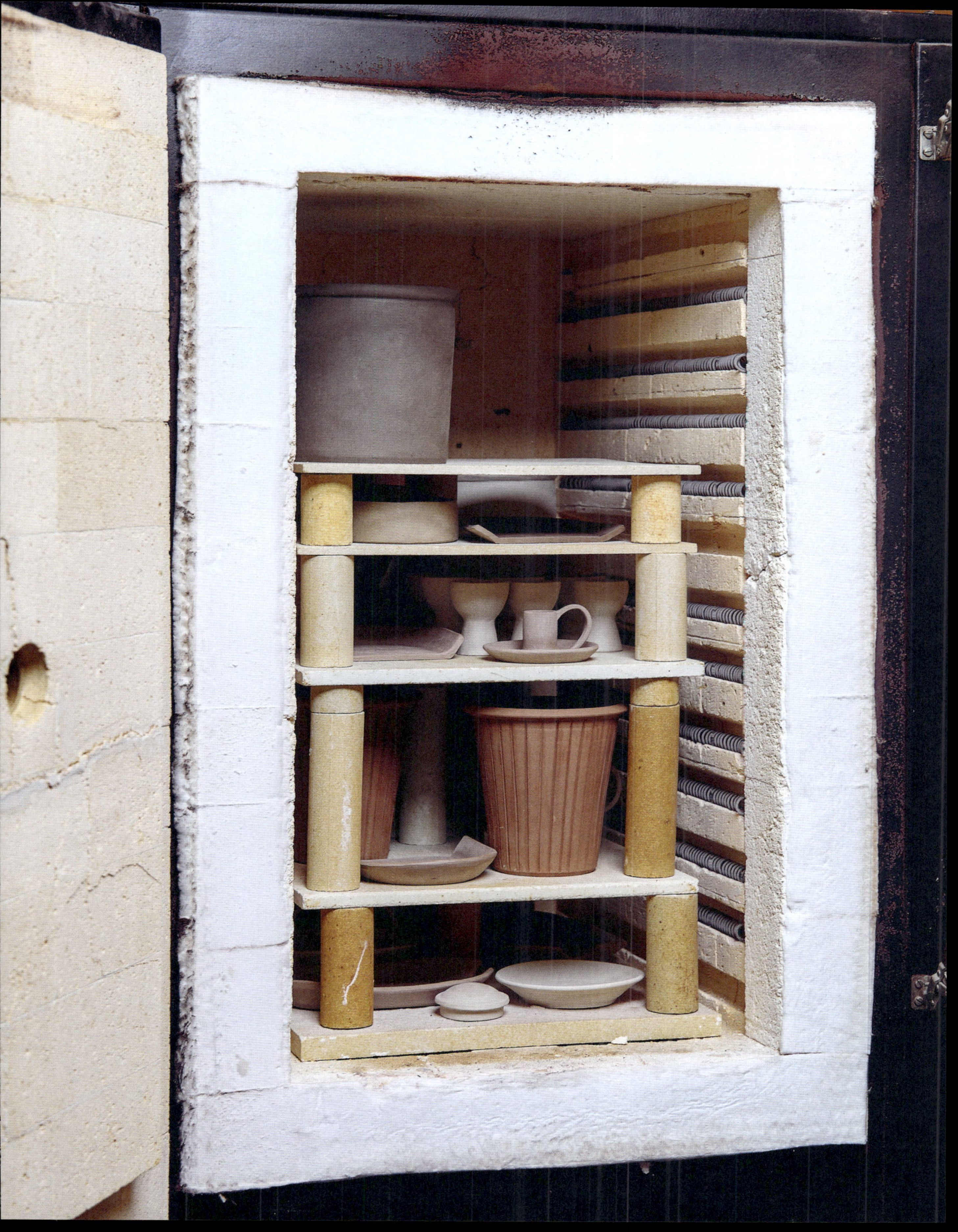

JUDGES' TIPS FOR SUCCESSFUL BISQUE FIRING

- Make sure your work is completely dry before firing.
- Stack pots on top of or inside other pots to maximize your kiln space – it does not matter if pots touch for bisque firing. Bowls can be stacked rim to rim or base to base, but make sure they are equally weighted – heavy pots sitting on lighter pots would cause problems!
- Don't wedge the bases of pots inside the rims of others – the clay needs space to shrink and will crack if it is restricted.
- Leave the bungs out of the kiln until 500°C (930°F) has been reached and the chemical water driven off. You can test this by holding a glass over the bung hole for a second or two. If it steams up, there is still water to be driven off so wait until the temperature has risen another 50°C (100°F) or so and then try again. (Warning – don't hold your hand too close to the hole because you could burn yourself. Wear protective gloves if possible.)

Once glazed, earthenware pots cannot touch in the kiln because they would fuse together as the glaze hardens in cooling. For safety you should be able to pass your hand between each item. However, they can be fired on star stilts to prevent the glaze coming into contact with the kiln shelf if the pots have been glazed all over. The stilts are easily knocked off after firing, leaving only tiny marks.

Low-temperature clays – earthenware

BISQUE FIRING

100–150°C (210–300°F) per hour to 500°C (930°F), then increase the rate of temperature rise by 150°C (300°F) per hour to 1060°C (1940°F).

Low-firing clays use a higher bisque temperature to reduce crazing in the glaze (a surface effect of tiny cracks that appear after firing). The clay remains sufficiently porous for glazing at this temperature. There may be some variations in the maturing temperature (the temperature at which clay and other materials in a clay body bond and become dense) of some low-firing clays, but your clay supplier will be able to advise.

GLOST FIRING

Most earthenware glazes fire to between 1060 and 1080°C (1940 and 1976°F), but occasionally higher.

Start the glost firing slowly – raising the temperature by 100°C (210°F) per hour to 450°C (840°F) – then accelerate the rise, turning the controller to the 'full' setting to reach the optimal temperature of the clay recommended by the manufacturer.

Most clay bodies fired to earthenware will remain porous, so need to be covered in glaze to make them waterproof. This is a important if you are making domestic ware, where hygiene is essential.

Once glazed, earthenware pots cannot touch in the kiln because they would fuse together as the glaze hardens in cooling. For safety you should be able to pass your hand between each item. However, they can be fired on star stilts to prevent the glaze coming into contact with the kiln shelf if the pots have been glazed all over. The stilts are easily knocked off after firing, leaving only tiny marks.

High-temperature clays – stoneware

High-fired stoneware glazes can be fired up to 1280°C (2336°F) or even 1300 (2373°F) in some cases. There is a trend for 1200°C (2192°F) glazes to save on fuel costs.

BISQUE FIRING

100°C (210°F) per hour to 500°C (210–932°F), then 150°C (300°F) per hour to 1000°C (1832°F) – or turn the controller to full.

GLOST FIRING

100°C (210°F) per hour to 450°C (842°F), then turn the kiln on full to the optimal temperature for the clay – the clay supplier can advise.

JUDGES' TIPS FOR STONEWARE GLOST FIRING

› All pots should have clean bases and feet, with all traces of glaze removed, otherwise they will stick to the kiln shelf.

› Don't support stoneware pots on stilts – place them directly on the kiln shelf to give adequate support. The clay can bend and slump at high temperatures if it is not on a firm base and will sink over stilts.

› Pots must not touch each other or the kiln walls during glaze firing, because they will stick together, so when you're packing your pots into the kiln, space them apart so that you can just pass your hand sideways between each item. This will also provide enough space to prevent any glaze bubbling or dripping from affecting surrounding items.

› A coat of batt wash (50% china clay, 50% alumina) will help protect the kiln shelves from glaze drips or runs.

TROUBLESHOOTING

Problem

The foot rings of pots seal onto the kiln shelf, even though it has been batt washed.

Solution

Try firing the pots on a thin layer of silica sand spread carefully over the kiln shelf. The particles of sand act like tiny ball bearings, allowing the clay to move easily as it shrinks and reaches its top temperature. Do not spread the sand too close to the edges of the kiln shelf, because it could fall onto the work on the shelf below and will ruin the surface of the glazes.

Problem

The pots seem to warp and crack excessively

Solution

This could be caused by several things:

› Uneven thickness in the walls of the pot will cause distortions as the clay shrinks – it does not particularly matter if the clay wall is thick or thin, as long as it is even.

› Uneven distortion of clay in the making process will cause distortions as the clay shrinks in firing, especially at high temperatures. This is because clay particles align in a specific way in the making process and, in much the same way that bent metal will never properly flatten again, clay will always revert to the shape it was first formed into once fired. Pay attention to the way you handle the clay in making – especially when slab building, where the potential for distortion is greatest.

› Very plastic clay will tend to warp more. Try adding sand or grog to even out the body prior to making. This will also reduce the shrinkage of the clay.

Health and safety

For safe practice, a few basic rules should be observed when working with clay and other related materials.

1. Never eat, drink or smoke in the workshop.
2. Always work in a suitably ventilated room with easy-to-clean, impermeable work surfaces and facilities for washing close by.
3. Avoid generating airborne dust – it is better to prevent dust than try to control it. To minimize hazards:

   › Clean up spillages when they occur. This applies to liquids as well as powders, because all materials become dust when they have dried. Spillage on the floor can also be a slipping risk.

   › Clean all tools and equipment at the end of the working day.

   › Use a vacuum cleaner with a filter, not a brush, to clean fine dust off all surfaces. After vacuuming, wash all surfaces.
4. Wear gloves when handling any colouring agents or oxides.
5. Wear a respirator (face mask) when handling powders.
6. Wear protective clothing, but try not to wipe dirty hands on aprons to avoid creating dust as it dries. Wash work clothing regularly.
7. Store dry materials in airtight plastic containers to avoid the possibility of bags breaking open and spilling dust into the air.
8. When sanding or fettling (trimming or cleaning) dry or bisque-fired pots, wear a respirator and goggles to protect your eyes.
9. Check that your tetanus immunization is up to date. Remember that clay is essentially dug from the ground and may carry bacteria that can cause infection in open wounds.
10. Keep a first-aid kit in the workshop and protect cuts and scratches from contact with any ceramic materials.

Beware

Certain materials used as colourants for clays and glazes can be harmful if breathed in or ingested and some studies suggest that some can even be absorbed through the skin. Be sure to wear the appropriate protection when handling materials.

Pottery suppliers should always supply the relevant health and safety data for their products and information relating to each material should be printed on its container – be sure to read it.

Glossary

Banding wheel A floor-standing turntable operated by hand and used for hand building and decorating.

Batt A plaster or wooden disc for throwing or moving pots without handling them, or for drying wares.

Batt wash A mixture of alumina and China clay used as a protective coating for kiln shelves.

Bisque (biscuit) Clay ware after the first firing, usually around 1832°F (1000°C).

Bisque firing The first firing of pottery wares to mature the clay and make it permanent.

Body The term used to describe a particular mixture of clay, such as earthenware body.

Ceramic A clay form that is fired in a kiln.

Coiling The technique of forming a pot from coils or ropes of clay. Variations include flattened coils.

Collaring The action of squeezing around a pot to draw the shape inwards, especially in the throwing process.

Earthenware Pottery fired at a relatively low temperature. The body remains porous and usually requires glazing if it is to be used for domestic ware.

Element The metal heating coil in an electric kiln.

Firing The process by which clay ware is heated in a kiln to harden or glaze it.

Firing chamber The interior of a kiln in which pottery is fired.

Firing cycle The gradual raising and lowering of the temperature of a kiln to fire pottery.

Flange A protruding rim or ridge that serves a variety of purposes – to give strength, to act as a locator for a lid or for simple decoration.

Foot The base on which a pottery form rests.

Foot ring A circle of clay that forms the base of a pot, elevating it from the surface and allowing it to stand evenly.

Glaze A thin, glassy layer on the surface of pottery.

Glaze stain A commercially manufactured colourant that is added to glaze.

Greenware Unfired clay ware.

Grog Fired clay that is ground into particles, ranging from fine dust to coarse sand. When added to soft clay, it adds strength, helps resist warping and reduces thermal shock.

Hand building Making pottery without the use of a potter's wheel, either by pinching, coiling or slabbing.

Kidney A metal, plastic, silicone or wood scraper.

Kiln A device in which pottery is fired.

Kiln supports/props Refractory pieces used to separate and support kiln shelves and pottery during firing.

Kneading A method of dispersing moisture uniformly through clay and removing air to prepare the clay for use.

Leather hard Clay that is stiff and damp but no longer plastic. It is hard enough to be handled without distortion but can still be joined.

Mould A plaster form used to shape clay.

Plastic clay Clay that can be manipulated without losing its shape.

Press moulding Pressing slabs of clay into or over moulds to form shapes.

Resist A decorative medium such as paper, latex or wax used to prevent slip or glaze from sticking to the surface of pottery.

Rib Often used as an alternative name for kidney; also a wooden or plastic tool used to lift the walls of thrown pots, among other things.

Scraper A thin metal or plastic tool used to refine a clay surface; it can be kidney shaped or straight.

Sgraffito Scratching through a layer of clay, slip or glaze to reveal a surface underneath.

Slabbing Making pottery from rolled slabs of clay.

Slip Liquid clay.

Slip trailing bulb A slip trailer is a small bulb shaped device made from rubber or plastic with detachable nozzles in different sizes for trailing fine lines of slip on the clay surface.

Sponging A decorative method of applying slip or glaze, or of cleaning the surface of pottery before firing.

Stilt A small stand used to support pots during firing to prevent glazed surfaces coming into contact with the kiln shelf.

Stoneware Vitrified clay, usually fired above 1200°C (2192°F).

Surform A rasp blade used to reduce the thickness of a clay wall or level a rim.

Terracotta Iron-bearing earthenware clay that matures at low temperatures and fires to a rich, red colour.

Toxic Any ceramic material – solid, gaseous, or liquid – that is injurious to health.

Trimming Removing spare clay from the base of a thrown pot using a sharp loop tool on the wheel.

Underglaze A colour that is usually applied to greenware or bisque-fired pottery and, in most cases, covered with glaze.

Vitrification point The point at which clay particles fuse together.

Vitrified Refers to clays that have been fired at high temperatures, fusing the particles together so they become glasslike.

Wedging A method of preparing clay for use, or mixing different clays together to an even, air-free consistency.

Whirler A hand-operated turntable that sits on the work bench; used for hand building and surface decoration of wares.

Index

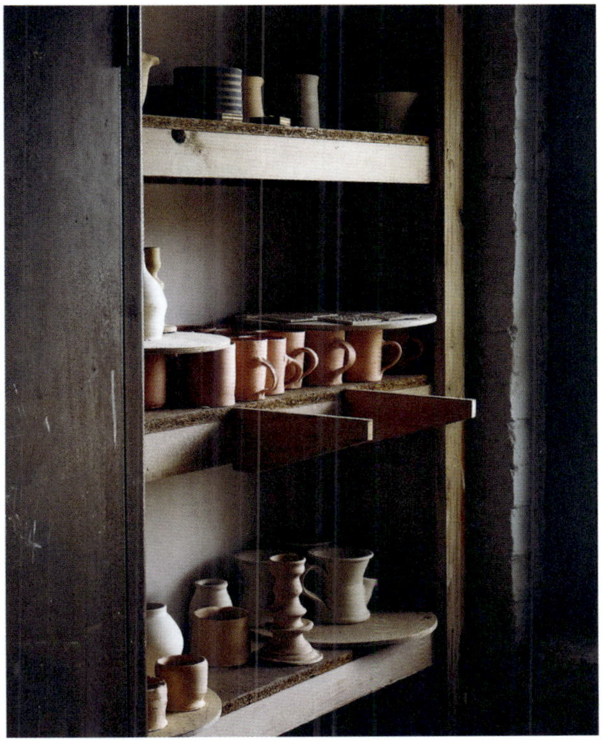

Acknowledgements

LOVE PRODUCTIONS would like to thank the author Jacqui Atkin, as well as the team at Quadrille for their hard work and dedication – Harriet Butt, Chelsea Edwards and Katherine Case. We would like to thank our brilliant judges, Keith Brymer Jones and Rich Miller for their knowledge and passion for all things clay, and our host Siobhán McSweeney for her enthusiasm and friendship to the potters. A big thank you to Josie and our challenge team, particularly Keiran Lea-Jones. Thanks to Channel 4, especially Deborah Dunnett. And finally, huge thanks to our brilliant potters, and our wonderful viewers.

JACQUI ATKIN would like to thank Quadrille and Love Productions for offering her the opportunity to become author of this book, but really special thanks go to her amazing photographer Phil Wilkins for his patience and expertise and to Simon Shaw, the brilliant thrower who makes it look all so easy.

About the author

JACQUI ATKIN creates bold artistic ceramics from her studio in north Shropshire. Here she looks out over the garden to the woodland beyond, which she says has the most enduring influence over her work, with its ever-changing seasons and rich colour palette and shapes. What makes her work distinctive is the way she interprets this into stylized designs incorporating botanical backgrounds and colourful bird imagery.

Jacqui has been working with ceramics for more than 30 years, has written many books on the subject and is a professional member of the Craft Potters Association. She was a guest judge on *The Great Pottery Throw Down* in series 7. Her work is exhibited in galleries and held in public collections in the UK.

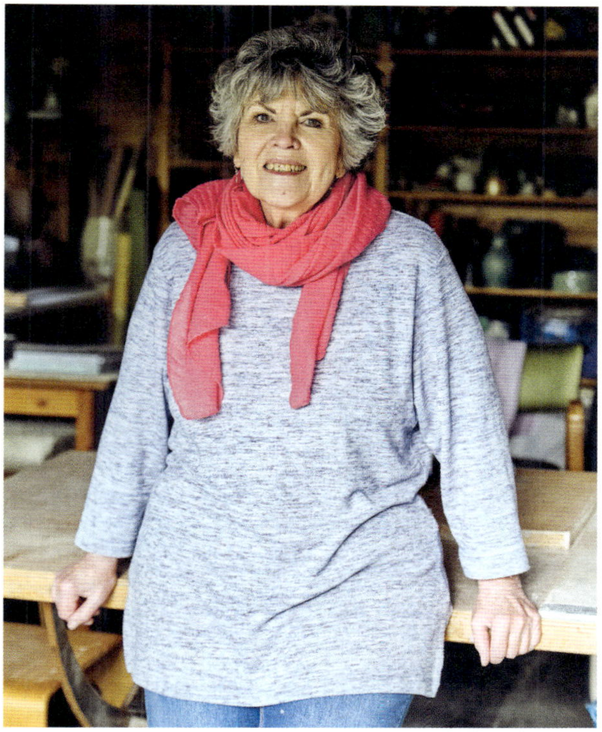

KEITH BRYMER JONES is a born-and-bred Londoner and a potter by trade. Many people know him as the judge on the popular Channel 4 show, *The Great Pottery Throw Down*, but his real job, and passion, is ceramics. Keith has been a ceramicist and design expert amassing both knowledge and experience for over four decades. Not only has he been successful with his own collection of ceramics, the award-winning 'Word Range', but he has also worked collaboratively with both British and international designers, artists, illustrators and fashion houses.

RICH MILLER studied ceramics at the Surrey Institute of Art and Design, graduating in 2003. For the last 19 years he's been running Froyle Tiles, a handmade tile company based in Surrey. Specializing in the bespoke production of high-fired stoneware tiles, it has carried out a range of commissions for a variety of notable architects and designers. These include a unique collaboration with Kate Malone and EPR Architects on 24 Savile Row and a collaboration with Jamie Fobert Architects on the new Pavilion at the Tate St Ives. Rich has a passion for clay and continues his own studio practice, exhibiting his ceramics at selected shows. Rich also a judge on the Channel 4 series *The Great Pottery Throw Down*.

This book is published to accompany the television series entitled *The Great Pottery Throw Down.*

Executive Producers Luke Byrne & Richard McKerrow
Series Producer Jennifer Morrison
Challenge Producer Josephine White
Head of Production Fin O'Riordan
On-set Photographer Patch Dolan
Production Executive Claudia Spofforth
Production Manager Scarlet Lindsey
Director of Legal & Commercial Affairs Rupert Frisby
Publicity Amanda Console, Shelagh Pymm
Channel 4 Commissioning Editor Deborah Dunnett

Quadrille, Penguin Random House UK, One Embassy Gardens, 8 Viaduct Gardens, London SW11 7BW

Quadrille Publishing Limited is part of the Penguin Random House group of companies whose addresses can be found at global.penguinrandomhouse.com

All project and set photography by Kim Lightbody except for pages 10–11 and the endpapers which were taken by Patch Dolan.

Published by Quadrille in 2025

www.penguin.co.uk

A CIP catalogue record for this book is available from the British Library

ISBN 978 1 83783 344 3
10 9 8 7 6 5 4 3 2

Managing Director Sarah Lavelle
Editorial Director Harriet Butt
Managing Editor Chelsea Edwards
Project Editor Sarah Hoggett
Proofreader Nick Funnell
Indexer Helen Snaith
Art Director & Designer Katherine Case
Project Photographer Kim Lightbody
Step Photographer Phil Wilkins
Head of Production Stephen Lang
Senior Production Controller Martina Georgieva

Colour reproduction by F1

Printed in China by C&C Offset Printing Co., Ltd.

The authorised representative in the EEA is Penguin Random House Ireland, Morrison Chambers, 32 Nassau Street, Dublin D02 YH68.

MIX
Paper | Supporting responsible forestry
FSC® C018179

Penguin Random House is committed to a sustainable future for our business, our readers and our planet. This book is made from Forest Stewardship Council® certified paper.

LOVE PRODUCTIONS is the award-winning production company that devised and produces *The Great Pottery Throw Down*. It also created and produces *The Great British Bake Off*, *The Piano* and *The Great British Sewing Bee*.

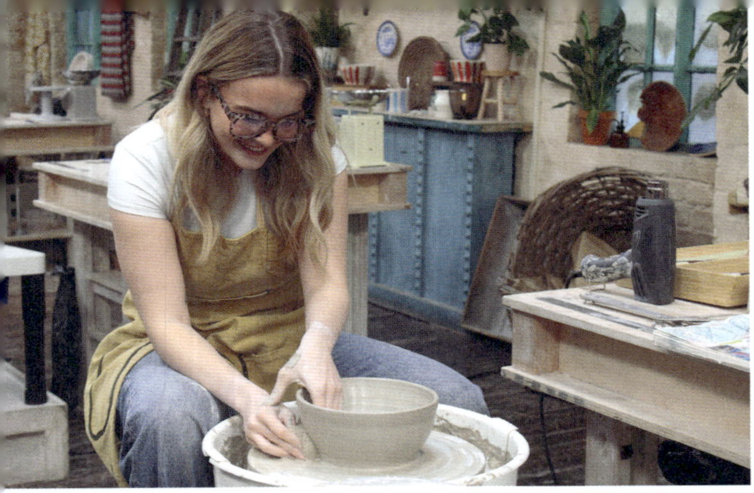
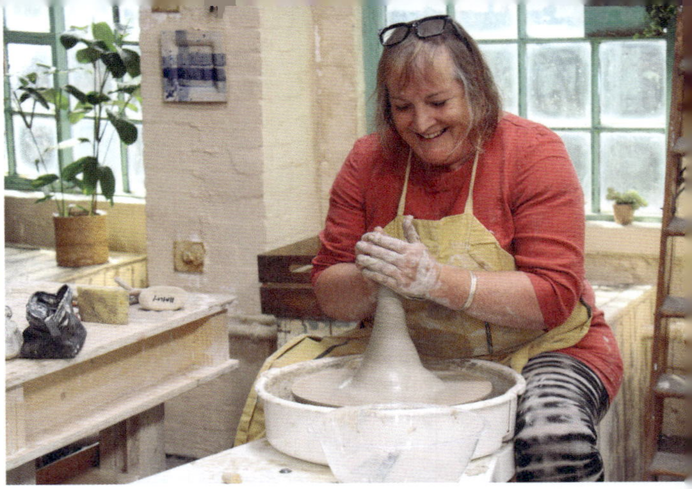
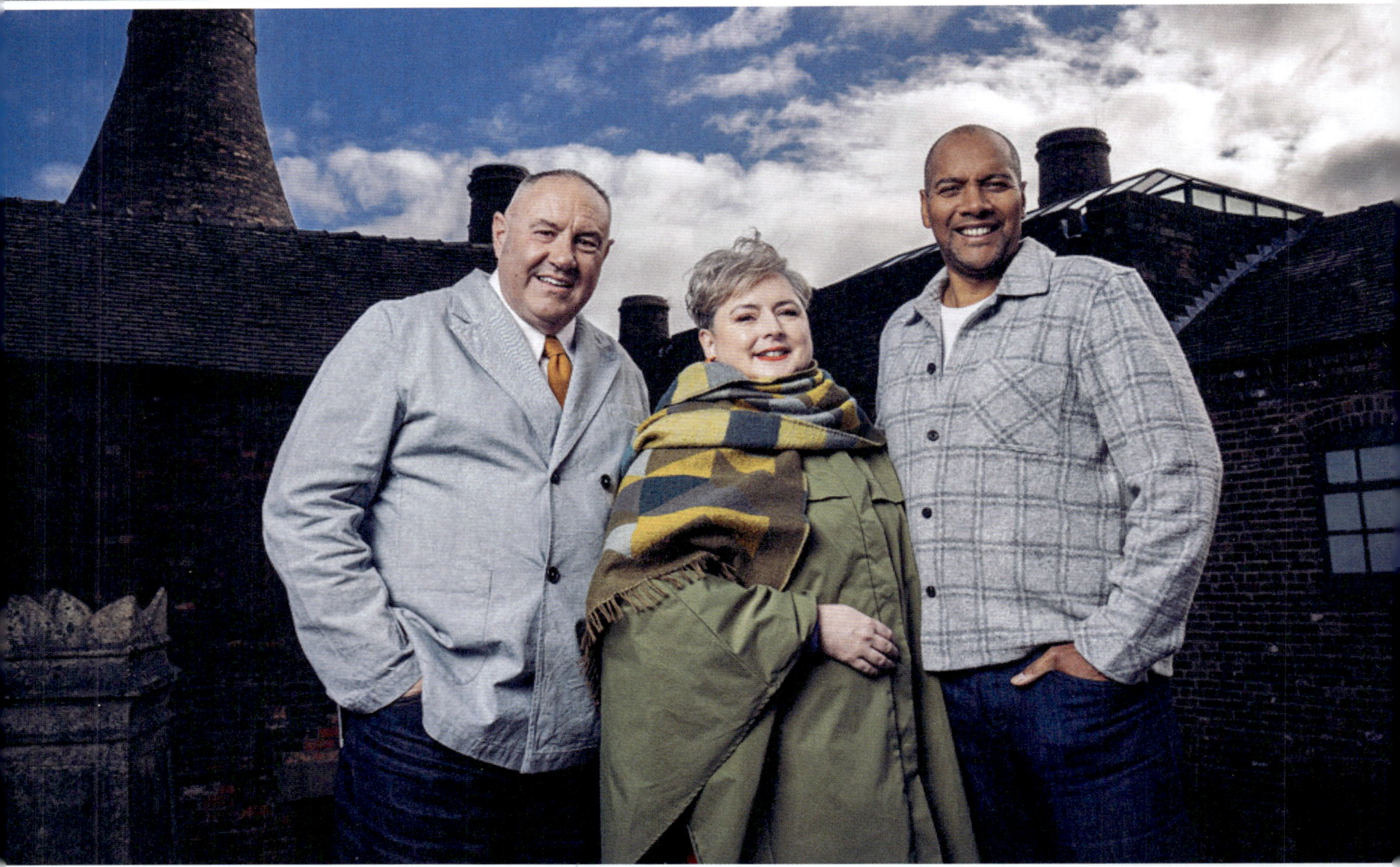
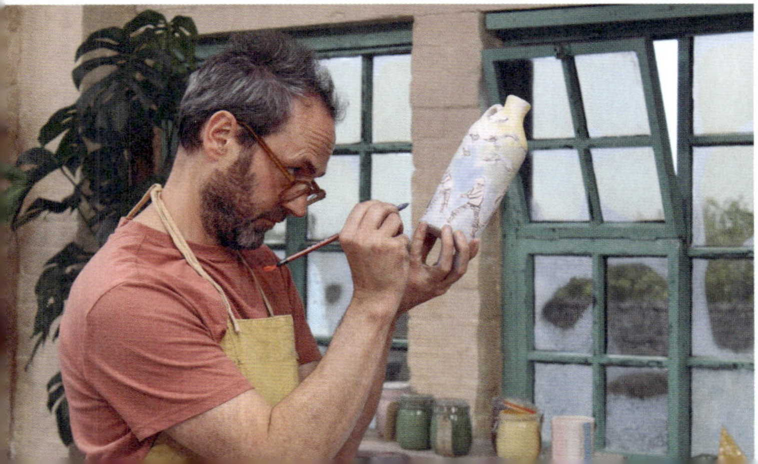
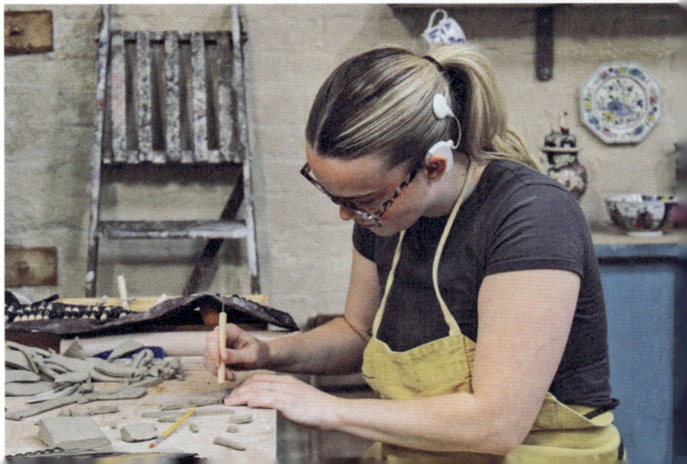